PUNISHMENT

DATE

PUNISHMENT

Gary C. Walters and Joan E. Grusec

UNIVERSITY OF TORONTO

W. H. Freeman and Company
San Francisco

Library of Congress Cataloging in Publication Data

Walters, Gary C
   Punishment

   Bibliography: p.
   Includes index.
   1.   Punishment (psychology)   I.   Grusec, Joan E.,
joint author.   II.   Title.
BF319.5.P8W3   155.4'18   76-30920
ISBN 0-7167-0366-1
ISBN 0-7167-0365-3 pbk.

to our families

One morning when I went into the parlour with my books, I found my mother looking anxious, Miss Murdstone looking firm, and Mr. Murdstone binding something around the bottom of a cane—a lithe and limber cane, which he left off binding when I came in, and poised and switched in the air.

"I tell you, Clara," said Mr. Murdstone, "I have been often flogged myself."

"To be sure; of course," said Miss Murdstone.

"Certainly, my dear Jane," faltered my mother meekly. "But—do you think it did Edward good?"

"Do you think it did Edward harm, Clara?" asked Mr. Murdstone gravely.

"That's the point," said his sister.

Charles Dickens
David Copperfield

The founders of a new colony, whatever Utopia of human virtue and happiness they might originally project, have invariably recognized it among their earliest practical necessities to allot a portion of the virgin soil as a cemetery, and another portion as the site of a prison.

Nathaniel Hawthorne
The Scarlet Letter

PREFACE

For a number of years we have both been concerned with the question of punishment, but from separate points of view. For one of us, interest has centered on the study of punishment processes in the animal laboratory; for the other, it has focused on the role of punishment in the socialization of children. Yet we have had a common research goal—to understand how punishment affects behavior. Occasionally, we discussed our research, at times discovering areas that seemed to overlap. But the differences in our conceptualizations of problems and in the questions that we considered to be of primary importance were more striking than the similarities.

We believed, however, that in our separate approaches there had to be areas of common concern, and so we decided to look closely at the research on punishment undertaken by learning and child-development psychologists to see whether it could be integrated. A result of that effort is this book. Attempts at such integration are not often made by psychologists. We can see why. They can be difficult and frustrating enterprises. However, we have also found that the experience can be immensely stimulating and even rewarding. It is instructive to have to describe and rationalize to a colleague concepts and approaches that one has generally taken for granted. Questions are asked that would probably never be asked by someone in one's own field, and not all are easily answered; some answers are based on assumptions that are not so readily granted by someone in another field. In the course of writing this book, each of us has closely examined the work done in the other's area; that has been invaluable in terms of how we now perceive our own areas.

It seems to us that many more endeavors of this kind should be undertaken by psychologists. Attacking problems from different points of view may often result in divergence, rather than convergence, of information. However, when it is time to determine what has been accomplished, common generalizations can be expected to emerge if the separate searches have been profitable. Should this prove not to be the case, then it becomes necessary to reassess what is being attempted and, if required, to rechart the course. This book represents our attempt to give the topic of punishment this kind of scrutiny. Although this book is intended for people who have had some background in psychology, anyone concerned about punishment and behavior can, we believe, benefit from our attempt to integrate results obtained by two differing approaches.

The topic of punishment covers a broad range, and in our writing we have had to be selective. For example, we have made only minimal reference to the vast body of information about behavior therapy. Much of the literature about this subject demonstrates that techniques that suppress responding in the animal laboratory also suppress responding in human beings. Where there is a relevant point to be made, it has been noted. But there are relatively few behavior-therapy studies that have actually *extended* our knowledge about the punishment process itself.

Several people have read and made valuable criticisms of earlier versions of the book: John Masters, Ross Parke, Marnie Rice, Phil Rushton, Richard Solomon, and Marty Wall. Although we know they would not agree with all that we have finally said, we are pleased to acknowledge our indebtedness to them for their interest in our effort.

Special thanks are also due to Christine MacAdam for organizing reference material for us, a task that she accomplished efficiently and cheerfully; to Ann Csink Zaduban and Fiorella Simiele for typing various drafts of the manuscript; and to Muriel Cook for assisting with some of the typing. W. Haywood Rogers, of W.H. Freeman and Company, offered patient encouragement throughout.

It is with great pleasure that we acknowledge our indebtedness to Robert Lockhart and Judy Walters, our respective spouses, for their intellectual and emotional support throughout the period during which the book was written. We have benefited greatly from their many suggestions and their constant encouragement.

Our research work through the years has been supported by grants from the National Research Council of Canada (NRC APA-161) and the Ontario Mental Health Foundation (OMHF No. 107 to GCW and OMHF No. 116 to JEG).

Additionally, we have both benefited from Canada Council Leave Fellowships, which allowed us to pursue our interest in this subject.

Historically, this book began while one of us (GCW) was attempting to write about punishment based upon studies of animal learning. At some point it became clear that this was not a sufficiently comprehensive approach. So, after a number of discussions, we decided to engage in a common endeavor that would paint a broader picture of punishment than could be done by a separate consideration of either of our areas. This endeavor started out as and has remained a genuinely cooperative one, and it is no longer possible for us to tell where the work of one of us leaves off and that of the other takes over; thus the order of authorship has been arbitrarily determined.

March 1977   Joan E. Grusec
                                                Gary C. Walters

CONTENTS

1

INTRODUCTION

A major task that parents have is to prepare their offspring for group living—to socialize them. And a great deal of this socialization consists of the suppression or elimination of behavior. Children are discouraged from engaging in such antisocial behaviors as lying, cheating, stealing, and aggression. Should the parents fail in the task of socialization, it is left to the group as a whole or its representatives to accomplish. Not all of socialization is so negative; children are encouraged to behave in prosocial ways as well. But clearly the suppression of antisocial behavior has traditionally been considered an important part of society's task.

Punishment is a tool upon which people have relied extensively to suppress behavior. "Spare the rod and spoil the child" is an old maxim that has guided many in their attempts to socialize children. Religious beliefs, although possibly less influential in recent times, have aided in the socialization process. Even though people were no longer under the surveillance and influence of their parents, they were still under that of God, with God's continued displeasure and wrath resulting in the ultimate punishment—eternal damnation. Although the Old Testament dictum of "an eye for an eye and a tooth for a tooth" has become less stringently applied, few people would deny that those who deviate from accepted behavior ought to experience some sort of unpleasant consequence. Punishment has even currently come into favor as a means of correcting certain behavioral abnormalities and has thus achieved the status of a therapeutic technique.

Given the universality of punishment, the behavioral sciences should surely have a great deal to say about it. Surprisingly, this is not the case. Although much research has been carried out by psychologists on the acquisition of behavior through positive reinforcement, much less is known about the elimination of behavior through punishment. A likely reason for the lack of a serious and systematic study of punishment is that punishment, in contrast to many other control techniques, is unaesthetic and unattractive. It is tainted by an association with brutality, child-battering, and control achieved by sheer force. People prefer to think of themselves as rational beings who are able to cope with the world in a reasonable, logical, and civilized fashion. Although this view may be mistaken, it has no doubt shaped the decisions of those who study human behavior about what ought to be the proper object of scientific study.

The aversion to control by force has permeated the way in which people view the socialization process. In child-rearing, the swing in the past fifty years has been toward greater permissiveness in coping with deviation. An example of this can be seen in a survey of trends in North America concerning advice given to mothers for controlling thumb-sucking, masturbation, and elimination and for weaning their children (Wolfenstein 1953). From 1914 to 1938 it was recommended that training be relatively severe. Thumb-sucking and masturbation were to be rigorously discouraged, with the emphasis shifting in the 1930s to early bowel training, regularity in all things, and a concern that a baby never have an opportunity to dominate its mother— the mother was not to yield even momentarily to any resistance the baby might show to her demands. The picture had changed quite markedly by the beginning of the Second World War. Weaning was to be carried out gently, with concern for the emotional impact it would have on a baby. Bowel training was to be done when the baby was ready, and the baby's happiness and the instillation of a desire to cooperate were to be of major concern. Leniency in regard to thumb-sucking and bowel- and bladder-training continued to increase in the 1940s.

The increase in permissiveness can be partly attributed to the increasingly important role psychoanalytic theories were playing in shaping North American thinking. In the 1930s, many individuals with psychoanalytic training had escaped from Nazi persecution to North America, and their influence was strongly felt among those concerned with problems of psychotherapy and child development. One of Sigmund Freud's major concerns was the detrimental effect of excessive punishment on personality development. His clinical observations had led him to believe that the punishment of children for yielding to natural impulses resulted in the growth of neurotic anxiety with its debilitating effects. The way to prevent neurotic behavior, then, was to minimize punishment in the socialization process and to allow children to express themselves and their needs freely. This approach was reflected in the child-rearing advice given to North American parents by such influential people as Benjamin Spock. It was strengthened by the contention of Edward Lee Thorndike, based on his laboratory studies of learning, that punishment was not a successful means of eliminating behavior. Although Thorndike did not address himself specifically to problems of feeding, elimination, and sexual behavior, his views had a great effect on educational philosophy. It is important to realize that the tenor of the times was such as to encourage a move away from punitiveness. The Second World War—a war that people were determined was to be the war to end all wars—was over; the hope was for a new world in which a premium was to be placed on peace, tranquillity, and goodness. The postwar atmosphere, then, was one that encouraged a rational, nonpunitive approach to the socialization process.

In the 1970s, the pendulum seems to be swinging back. Although it would be incorrect to conclude that punishment has come back into favor as a method of control, the trend does seem to be away from the permissiveness of the 1950s. What may be pessimistically viewed as a deterioration of the human situation suggests that permissiveness is not the answer either. Current thinking embraces moderation in which a degree of control, discipline, and even punishment is deemed appropriate in child-rearing. This has been documented by Ross Parke (personal communication), who reports that information about child-rearing, collected as part of a longitudinal study by the Fels Research Institute in Ohio, reveals a marked increase between 1960 and 1970 in the severity of parental discipline and restrictiveness.

Two Approaches to the Scientific Study of Punishment

Information about punishment as a behavioral-control technique comes largely from two sources: one is a relatively systematic body of empirical data from experimental psychology dealing primarily with the effects of punishment on non-human organisms, although studies of humans are also included; the other is what has been discovered about the effects of discipline and punishment on child development and the socialization of the child. Although it is reasonable to expect that the lines of research from the learning and child-development areas might have converged on the general problem of punishment, there has in fact been little effort to coordinate them—the two have developed and continue to move in parallel streams, overlapping only occasionally.

The emphasis in learning studies has been to investigate variables that influence the effectiveness of punishment and to describe the characteristic behavioral changes produced by prototypical punishment procedures. There has been great concern with the generation of empirical data and the resolution of methodological problems, but very little theory-based hypothesis-testing. Although a great deal of data has been accumulated owing to an increase in the number of empirical investigations of punishment in the last decade, little work has been done in evaluating and using the data to develop theories.

The emphasis in child-development studies of punishment has been on the practical problem of how moral standards become inculcated into a person—the development of an internalized value system or conscience. There has been much interest in how a child comes to inhibit the expression of certain behaviors, not because of fear of punishment, but because of anxiety over self-inflicted punishment, or guilt. Unlike those working in learning, researchers in child development have spent little time looking at the short-term suppressive effects of punishment. Instead, they have concentrated on investigations of the conditions under which behavior continues to be suppressed even in the absence of a socializing agent (i.e., the person who administered punishment). In contrast to learning studies, child-development studies of punishment have consisted largely of theory-based hypothesis-testing with little parametric investigation. Emphasis is on how internalization may best be accomplished rather than on systematic studies of variables affecting internalization.

How is it that two lines of research within the same discipline could approach the study of a common problem, punishment, in such different ways? The answer becomes evident by looking at their only occasionally overlapping historical antecedents.

Behaviorism and Learning Approaches

The main contribution of the behaviorists was the introduction of a new methodology, a new way of approaching the study of man. The founder of behaviorism, John B. Watson, reacted against the introspectionist legacy of Wilhelm Wundt with its emphasis on the study of mental events such as thoughts and images. Fortified with exciting new experimental results on conditioning from Pavlov's laboratory and supported by a growing wave of disenchantment with introspectionist data, Watson had an ideal climate for producing an about-face within experimental psychology. Pavlov had even supplied him with a response unit with which to objectify behavior, the reflex. Against this background, in 1913 Watson produced a tremendously influential article in which the credo of the behaviorist was spelled out.

The goal of an objective science of psychology was the prediction and control of behavior. Man, for all his complexities, was only one of many organisms to be studied and, in the behaviorist scheme of things, not to be treated as something special but to be investigated like other animals. Thus, the introspectionist study of consciousness was rejected, both in methodology and substance, as a subject matter for psychology. Watson urged his colleagues to purge psychology of the study of the mind and turn instead to the proper business of a scientific psychology, the study of behavior. In the tradition of British associationism, Watson also pressed the view that people are eminently malleable organisms whose modifiability through experience was to be taken as an unquestioned premise. It was this premise that underlay the search of most learning theorists for a general theory of human behavior. The behaviorist approach was to remain dominant for almost five decades and, in a variety of versions, is still a major force today.

Watson himself engaged in very little laboratory investigation in the course of his career, although his experimental investigation, with Rosalie Rayner, of the development of emotional responses in children was a seminal one. He was more concerned with making general pronouncements than with the empirical study of learning. In contrast, his contemporary, Thorndike, did set out to discover the laws of learning. Thorndike's work marked the beginning of the laboratory study of punishment. He had been studying learning in laboratory animals well before Watson's plea that psychologists reject mentalistic notions. As early as 1898, he announced that, from the results of his experiments with a variety of animals, he had discovered a general law of learning, the Law of Effect. This law stated that organisms tend to repeat those responses that are followed by satisfying states of affairs (rewards). There was no mention at that time of the effects of punishment, although Thorndike did suggest that responses that brought no satisfaction would not be repeated. By 1911, he had substituted "discomfort" or "annoyance" for "no satisfaction" and argued that organisms tend not to repeat those responses followed by annoying states of affairs (punishments). Because of his prestige in American educational circles, Thorndike's then symmetrical Law of Effect was widely accepted. Thorndike's greatest influence, however, was yet to be felt. In his Law of Effect, he conceptualized the learning process in terms of relationships between stimuli and responses. Punishment worked because it was able to weaken those relationships. Although this negative side of the Law of Effect seemed logical, it became apparent to Thorndike through the years that it did not square with experimental fact. Punishment, so far as it was used in the laboratory, did not seem to him to eliminate undesirable responses or weaken their assumed connections. Finally, in 1932, Thorndike discarded the idea that punishment could be a determinant of learning. His changed view was quickly adopted by teachers' colleges, and an era of permissiveness in educational philosophy followed. Newspapers and popular magazines took up the idea, and parents were told that they were not supposed to punish children for misbehavior because it was simply not effective. This new belief was strengthened by the negative view of punishment espoused by psychoanalytic theory.

What led Thorndike to form his conclusions about the ineffectiveness of punishment? He had conducted several experiments with college students in which they were asked to select one of five Spanish words that might mean the same as an English word appearing beside them. As many as two hundred such choices might have been included in an experiment. If subjects made the wrong choice, Thorndike punished them by saying, "Wrong." Examination of the data showed that saying the word "right" improved performance, whereas saying the word "wrong" or saying nothing at all did not improve it. In fact, the extent to which saying "wrong" had any effect on performance was that it tended to be followed by repetition of the incorrect choice. Thorndike concluded from these data that punishment was ineffective in the modification of behavior. But was saying the word "wrong" to a college student under such circumstances punishment? Certainly the punishment, if it was that, was very mild. What about stronger punishment? There are two early studies that bear on this question, both of which support the view that punishment is not effective in eliminating a response.

Skinner and Estes on Punishment.   In 1938 B. F. Skinner reported the results of his investigations of punishment in laboratory rats. The animals were trained in restricted environments to press a lever in order to receive food reinforcement. After the rate at which a rat pressed the lever had become stable, an extinction procedure was introduced in which pressing the lever was no longer followed by reward. Further, some of the rats received punishment in the form of a hard mechanical slap to their paws when they pressed the lever. Thus, Skinner was able to compare the degree of response suppression produced during extinction with punishment with that produced without punishment. If punishment were an effective method of eliminating learned behavior, the slap would be expected to reduce the rate at which the rats pressed the lever. Skinner did indeed find that punishment and extinction depressed response rate more than extinction alone but did so only as long as the punishment was administered. When punishment was terminated, there was a sudden, short-lived increase in response rate. At the end of the extinction procedure, the number of responses emitted was the same for both punished and unpunished animals. Thus, although Skinner's punishment procedure yielded short-term effects while it was being employed, it produced no lasting changes.

Several years later William Estes (1944) conducted a series of experiments in which electric shocks were used as punishment. He wished to see whether intense stimuli yielded effects comparable to those produced by rewards in terms of their permanence and magnitude. As had Skinner, Estes first trained rats to press a lever in order to obtain food reinforcement. After the lever-pressing response was established, the reinforcement procedure was terminated and the rats were shocked every time they touched the lever during the first ten minutes of each testing session. Estes reported that the lever-pressing response was reduced to zero. However, after a period of rest, the rats would again approach the lever and behave just like rats who had not been shocked. Longer rest periods were necessary as the punishing shocks became stronger, but the animals always resumed lever-pressing. Punishment, Estes concluded, did not weaken relationships between stimuli and responses, nor did it eliminate behavior; it simply suppressed the response temporarily. The import of the work of Skinner and Estes was to confirm Thorndike's original conclusion by supplying apparently strong experimental evidence that punishment was indeed ineffective in eliminating behavior.

The stage was thus set for the introduction of value judgments concerning the usefulness of punishment. Because punishment apparently did not eliminate prohibited behaviors, educators and child psychologists believed that its only possible function was to vent the anger of the punisher. Their opinion added support to the popular notion, derived from the formulations of Freud and Thorndike, that punishment was an ineffective disciplinary tool. Given the information available to the "experts," this advice was reasonable. What in retrospect seems less reasonable is that behavioral scientists, whose job it is to obtain information about factors that affect the modification of behavior, virtually ceased serious systematic investigation of the effects of punishment. Discussions of punishment were limited to the popular interpretation of Estes's work—that is, that punishment is not an effective technique for modifying behavior. This is, incidentally, a generalization that Estes himself has criticized as a misinterpretation of his views (Campbell and Church 1969).

It was not until the publication of O. H. Mowrer's two-volume work on learning theory in 1960 that punishment received serious consideration in textbooks about the experimental study of learning. His assessment of the understanding of punishment at that time is worth noting:

> The remarkable thing is that, even now, our knowledge in this area cannot be said to represent much of an advance over common sense. . . . What appears to be progress within the confines of scientific psychology is, therefore, little more than a recovery from the confusion into which the field was thrown by dramatic, but inadequate, earlier formulations. [1960a, p. 47]

The apparent lack of interest in the experimental study of punishment through the years has been documented by Boe (1969) in a survey of articles published between 1902 and 1966. He determined two things: the number of punishment studies had dramatically increased in the early 1960s and the increase reflected an increased interest in the study of punishment specifically (it was not merely part of an overall increase in experimental studies in the general area of learning).

Three events were indications of this new interest in the study of punishment. In the late 1950s several experimental psychologists, working within the tradition of the operant analysis of behavior, began conducting parametric investigations of punishment in animals. This work, much of which was performed by N. H. Azrin and his colleagues, yielded the beginning of a solid data base for later integrative views of punishment. Next, the first contemporary review and general reassessment of the problem of punishment by an experimental psychologist was done in 1963 when Russell Church called attention to the complexities of the effects of punishment on behavior; it was becoming clear that punishment was more interesting than the textbooks had led many to believe. And, finally, Richard Solomon, in a presidential address to the Eastern Psychological Association in 1964, called for a review and reassessment of the experimental literature on punishment. By the mid-1960s, the study of punishment was returned to the laboratory, and psychologists studying learning were searching for answers to questions long overdue. The first systematic analysis of punishment had begun.

Child-Development Approaches

Historically, the scientific study of the discipline of children has, as noted earlier, been separate from the study of general learning principles. As long as people believed that behavior was predetermined, there was little reason for concern about techniques of control. But as soon as they began to consider themselves modifiable organisms, there was reason to inquire into how behavioral changes might be brought about. The doctrine that man was shaped by his experience was formalized by John Locke, whose main contribution to psychology is not in content but in his conceptualization of man's basic nature. In speculating about the most effective way to shape behavior, he stressed the importance of experience alone, likening a young child to a blank slate upon which the events of life left their imprint, and made some surprisingly modern suggestions about the use of reward and punishment (Kessen 1965). He maintained that discipline should be what is today referred to as *psychologically oriented*—that parents should rely on esteem and censure as methods of control rather than material reward and physical coercion. This is a position that has also been taken by many psychologists in the past twenty-five years, but it has as its basis the results of empirical studies. Another recommendation of Locke's was that children not be burdened with rules and precepts, many of which, he maintained, are not understood and are therefore ineffective. A more effective way to alter behavior is to have the child repeat an action over and over until it can be done perfectly. This is a thesis about which there is currently some disagreement among child-development psychologists; however, a young child is probably better socialized by the judicious use of reward or punishment after an action than by an adult's statement of its appropriateness or inappropriateness (e.g., see Grusec, 1973). We have no way of knowing how influential Locke's ideas on child discipline were, but they have been discussed at some length here because they are of historic interest.

Freud, like Locke and Watson, greatly influenced our notions of human nature, but his ideas also helped to shape both popular and scientific views about punishment and child socialization. He described the moral aspect of personality—the superego—as being composed of two parts: the ego-ideal and the conscience. The ego-ideal comprised those aspects of behavior that were acceptable to society and was built up by means of rewards. Conscience was that part of the superego that curtailed unacceptable behavior, and punishment was the mechanism for its development. Punishment for misbehavior was initially administered by a parent or other socializing agent, but the aim of socialization was to have children adopt the standards of others as their own—the concept of internalization—and punish themselves for any deviation from them. And this, of course, is the basis for one of the major sources of difference between the child-development and learning approaches to behavior elimination. The purpose of discipline is generally conceived to be the building of conscience—of teaching a child to avoid deviation not through fear of punishment by an external agent but through feelings of guilt or anxiety. This anxiety about deviation is a form of self-punishment that can be personally devastating in its discomfort; it can occur even when there is no apparent chance of detection or punishment by an external agent.

Freud's theory influenced later thinking about punishment in several ways. As noted earlier, he believed that the punishment of children by their parents could have a crippling effect on the children. Because much of it was administered for manifestations of psychosexual needs in the form of oral, anal, and genital activities, conflicts were generated between the desire to gratify these basic needs and the desire to avoid parental and self-inflicted punishment. Thus punishment interfered with the natural development of a child if, indeed, it did not seriously distort it. Freud speculated that children suffering from such conflicts would grow into adults who could not function because of debilitating anxiety, or who would exhibit bizarre behavior because they were employing defense mechanisms to cope with the anxiety. Even worse, people could punish themselves simply for thinking of a misdeed. Thus it was possible to lead an exemplary existence and yet be torn apart by the pangs of conscience. The outcome of these views was to urge limited use of punishment in child-rearing and, in the study of child psychology, to seek alternative methods of response elimination.

Freud's observations, made as they were from clinical studies of neurotic patients, lacked the support of rigorously conducted research. Nevertheless, they greatly influenced scientific thinking about punishment. Further, they encouraged child-development researchers to look for techniques of response elimination that would have less harmful effects on personality. This produced an interesting similarity between the learning and child-development areas. Although learning researchers differ from child-development researchers in that they tend to be more questioning of basic assumptions and less receptive to a global conceptualization of a problem, researchers in both fields were very willing to accept evidence that punishment is ineffective and even harmful. The nature of the evidence and its scientific respectability differed, but the eagerness to accept the conclusion was the same.

Watson's attitudes contrasted sharply with those of Freud. His influence on modern child study, however, has been no less marked than Freud's and has been described by Kessen (1965) in the following way:

Watsons's simple dogma of the limitless power of man to change his fellow man was met with the unreasoning support and unreasoning opposition that builds cults and newspaper copy. It was Watson's dedication to the principle of man's modifiability by experience that made him a child psychologist and changed the tone of child psychology in the United States for several decades. . . . Watson's lasting contribution to our knowledge of children is centered on his studies of the infant and on his startling and exciting proposal that parents could make of their children what they willed . . . [but] his dogmatism imposed constraints on academic child psychology that it did not throw off for many years. [pp. 229–232]

Watson's emphasis on the importance of environment, on the behavioristic approach to the study of psychological functioning (without concern about intrapsychic conflicts or the dynamics of personality), and his belief that the nature of human development can be understood through the study of lower organisms have influenced both learning and child-development research.

Parenthetically, it should be noted that, besides setting the stage for an academic revolution within psychology, Watson's influence extended to the home. He was responsible, at least in part, for the strictness in child-rearing practices in the late 1920s and 1930s that was mentioned earlier. In his popular writings, he stressed that infants should not be given too much attention and affection lest they become spoiled and learn to demand attention. And because Watson was associated with a scientific approach to the study of man, his pronouncements had the aura of respectability that laboratory research carries with it. In putting forth this point of view, Watson tacitly approved of the use of punishment in child-rearing, although he had no scientific evidence that it was an effective disciplinary technique. In fairness to Watson we should acknowledge, as Mary Cover Jones

(1974) has recently reminded us, that by 1936, when he wrote his autobiography, he regretted his earlier child-rearing recommendations. In discussing his book *Psychological Care of Infant and Child,* published in 1928, Watson said, "I feel sorry about [this book] . . . because I did not know enough to write the book I wanted to write."

Research in the 1950s and 1960s. Freud and Watson were primarily responsible for the somewhat peculiar turn of events in certain areas of psychology in North America in the 1940s and 1950s. Psychologists, particularly those in clinical psychology and child development, were attracted to Freud's theories because of the satisfying and comprehensive view of the complexity and richness of human life that these theories gave. But they also found the rigor and respectability of Watsonian behaviorism appealing. Thus, they attempted to bring together the two theories—one a general theory of psychological functioning based on inadequate scientific evidence and the other an admittedly less complete and barren general theory of conditioned responses, but based on laboratory research. Such a pairing was not so difficult as it might seem. The theories were compatible in several ways: both included concepts of drive and drive reduction, of satisfying or reinforcing events, and of behavior as determined by experience. In other ways they were quite incompatible: for example, in criteria for verification. In spite of this incompatibility, however, the kinds of behavior that researchers investigated, and the hypotheses they tested, were very much dictated by Freudian theory, although the language that was used to state their hypotheses and describe their findings was that of learning theory. Their methodology was a compromise between the limitations of clinical inference and the artificiality of laboratory experimentation.

In the 1950s, there were many attempts to study the effects of early punishment on personality in childhood and in later life (e.g., Bernstein, 1955; Thurston and Mussen, 1951; Wittenborn, 1956). In addition, there were a number of attempts to discover the child-rearing correlates of juvenile delinquency (Bandura and R. Walters 1959; Glueck and Glueck 1950; McCord, McCord, and Zola 1959). The first extensive effort to assess the effects of the disciplinary practices of parents on a child's behavior was that of Sears, Maccoby, and Levin (1957). Their study is less strongly couched in theoretical terms than many others: for example, Whiting and Child's (1953) study of cross-cultural child-rearing practices. Other investigations (e.g., Sears, Rau, and Alpert, 1965) extended these early efforts, the researchers continuing to interview parents about their child-rearing techniques and correlating the methods they used with various observer ratings and projective and behavioral assessments of conscience. By "conscience" researchers meant such disparate—and uncorrelated—events as resistance to temptation and as guilt, the latter translated into such behaviors as attempts at confession and restitution for the harm caused by deviation.

Although the discussion of data and their interpretation were strongly influenced by the principles of learning theory, there seems to have been little interaction between the child-development and learning areas, largely because virtually no research was being done on punishment in learning laboratories. In the late 1950s, Solomon began to study conscience in dogs, and to assess experimentally the effects of different punitive interventions on what he referred to as resistance to temptation and as guilt (Solomon, Turner, and Lessac 1968). But this highly imaginative work had little effect on the activities of learning researchers at the time, influencing, instead, much of the child-development research that is described in Chapter 3. It is interesting to note that Solomon's original studies on the development of conscience in dogs were carried out at Harvard University, where studies of the development of conscience in children were being conducted by other researchers at the same time (e.g., Sears, Whiting, Maccoby, Levin, and Burton).

By the 1960s, Skinner's influence had become important in the area of child development. Unlike many other learning theorists, Skinner had a great deal to say about practical human problems, and this attracted the attention of human-development researchers. This was the beginning of a new approach in the application of principles of learning theory to social behavior—for psychoanalytic theory did not play a part in Skinner's writings. His beliefs about punishment were part of a general approach that was fairly widely adopted. Thus Skinner maintained, as he still does (Skinner 1971), that punishment is ineffective as a technique for the elimination of responding. In 1963, Albert Bandura and Richard Walters published a book on social learning and personality development that was well within the new approach. The legacy of Freud is evident in this book, for the aspects of child development on which researchers had concentrated their efforts—aggression, dependency, and morality—were those that Freud had designated as being of primary importance. But their analysis was strictly within a behavioral framework. Especially noteworthy is that, in addition to principles established through the study of human and animal learning in nonsocial situations, Bandura and Walters included principles established through the study of human behavior in group or social situations. Thus, much of their book deals with imitation, or observational learning. It also reveals the beginning of another trend in child-development research—the use of the experimental method and an attempt to simulate real-life situations in the laboratory. Bandura and Walters describe punishment as having limited effectiveness and side effects that can be detrimental, an indication of their adoption of the Skinnerian position. However, researchers subsequently working within the same social-learning framework seem to have been less convinced of the detrimental nature of punishment, influenced no doubt by evidence from the research of learning psychologists that punishment is effective.

Integration of the Two Approaches

In the 1960s, child-development research underwent several changes, some of which would certainly seem to have enhanced the possibility of integrating the research being done on learning and child development, particularly as it relates to the elimination of behavior. The first change was to rely less on psychoanalytic theory and to adopt more completely the behavioristic or neobehavioristic model for the understanding of human development. The theoretical bases for the two lines of research thus have more in common than they once did. The second change was to use experimental methodology, which makes it easier to take the same kind of parametric approach to the investigation of problems that has characterized research in learning for the past thirty years.

Another development was one that seems to have moved the two lines of research apart, and that is the extensive work done on observational learning. It is possible to suppress a given behavior in young children, for example, by having them watch someone else engage in that behavior and then be punished for it (Bandura, Ross, and Ross 1963b). Although vicarious learning has been demonstrated in monkeys (e.g., Myers, 1970), it does not fit easily into the theoretical framework generally employed by learning theorists. The cognitive explanations given for the effects of models on observers go beyond the associationistic ideas that, at least until recently, have dominated learning research.

It is the concepts of thinking and cognition that seem to pose some difficulty for a complete resolution of the two approaches to psychological research in learning and child-development. Learning psychologists have attached little importance to the study of cognitive processes—such a pursuit was shunned by Watson and avoided by most neobehaviorists who followed him. This neglect of mental events is probably the major reason why learning has, in the past ten years, fallen out of favor with some psychologists. Thinking, ideation, the processing of information—which have recieved so much attention of late—have been ignored. Child-development research, on the other hand, has been strongly influenced by cognitive theory, with emphasis on such topics as development of moral judgments and their effect on behavior. Studies of child discipline stress the usefulness of reasoning, of explaining the consequences of children's behavior to them. Social-learning theorists of the Bandura and Walters persuasion are no longer known by that label; they have become "cognitive social learning" theorists (e.g., Mischel, 1973). In several ways, however, the concepts of thinking and cognition are less of a problem in resolving the differences in approach of the two lines of research than they seem to be. The data from the learning laboratory remain valid no matter what kind of theoretical basis is used to account for them. And there is beginning to be an interest on the part of some contemporary learning theorists (e.g., Bolles, 1975a) in cognitive explanations of learning and a return to some of the cognitive notions espoused by Edward Tolman in the 1930s.

When research is promoted by one kind of theory, there is always the risk that it may be peripheral to the data requirements of another theory. It may even be irrelevant to the kinds of questions that should be asked in order to gain a reasonable understanding of behavior. Is there really any reason to suppose that data generated by research in the animal laboratory, which has been guided for so long by an approach that excludes cognition, will be of any help in understanding the effects of response-elimination techniques on organisms that are clearly capable of complex cognitive activities? We think there is. For one thing, learning theory has traditionally dealt with problems that seem to be very relevant to personality development. Watson and Rayner (1920), for example, using a conditioning paradigm, showed how fear of a previously neutral stimulus could be developed in a young child. From this demonstration, they went on to theorize about how such words as "bad," "don't," and "dangerous" could, through conditioning, arouse anxiety and thus serve to suppress behaviors with which they were paired. Aside from the face validity of this approach, there have been practical demonstrations of the usefulness of applying the principles of respondent and operant conditioning to personality development. The success in recent years of behavior therapy, with its extensive reliance on learning principles to modify maladaptive behavior, suggests that this may indeed be a fruitful approach to the understanding of personality.

Human beings, obviously, engage in more complex cognitive activities than do animals. They use language, they can be reasoned with (sometimes), and their perceptions can be reorganized by means of simple instructions and information. Not much of the data generated in the animal laboratory seems pertinent to this, nor is there any reason to believe that attempts should or could be made to gather additional data that might be pertinent. In dealing with research in child development in this book, we shall of necessity talk about phenomena that are not considered in learning research. But there are data from the learning laboratory that bear upon certain important aspects of socialization, especially that of young children, whose cognitive facilities are less well developed than those of adults. However, adults also often react to environmental events in ways that can be explained using conditioning principles alone.

Given that punishment has been a subject of study for both child-development and learning researchers and that events, particularly of the past ten or fifteen years, seem to have made the integration of the two lines of research a possibility, why has the research on punishment that the two have generated seldom coincided and never merged? One answer is obvious. Generally, people working in the two lines of research have had different interests and areas of concentration. And psychologists are not particularly eager to encroach upon the territory of other psychologists: integration of different approaches is usually a forbidding task at best, especially where real or apparent differences in methodology, in degree of control over variables, in definitional problems, and in the conceptual issues and goals loom large. Child-development researchers have been concerned with seemingly complex phenomena involving cognitions and feelings such as guilt. They have had to explain events not easily handled within a conditioning framework. For example, why do people avoid deviation when there is no chance of their being found out and therefore no chance of their having to experience the unpleasant consequences that take the form of punishment administered by an external agent? The parallel between questions of this kind and questions that arise from the study of a rat pressing a lever in a Skinner box is not immediately clear.

Considerations of this sort should not discourage attempts at synthesizing research that deals with the same phenomenon. Only by testing the fit will we know how good it is, and the testing itself may supply information and give direction not previously apparent.

2

BASIC CONCEPTS, DEFINITIONS, AND METHODS

Punishment: Response Elimination or Response Suppression?

The purpose of any punishment technique is to remove an unwanted response from an organism's behavioral repertoire. Recall Thorndike's original suggestion that punishment weakens associative bonds, with its clear implication that punishment is capable of undoing the structure of learning. He later reversed his position, arguing that punishment could have indirect effects on behavior but did not function as a primary process to weaken habits. Judging from the variety of pronouncements on this topic through the ensuing years, the fundamental issue of whether punishment can serve to eliminate a response or whether it produces only temporary suppressive effects has still not been resolved. Consider the following statements:

> Annoyers do not act on learning by weakening whatever connection they follow. If they do anything they do it indirectly. [Thorndike, 1931, p. 46]

> It is difficult to designate the empirical criteria which would enable us to know on those occasions when punishment for a response results in a weakening of performance of that response whether a habit was indeed weakened or not. How can one tell whether . . . the punished response habit is itself weakened by punishment? [Solomon, 1964, p. 195]

> We must conclude . . . that punishment really does "weaken" behavior. . . . The empirical basis for the alleged ineffectiveness of punishment appears subject to reinterpretation. [Azrin and Holz, 1966, pp. 436 and 439]

> As implied by the term "response suppression," punishment puts down a response by force and tends to conceal it from public view. Neither punishment nor any other technique serves to eliminate a response after it has been established. [Church, 1969, p. 111]

> Accumulating evidence [is] against a theory . . . which would attribute to response-contingent punishing stimuli a unique property of weakening stimulus response association. [Estes, 1969, p. 79]

> We still do not know whether Thorndike was correct 60 years ago when he said that punishment weakened an S-R [stimulus-response] connection or whether he was correct 20 years later when he said that punishment does not weaken S-R connections but has only indirect effects on behavior. [Bolles, 1975b, p. 393]

It is apparent from these statements that there is no consensus on whether punishment weakens behavior. Part of the problem is that it is difficult to determine what "weaken" means when this term is applied to the action of punishment. Certainly, there is no strong support for the assertion that punishment, by itself, produces permanent effects. Rather, the evidence available at this time suggests that punishment techniques promote varying degrees of response suppression. And "suppression" connotes not only the holding down of a response by force, but also the temporary or conditional quality of such action. It is important, therefore, in dealing with the topic of response "elimination" to distinguish carefully between intent and demonstrated effectiveness.

The thrust of contemporary punishment research is to consider the permanency of effect in terms of isolating the variables that control the degree of change in behavior. In the final analysis, it is a consideration of these variables that will supply information about the effectiveness of punishment or any other response-elimination procedure.

The Language of Punishment

A technical language has been developed by investigators studying aversive control in the learning laboratory, and it is essential to know its basic vocabulary. However, there is not always total agreement on the use of terms employed in learning studies of punishment and response elimination. Indeed, at a conference on punishment and aversive control held in 1967 (see Campbell and Church, 1969), the twenty-one participating experts were unable to decide upon a definition of the very thing they were talking about. Similar problems with language are not as evident in the child-development literature, in which the use of terminology tends to be much less precise.

Definitions of Punishment

Attempts to define punishment usually begin with one or the other of two general approaches, neither of which is perfectly satisfactory. One suggests that punishment consists of the presentation of an aversive stimulus when a specified behavior occurs. The other bypasses the notion of aversiveness by viewing punishment as the presentation of any event that serves to reduce the probability of responding.

Punishment as an Aversive Stimulus. If punishment is defined as the presentation of an aversive stimulus consequent upon the performance of a given behavior, then it is necessary to know how it can be determined that a stimulus is aversive. For child-development researchers this is not a difficult question. They know what is unpleasant for them, and they assume it is unpleasant for others. If their assumptions are wrong, their subjects can tell them so—babies cry and children protest verbally. Determining what is unpleasant, or aversive, for a rat or pigeon, however, is more complex, requiring learning researchers to strive for a precise delineation of the term. Defining aversive stimuli as painful or noxious only begs the question. Rather, the determination of whether a given stimulus is aversive has rested upon the *demonstration* of its unpleasantness: for example, if an organism seeks to escape from the stimulus then, by definition, that stimulus is said to be aversive or noxious. Any set of circumstances that causes the organism to remove, or attempt to remove, itself from its effects can be classed as unpleasant.

Although this definition may seem to be straightforward, there are problems with it that have made it unacceptable to many psychologists. Perhaps the most serious difficulty is that some stimuli have been demonstrated to be capable of suppressing a response when they are made contingent upon the performance of that response, yet the same stimuli do not support escape behavior. Rachlin (1969), for example, has pointed out that, although electric shock can suppress behavior, very severe shocks interfere with the learning of an escape response, and Church (1969) has found that animals are unable to learn to escape if shocks of short duration are used. Another obstacle to the universal acceptance of this definition is that, according to one major theoretical approach to the study of punishment, what the punished organism learns is to avoid behavior for which punishment is likely to be the consequence. Psychologists who accept this view of punishment would require a demonstration not only of escape behavior, but also of avoidance behavior for a satisfactory definition of punishment. Moreover, experimental parameters such as the intensity and duration of the punishing stimulus would have to be identical in both demonstrations. For example, just because an organism learns to escape from an electric shock that is continuously present does not insure that a shock of the same intensity would have punishing properties if it were applied for a very brief period.

Unfortunately, few researchers in either child development or learning ever attempt to demonstrate that the conditions implied by the definition of an aversive stimulus have been met. Yet punishment defined as the presentation of an aversive stimulus consequent upon the performance of a behavior clearly requires such a demonstration (see G. Walters and Glazer, 1971). Typically, researchers are satisfied that a stimulus is aversive if its presentation results in a decrease in the behavior that it is intended to suppress. The precision and elegance of elaborately reasoned definitional and conceptual matters are reserved mainly for seminars, scholarly papers, or conferences and do not always influence the way in which researchers work in their laboratories.

The Functional Definition of Punishment.   In the functional definition of punishment, the notion of aversiveness is disregarded altogether, and punishment is defined in a way similar to that in which reinforcement is usually defined. Reinforcement is identified as any event, consequent upon a response, that functions to increase the future probability of occurrence of that response. Punishment, then, becomes defined in an analogous but opposite way; that is, any consequence of behavior that *reduces* the future probability of occurrence of that behavior. Azrin and Holz (1966) have defined punishment more fully as ". . . a reduction in the future probability of a specific response as a result of the immediate delivery of a stimulus for that response." Further, they specify that the stimulus in this definition is a *punishing stimulus*[1] and expand upon their definition of punishment:

> The definition is not in terms of a subjective feeling or a state of being. Therefore, it will be incorrect to designate a stimulus as a punishing stimulus simply because that stimulus leads to a statement of unhappiness or to an emotional state. Secondly, a specific event must be produced by a specific response in order to be considered a punishing stimulus. A simple decrease in responding is not a sufficient reason for classifying a procedure as punishment. Satiation, extinction, drugs, disease, stimulus change, etc., also may reduce responding. . . . Only when a reduction of responses results because the responses produce a specific stimulus do we designate the process as punishment. A corollary to this definition is that it is contradictory to speak of punishment for not responding since no specifiable response produces the punishing stimulus. . . . A third critical aspect of this

---

[1]Another term frequently used to designate the punishing stimulus is *punisher,* but it also refers to the agent applying the punishing stimulus. In this book, its use will be restricted to mean the latter.

definition is that it specifies the future probability of a response. The reduction in responding during the actual presentation of a stimulus is not indicative of punishment. . . . The change in response frequency *subsequent* to a stimulus defines the reinforcing or punishing properties of that stimulus. For this reason, our definition of punishment is in terms of a reduction in the future probability of the punished response. [pp. 381–382]

Dealing with punishment in this way allows for its definition in terms of the directly measurable characteristic of response reduction instead of a derived process that requires the prior definition of an aversive stimulus. However, this definition, like that in which punishment is described as an aversive stimulus, is not without problems. For example, if a punishing stimulus must produce response suppression, then, if suppression does not occur, punishment by definition has not taken place. And what about a situation in which a punishment procedure previously found to be effective later proves to be ineffective? Azrin and Holz argue that this demonstrates that the punished response is being maintained by reinforcement and motivational variables that are capable of overriding the influence of the punishing stimulus at any time. However, this argument is only as powerful as the researcher's ability to identify such variables.

Some punishing stimuli, such as shock, may facilitate, rather than suppress, the punished response so that it increases in rate or vigor. Most explanations for this phenomenon have included the notion that the effects of any stimulus are relative to the ability they have acquired to affect behavior. For example, electric shock is not only an aversive stimulus: under certain conditions it can also serve as a signal for positive reinforcement, thus functioning like any other cue, such as a light or tone, that has been paired with reinforcement. Another example of a punishing stimulus that can facilitate the punished behavior is the spanking of a child who engages in "negative attention-seeking"; that is, who behaves in a way that will predictably lead to punishment. One way of understanding this behavior is to say that the child engages in unacceptable behavior because the punishment that follows is coupled with attention: temper tantrums, for example, lead to spanking, which requires the parent to pay attention to the child. If such attention is sought by the child, if there is no other way to obtain it, and if the spanking is not *too* severe, spankings may facilitate the behavior they are intended to suppress.

Just as a punishing stimulus can take on reinforcing properties, so can a potentially positive reinforcer acquire those of a punishing stimulus. For example, under certain circumstances, if the presentation of food is paired with electric shock, then food can become a signal for shock.

Procedure and Process Definitions Compared. The most striking difference between the two attempts at definition that have been considered here seems to lie in whether the emphasis is on procedure or on the results it produces. In defining punishment as the application of an aversive stimulus, the emphasis is on a specific procedure, whereas the Azrin and Holz definition emphasizes the outcome of the procedure—the behavioral process of response suppression. Separating a procedure from its expected outcome is a common way of dealing with the concept of reinforcement. For example, reinforcement may be thought of in terms of a set of the specific procedural details of its operation—the presentation of a positive reinforcing stimulus contingent upon the performance of a given behavior. The behavioral process of reinforcement, however, refers to the results obtained by means of this procedure—an increase in the probability of occurrence of the reinforced response. Defining a punishing stimulus by linking it to the occurrence of a process is circular, as is the analogous definition of reinforcement. Although there have been several attempts made to resolve this problem, none has proved very successful (see Fowler, 1971; Rachlin, 1970). The circularity of process definitions of reinforcement and punishment seems to be unavoidable.

It is our view that the distinction between procedure and process (behavioral outcome) is important. The introduction of a punishment procedure, even one that has been effective in the past, does not necessarily allow the assumption that the behavioral process (namely, response suppression) typical of a punitive intervention will always occur. However, it is not so important that one or the other definition—either procedure or process—be considered more acceptable. The usefulness of any definition cannot be legislated; nor does its acceptance, at least in the study of punishment, seem to affect the choice of research strategy. Accordingly, we shall use the terms punishing stimulus and aversive stimulus interchangeably, solely as descriptive terms, without particular reference to either definitional approach.

Other Terms Defined

Several distinctions between terms must be made in order to distinguish punishment from related concepts and procedures. A punishing stimulus is to be distinguished from a *negative reinforcer,* the latter term referring to a stimulus that serves to strengthen an ongoing behavior whenever that behavior results in the removal of the stimulus or the prevention of its presentation. Thus, negative reinforcement is said to function in escape and avoidance learning.

Another distinction to be made is between primary and secondary punishment. *Primary punishment* refers to the operation of stimuli that have punishing properties in and of themselves (e.g., stimuli such as electric shock) and do not require association with other stimuli in order to serve as punishing stimuli. *Secondary punishment* designates the operation of stimuli that have taken on punishing properties either by having been paired with primary aversive stimuli or by having been associated with the loss of opportunity to obtain reinforcement. Secondary punishing stimuli will be described in greater detail later in this chapter in a discussion of the varieties of punishing stimuli available to researchers. For now, it should simply be noted that secondary punishing stimuli operate in real life to a much greater extent than do primary punishing stimuli. For this reason it is important not only to understand how such stimuli acquire their punishing properties, but also to consider the variables that influence their effectiveness. Unfortunately, relatively little attention has been given to the study of secondary punishment in the learning laboratory.

It is also useful to distinguish other forms of aversive control from punishment procedures. In *escape learning*, aversive stimulation is presented and remains in effect until the organism responds in a designated way. The organism is then said to have escaped the aversive stimulation and, with repetition of the procedure, the time taken to escape decreases in an orderly fashion—escape learning has occurred. If the experimenter then introduces a signal, such as a light or tone, into the procedure in a way that will make the signal become predictive of the onset of aversive stimulation, the organism may learn to perform a response to terminate the signal itself. This is the basic procedure for demonstrating *discriminative avoidance learning*.

Escape and avoidance learning are reconsidered in a discussion of punishment theories in Chapter 3, since one type of theory states that an organism in a punishment situation learns to avoid responses that lead to the presentation of the punishing stimulus. Mowrer (1960a) has made a distinction between *active avoidance learning,* in which an organism learns to act in such a way as to prevent the onset of aversive stimulation, and *passive avoidance learning,* in which the organism learns what not to do in order to prevent its occurrence. Passive avoidance, then, is another way of describing response suppression (see also Solomon, 1964).

A Prototypic Punishment Procedure

Of the procedures employed by child-development researchers in their studies of punishment, none can be said to be "typical." However, they often use variations of a resistance-to-deviation paradigm first used by Solomon with dogs. In one variation, children are asked individually to choose between one of two toys to play with and punished—often by subjecting them to the harsh tone of a loud buzzer—for selecting the one they prefer: that is, whichever one they select becomes the "forbidden" one. The children are then left alone and the amount of time they play with the forbidden toy is recorded by a hidden observer. Although the effects of a number of parameters of punishment have been assessed through the use of this general paradigm, it cannot be considered representative because so much of the information collected by child-development researchers on punishment has been obtained through the use of other procedures.

In learning research, most of what is known about punishment has been obtained from one type of procedure, and so it seems most appropriate to discuss that one in detail. Assume that, in the learning laboratory, we wish to determine the effects of a punishing stimulus on behavior. The most commonly used punishing stimulus is electric shock, which is usually applied to a rat's feet through a series of parallel metal rods that constitute the floor of the experimental chamber. The source current to be used might be of an intensity of 0.20 mA at a constant duration of 200 msec per shock, delivered to the rods by means of a scrambling device, which insures that the shock presented is inescapable. Because the rats have to be engaging in some sort of to-be-punished behavior before the punishing stimulus is presented, they are first trained, on an intermittent schedule of response-contingent reinforcement, to press a lever for food when hungry. The use of an intermittent reinforcement schedule allows for the punishment of nonreinforced as well as reinforced responses later. After the animals' responses have stabilized, the punishing stimulus is introduced, each lever-press being followed immediately by a shock. (Shock need not always be presented for every lever-press in this type of procedure: it could be presented for every other one, every third, and so on.) With the punishment parameters employed in this sample study, a rapid suppression of responding can be expected for most animals in the first few punishment sessions. But after the first few sessions, even with the punishment contingency still in effect, most animals resume behaving the way that they did before punishment to some degree. After the punishing stimulus has been removed from the experiment, all of the animals resume that behavior.

There are several points worth noting about this procedure. The first is that the punishing stimulus is both contingent on and contiguous with the response of lever-pressing. By *contingent* is meant that punishment is a consequence of responding, rather than being delivered independent of it. By *contiguous* is meant that punishment follows the response immediately. It is important to realize that contingency and contiguity are both continuous notions. In any given situation the probability that a particular response will be followed by punishment can range from 0 (noncontingent) to 1. Similarly, the delivery of the punishment can follow the response immediately or it can be delayed (noncontiguous).[2] The two variables of contingency and contiguity can be confounded in animal punishment studies, given that a punishing stimulus that was intended to be noncontingent may occasionally follow the response in question immediately. Although this is a problem that is difficult to solve in studies using animals, it can be easily solved in child-development studies: children can be told that a particular aversive stimulus has been presented because they have responded in a certain way, or that its presentation is independent of what they are doing—a luxury denied those dealing with rats and pigeons.

A series of questions can now be asked about the prototypic punishment procedure used in the learning laboratory. Note that positive reinforcement remains in effect after the punishment contingency has been introduced. Would there be faster, more complete, and perhaps longer-lasting suppression of the punished behavior if an extinction procedure were introduced simultaneously with the punishment procedure? Does the schedule of reinforcement supporting the punished behavior influence the effect of punishment? Is there a relationship between the magnitude of reinforcement and amount of pre-punishment training and the effect of punishment? And how does the punishment schedule affect the results? Would they

------

[2]More attention has been given to contiguity than to contingency in punishment studies in the learning laboratory. The manipulation of contingency as an independent variable in free-operant punishment studies is problematic. How, for example, can a study having a 100% punishment contingency (easily programmed) be compared with one have a 75% contingency in which the remaining 25% of shocks are independent of an animal's behavior? Given that the animal is responding freely and probably at a high rate, the problem is one of programming the delivery of 25% of the shocks so that the response is not predictive of the shock. One way to accomplish this is to delay the presentation of any noncontingent shock occurring within t seconds of a response, but this may set up an avoidance procedure in which the animal learns to respond in order to postpone shock delivery (Sidman avoidance).

be different if the punishing stimulus were presented on a variable-interval schedule or some other intermittent schedule? Is punishment for every response more effective than intermittent punishment? Another consideration is the selection of variables that affect the severity of the punishment, such as the intensity and duration of the punishing stimulus. How do these variables affect its effectiveness?

What would happen if the punishing stimulus were presented after the performance of a behavior other than pressing the lever. A simple chain of behaviors that the animal engages in might be: approaching the lever $\longrightarrow$ touching the lever $\longrightarrow$ pressing the lever $\longrightarrow$ approaching the food-cup $\longrightarrow$ consuming the food pellet. If the goal is to suppress lever-pressing, is it necessarily correct to assume that the most effective procedure is to punish the animal for pressing the lever? Perhaps punishing it for approach behavior or for consuming the food pellet would be more effective in reducing the lever-press response.

In the prototypic procedure described, the effectiveness of punishment is measured by changes in the frequency of responding, but there are other things that could also be measured. For example, the time between responses might be recorded to obtain the precise distribution of responses in each punishment session. More important, the procedure could be arranged so as to permit the measurement of behaviors in addition to lever-pressing that are exhibited in the prepunishment, punishment, and postpunishment phases of the experiment. Information on what an animal is doing when it is not pressing the lever could be important for both descriptive and theoretical accounts of punishment. For example, how much is known about the generalization of punishment? In the simplest case, a behavior controller may wish to eliminate behavior "A" from an organism's repertoire but not necessarily any other, even related, behaviors. Would the rat in our prototypic procedure press a lever that was shaped differently from the one it had been punished for pressing? The question is particularly relevant to the study of socialization: would punishment for inappropriate talking in a classroom, for example, affect a child's verbal behavior outside the classroom? If so, to what extent and under what conditions? An overall approach to the problem of how punishment affects behaviors other than the target response has been suggested by Dunham (1971). Although his suggestion is addressed to those working in the operant tradition, it can be applied to studies of punishment within other frameworks. Dunham recommends that operant punishment researchers combine their procedures with those used by ethologists in such a way as to retain the experimental rigor of the laboratory while observing and recording a number of different kinds of responses. In this way, an experimenter can assess the effects of punishment on a larger part of an organism's repertoire than the punished response alone.

Finally, what would happen to the punished response if the animal had available an alternative response that produced the reinforcer unaccompanied by punishment? Would the use of an alternative reinforced response facilitate the suppression of lever-pressing and, more important, would it affect the recovery of the original response?

Our seemingly straightforward punishment experiment turns out to be not so simple. There are many variables that have to be considered. What if, instead of punishing the animal for an arbitrary behavior such as lever-pressing, we had punished it for some "naturally occurring" behavior (i.e., one that the animal had not been deliberately trained to perform such as grooming, posturing, or exploring)? Or, what would happen if the behavior to be punished required that the animal be trained, but, unlike lever-pressing, was one that was

already part of, or related to, a pre-existing natural response—
an operant behavior such as licking at a metal tube? Certainly,
a rather complicated picture is emerging in which a multitude
of factors may be considered to play a role in the suppression
of behavior by punishment.

Selection of the Punishing Stimulus

Generally, the basic punishment procedure is quite straightforward: the occurrence of the to-be-punished response is followed
by the presentation of a punishing stimulus. In real life, selecting
the response that is to be punished is not difficult—it already
occurs at a high enough rate for the socializing agent to have
decided it is in need of modification or elimination. In the laboratory, the experimenter can select a naturally occurring response, or build in a new response, and then proceed to study
variables that are influential in determining the degree and durability of response suppression. However, how does one select the
punishing stimulus employed to achieve this end? What should
its characteristics be if it is to reveal something about the nature
of punishment? How easily are these requirements met both in
controlled experimentation in the laboratory and in naturalistic
studies? Azrin and Holz (1966) have listed several requirements
that an "ideal" punishing stimulus should meet, the most important of which are:

1. The punishing stimulus should be capable of precise
physical specification. An experimenter may wish to employ a
range of values of intensity and duration of the stimulus,
much as pharmacologists do when they wish to demonstrate
the dose-effect relationship of a drug. If the punishing

stimulus is not quantifiable, the experimenter must resort to general terms such as low, moderate, and high punishment, and these terms are relative at best and often meaningless. Yet such descriptions of the severity of punishment are frequently found in both learning and child-development studies.

2. Subjects should be permitted no unauthorized escape from the punishing stimulus, nor should they be able to minimize its occurrence. If the subjects are able to engage in behaviors that allow either of these conditions to occur, precise specification of the punishing stimulus delivered by the experimenter is misleading in terms of the effect it has on the subjects.

3. The punishing stimulus should produce minimal skeletal reactions, such as intense withdrawal or approach. Such reactions may be incompatible with the performance of a given punished response, not because of a punishing effect, but merely as a result of the elicitation of competing skeletal responses. This point is nicely demonstrated in a study by Fowler and N.E. Miller (1963) in which rats were trained to traverse an alleyway for food reward. Upon completion of training, the animals received shock in the goal box, some of them shocked on only their hind paws and others on only their forepaws. Shock on the hind paws elicited a skeletal reaction of lurching forward, whereas that on the forepaws caused the rats to jump backward. Rats receiving hind-paw shock demonstrated greater persistence in approaching the food than did those given forepaw shock. Thus, even though the aversiveness of the punishing stimulus was presumably identical for both groups of rats, the elicited skeletal reactions produced a difference in the degree to which the response was suppressed—a difference accounted for not by the aversiveness of the punishing stimulus, but by the way in which it was applied (see also Bolles and Seelbach, 1964).

Varieties of Punishing Stimuli

Primary Punishing Stimuli. As previously noted, primary punishing stimuli are those that are thought to be inherently aversive—stimuli such as electric shock, loud noises, physical slaps, and so on. Air blasts, bar slaps, toy snakes, bright light, forced running in a motor-driven wheel, and intracranial brain stimulation have been employed in isolated studies with animals, but their occasional use is not enough to assess their general effectiveness. Electric shock has been the stimulus of choice in the learning laboratory, probably because it meets the requirements of an "ideal" punishing stimulus. However, even the use of electric shock is problematic. For example, its effects depend on its application: shock applied through electrodes attached directly to an organism is different from that applied through the grid floor of an experimental chamber.[3] Everything considered, however, electric shock is a very effective punishing stimulus, and a great deal is known about the effects of such variables as the intensity, duration, time of onset, and schedule of its presentation on the suppression of certain kinds of responses in laboratory animals.

The careful and systematic investigation of electric shock or any other primary punishing stimulus has not been undertaken by researchers working on child discipline. Generally, the kinds of punishing stimuli that have been studied by developmental researchers are quite different from those studied in the animal laboratory.

Although electric shock has not been used very much in experimental investigations of response suppression in children, it has been employed in the treatment of autistic and retarded children to increase social behavior (see Lovaas, Schaeffer, and

---

[3]The reader interested in a more detailed discussion of these complexities should refer to Azrin and Holz (1966) and to Campbell and Masterson (1969).

Simmons, 1965), to decrease such maladaptive responses as self-destructive behavior (see Lovaas and Simmons, 1969), and to decrease inattention and increase learning (see Kircher, Pear, and Martin, 1971). Such use raises ethical questions; however, the application of electric shock to suppress self-mutilating behavior can certainly be justified. It is surely better to put a child through a brief painful procedure than it is to tie the child to a bed or place it in a straitjacket for most of the time. Nevertheless, the employment of shock as a punishing stimulus under any other circumstances would not be condoned by most people. In fact, the use of any kind of corporal punishment in the laboratory is generally not permitted. On the other hand, society considers it acceptable for parents to employ corporal punishment, perhaps because it is believed that they will use it in a more responsible way (this does not always happen, of course), or because of an unwillingness to interfere in parent-child relations. It is in a naturalistic setting, then, that the effects of corporal punishment on response suppression can be studied: although parents do not apply electric shock to their offspring when they misbehave, they do spank and slap them. It is by no means obvious that we have arrived at the ultimate moral position in terms of how we view the ethics of various punitive interventions. As far as punishment research is concerned, however, it is evident that experimenters have to work within the confines of society's current beliefs about the acceptability of any given form of punishment.

It is for this reason that experimenters studying punishment in children have turned to primary punishing stimuli that do not cause physical pain. For example, loud noise, which is annoying but presumably not painful at the sound levels employed, has been used successfully in the suppression of behavior (e.g., R. Walters and Demkow, 1963; Parke and R. Walters, 1967). Yet, its apparent effectiveness as a punishing stimulus may be due to the fact that it draws a child's attention to what the punishing agent considers to be correct behavior. For example, Sajwaj and Hedges (1971) found that a loud blast from a bicycle horn helped a retarded child to eliminate responses that interfered with cleaning-up. However, to maintain the cleaning-up, it was necessary to praise the child, and the praise had to come from the child's parent, who used the horn. It may be that, instead of suppressing behavior, the effect of blasting the horn was to cause the child to look at the parent and thus respond to the praise. Thus, the potential usefulness of noise as a punishing stimulus for child-development studies is limited. In learning studies it has been found that animals adapt to its repeated presentation and its effectiveness is less than that of electric shock—nondamaging levels of noise have been found to be less aversive than electric shock at the intensities typically used in laboratory research (Campbell and Bloom 1965).

Foxx and Azrin (1973) have used *overcorrection* as a punishing stimulus. Subjects are required, if the circumstances permit, to make restitution for their misbehavior by having not only to restore the situation to what it was before disruption, but to improve it and to practice correct behavior. For example, children who put objects into their mouths have their mouths washed out with antiseptic solution, with the accompanying explanation that their behavior results in exposure to harmful germs and that hygienic precautions must therefore be taken. Or a child who overturns a table would have to right it, dust and wax it, and straighten and dust all other tables in the room.

Secondary Punishing Stimuli. As mentioned earlier, secondary punishing stimuli are those stimuli that are not intrinsically aversive but acquire their punishing properties as a result of having been paired with aversive stimuli. For example, a tone or a verbal command such as "No" paired with a physically painful stimulus such as an electric shock or a slap can itself become a punishing stimulus. Likewise, an otherwise neutral event that results in the loss of an opportunity to obtain positive reinforcement can serve as a secondary punishing stimulus; this loss of opportunity is referred to as *time-out*. There are a variety of time-out procedures ranging from the physical removal of an organism from the experimental environment to the restructuring of that environment in such a way that there is a period in which a given response is reinforced and one in which it is not. What all time-out paradigms have in common is the withdrawal of an opportunity for an organism to emit a response for which it expects to receive positive reinforcement (Ferster and Skinner 1957). Thus, if an organism is reinforced for responding in the presence of one stimulus but not in the presence of a second, then, strictly speaking, the latter event can be termed a time-out. The important point is that making time-out contingent upon a particular response may lead to a reduction in the future probability of occurrence of that response, particularly if an alternative way of obtaining reinforcement is also available; thus time-out satisfies our definition of a punishing stimulus.

Taken as a whole, the evidence indicates that time-out does have punishing properties. There are a variety of demonstrations of its usefulness both experimentally and practically. For example, time-out has been shown to suppress a pigeon's key-pecking response for food (Thomas 1968), to hasten the extinction of avoidance responses (Nigro 1966), to suppress schedule-induced drinking (polydypsia) in rats (Flory and Lickfett 1974), and to reduce the incidence of aggressive and destructive behavior in retardates (J. Hamilton, Stephens, and Allen 1967).

McMillan (1967) has compared the effectiveness of time-out with that of shock punishment on the lever-pressing, maintained by food reinforcement, of monkeys. He found that, although these two punishing stimuli reduced responding to approximately the same degree, several striking differences emerged. For example, toward the end of any given experimental session, monkeys tended to resume, at the prepunishment rate, the responding for which they were being punished with electric shock, whereas those receiving time-out punishment maintained the same low rate of responding throughout the entire session. On the other hand, Leitenberg (1965), in his review of time-out studies, concluded that shock punishment is a more effective suppressor of behavior than time-out, and Risley (1968) has related that time-out failed to suppress the potentially harmful climbing behavior of an autistic child, whereas the use of electric shock suppressed it rapidly. This is especially interesting in view of the fact that time-out was used successfully in controlling other kinds of behavior exhibited by the same child.

The evidence that time-out is capable of producing suppression of ongoing behavior is impressive, but it is difficult to explain exactly why it fails to suppress responses in certain cases. Time-out is an important, though not well understood, punishing stimulus. Its use in clinical and institutional settings is quite common. It has obvious advantages over corporal punishment and, in nonexperimental circumstances, is more easily employed than, say, an extinction procedure that depends on both the identification and the manipulation of a known reinforcer, which is not always possible outside the laboratory.

Time-out is probably the most common secondary punishing stimulus used in the learning laboratory. Child-development researchers, however, have relied heavily on additional secondary punishing stimuli, including verbal criticism (e.g., "No" or "That's wrong"), withdrawal of approval or love (e.g., "I'm disappointed in you"), and withdrawal of material reward. In the laboratory, the withdrawal of reward may consist of taking away chips, tokens, or points that have purchasing power. The procedure is called punishment by *response cost.*[4]

Love-Oriented and Power-Assertive Discipline. In child-development studies, punishing stimuli have been separated into two classes: *power assertion,* which includes physical punishment, the withholding of material rewards and privileges, and verbal derision; and *love-oriented* techniques, which include expressions of disappointment and hurt, social isolation, and so on. The distinction is not made on the basis of type of punishment—power-assertive punishing stimuli may be either primary or secondary, and love-oriented techniques include both time-out and response-cost procedures. The two classes of punishment, however, have been assumed to differ in their effects on response suppression, as well as on such so-called indexes of moral development, or conscience, as a sense of guilt and confession. There are several bases for this assumption. The psychoanalytic account of moral development holds that guilt, which is dreaded because of its resemblance to anxieties about punishment and abandonment, is more likely to be engendered by discipline that arouses anxiety over loss of love than by physical pain. According to Allinsmith and Greening (1955), those who use power-assertive techniques on children supply them with models for the open expression of anger, whereas those who use love-oriented techniques do not. The latter facilitates the turning inward of anger, and it is this internal anger that forms the basis of a capacity for guilt. Sears, Maccoby, and

---

[4]Response-cost punishment should be distinguished from an extinction procedure. The frequency of performance is decreased in an extinction procedure by *withholding* reinforcement for responding, whereas in a response-cost procedure, an already acquired reinforcer is *taken away* from an organism contingent upon the performance of a response.

Levin (1957) suggest that children punished by the withdrawal of parental love would have to emulate parental attributes, including value judgments, in order to replace the withdrawn reinforcement. And according to cognitive dissonance theory, power assertion is less likely to promote permanent adoption of parental values because children recognize that their compliance with parental dictates is the result of external pressure. When love is withdrawn, the reason for conformity is less obvious and so conforming behavior may be attributed to a personal decision to behave in a specific way: this is much more likely to lead to an enduring change.

A number of naturalistic studies support the hypothesis that love-oriented techniques can be used with greater success than the assertion of power in developing moral values in a child, but the evidence obtained from these studies may be confounded by the parental reasoning that is often a part of such techniques. When reasoning (i.e., explaining to a child why a particular behavior is undesirable) is removed, there seems to be no relationship between love-oriented techniques and various indexes of moral development (Hoffman 1970b). Moreover, relying solely on data obtained from naturalistic studies as a way of demonstrating the differences in effect between the two classes of punishing stimuli is open to question: for example, are the two classes of punishing stimuli administered in the same way? The withdrawal of love may last much longer than physical punishment and thus be more severe in its effects, with a concomitant increase in the behavior desired by the socializing agent. Withdrawal of love may be more likely to last until some sort of reparative response or renunciation is made (Hill 1960). Indeed, when the termination of either withdrawal of material reward or withdrawal of love is contingent upon self-criticism, the strength of the response increases under both conditions of punishment (Grusec and Ezrin 1972).

The theories of the effectiveness of punishment cited herein are also based on the assumption that different indexes of moral development are related. The avoidance of guilt, for example, should lead to the suppression of responses that would generate that guilt. There is abundant evidence, however, that such relationships do not exist. Solomon, Turner, and Lessac (1968) report that puppies trained in a way that facilitated resistance to temptation showed little evidence of "guilt" when they did deviate and, contrarily, those who showed little resistance to temptation appeared guilty after deviation. Cheyne and R. Walters (1969) found in studies of children that those who deviated least were also more likely than the others to deny it when they did deviate. And children who are self-critical after deviation show less emotional upset than those who have not been trained to use a self-critical response (Grusec and Ezrin 1972). We shall have little more to say about these interrelationships because our main concern is with suppression of responding—that is, resistance to temptation or deviation. The point is that any findings reported with respect to indexes of moral development must delineate the relationship between certain child-rearing practices and a specific behavior—such as the suppression of the punished response—very precisely.

Comparing Punishing Stimuli. Because child psychologists have studied a variety of punishing stimuli and learning researchers have concentrated most of their efforts on only one, comparing the findings from the two lines of research is hampered by the different kinds of stimuli used—not all punishing stimuli have equivalent effects. It is necessary to determine, for example, whether loud noises and electric shock have similar effects on behavior. And whether the effects of response cost parallel those of electric shock and time-out. These are the kinds of questions and comparisons dictated by socialization studies.

The fact that they have not been of great concern to learning researchers is a reflection, again, of different emphases in the two research traditions.

In order to compare different kinds of punishing stimuli, their quantitative differences, such as degree of aversiveness, duration, and frequency of application, must be taken into consideration. For example, the withdrawal of love may be more subjectively painful than spanking; parental disapproval may persist for several hours, whereas corporal punishment may last for only a matter of seconds; verbal disapproval may be applied every time a child engages in a given behavior, whereas spanking may not be. Such quantitative differences have been systematically explored by learning researchers, but have been virtually ignored by child-development researchers.

Selection of the Behavior to Be Punished

Before undertaking an analysis of punishment, a researcher must decide on the behavior to be modified. The choice is sometimes dictated by a primary interest in the behavior itself rather than the punishment process. Child psychologists interested in the study of aggression may be concerned with the influence of punishment on aggressive behaviors, for example, although their fundamental concern is understanding aggression. However, an investigator whose primary interest is to understand the punishment process itself typically selects a specific response from a given class of behaviors and uses some measure of response change as an indicator of the effects of punishment. On what basis does the investigator choose a class of behaviors to study and a specific response within that class? Are there criteria that lead to the choice of one response over another? Does it make any difference which response is chosen; that is, would the nature of the response affect the way in which variables work, and would it affect the conclusions drawn about the effects of punishment?

There are three criteria that make some responses more desirable to study than others. First, the prepunishment rate of occurrence of a response that is to be punished should be high enough to accommodate the observation of any suppressive effects of the punishing stimulus. Second, the rate at which the response occurs throughout the period of observation should be relatively uniform. If the response rate fluctuates because the experimenter lacks control over the behavior being studied, attributing changes in response frequency to the punishment procedure becomes complicated. And, third, the response should be one that is sensitive to changes in the characteristics of the punishing stimulus.

The choice available to researchers attempting to satisfy these criteria in their investigations of punishment is between behavior—either innate or learned—already in an organism's repertoire and arbitrary behaviors that are built into its repertoire under controlled laboratory conditions for the purpose of studying the effects of punishment on them. Researchers in child development and child socialization have virtually restricted this choice to those behaviors that children already have in their repertoires, often giving little thought to how the behaviors came into existence. Subjects are punished for playing with attractive toys, for not attending to a boring task, for making the wrong choice in a discrimination task, for engaging in disruptive behavior in the classroom, for having temper tantrums, and so on. In naturalistic investigations, the emphasis is on behaviors that socializing agents consider to be worth changing, such as disobedience, a lack of concern for others, and damaging property. In every case, advantage is taken of the fact that the children being studied already behave in ways that satisfy, at least to a degree, the criteria of high frequency, stability, and sensitivity. On the other hand, those working in learning laboratories, particularly with animals, have focused on behaviors that are first acquired under controlled laboratory conditions. Moreover, they have emphasized the study of one kind of learned response, the arbitrary operant. Experimenters select a response that would probably never occur under normal circumstances (e.g., lever-pressing or key-pecking) and build it into the organism's behavioral repertoire using positive reinforcement. Then they introduce a punishment procedure and assess its effects.

The reason that this approach has dominated the study of punishment in the animal laboratory is that it enables the investigator to select a response that satisfies the three criteria of response selection. It has not been adopted by child-development researchers, perhaps because of a concern with "relevance" and with real-life situations, and because of a history less dominated by the traditions of operant technology. Yet the remarkable degree of control and precision that is achieved by means of this technology makes the use of arbitrary operants in punishment research extremely attractive. The assumption underlying their use is that one response is as good to work with as another for the purpose of deriving general principles of learning. Indeed, the very arbitrariness of the response seems to make it less complicated to deal with than other behaviors whose origin is either unknown or, as is true of species-specific behaviors, not completely understood. However, what kinds of limitations have been imposed on the ability of psychologists to make generalizations about punishment by relying on one kind of learned response in the animal laboratory and on a variety of responses in studying child socialization? Does the choice of behavior make a difference? The answer seems to be that it indeed does. In an analysis of experimental studies of punishment, Solomon (1964) stated that "to predict in even the grossest way the action of punishment on a response, one has to know *how* that particular response was originally inserted in the subject's repertoire." Solomon was stressing the importance of understanding the relationship between the effect of punishment and the nature of the punished behavior. For a given punishment procedure to be effective, an investigator must have information not only about how to administer the punishment, but also about the nature of the particular behavior it is intended to eliminate. To illustrate this, Solomon briefly surveyed the effects of punishment on five classes of response: (1) those established by positive reinforcement, (2) consummatory behavior, (3) sequential patterns of instinctive acts, (4) discrete reflexes such as the patellar tendon reflex, and (5) those established earlier by exposure to aversive stimuli, such as escape, avoidance, and previously punished behavior. Although little was known in 1964 about the effects of punishment on the last four classes, it was clear even then that there were interactions between punishment and the nature of the behavior to be punished. Solomon points out, for example, that there is reason to believe that the same punishment that very successfully suppresses consummatory behavior has not nearly so devastating an effect on instrumental acts, and that the suppression of avoidance responding can be very difficult if the punishing stimulus is the same as that which was used to establish the avoidance response.

A similar concern has been expressed by Myer (1971):

> Almost all of our current knowledge of the effects of punishment is based upon studies of the effect of electric shock contingent upon food-motivated instrumental responding by domestic rats. . . . It is difficult to understand why lever pressing or running down an alley should be regarded as more useful in gaining an understanding of behavior than feeding, copulation, or attack behavior; why hunger should be considered the fundamental motive underlying behavior; or why the domestic rat should be regarded as the prototypic organism. Until the scope of research is broadened to include a greater variety of stimuli, responses, and organismic conditions, any conclusions about the mechanisms un-

derlying the suppressive effects of punishment must be highly tentative. [pp. 527–528]

Nor has the problem of punishment-behavior interactions been dealt with in a systematic way by child-development researchers. Some clinicians do warn that it is useless to punish certain behaviors because they arise from some unfilled need and will not disappear; or they will reappear in some other form until that need is satisfied. But concern with the behavior-punishment relationship goes little beyond this. In fact, a basic tenet of behavior modification is that knowledge of the origin of a behavior is unnecessary to any attempt to change it. There are a few exceptions, however: for example, it would be difficult to find any therapist, regardless of theoretical persuasion, who would attempt to eliminate the phobic behavior of children by punishing them for being fearful or for avoiding the anxiety-producing situation.

Of major importance is the extent to which current findings, and the generalizations drawn from them about punishment effectiveness, are going to forecast the results of future punishment research. To the extent that such generalizations are made from findings obtained by using an operant model, they may be inadequate. The slight concern with establishing the origin of the punished behavior that is evident in child-development research also limits the conclusions that can be drawn about punishment.[5]

---

[5]Unfortunately, few psychologists agree on how responses should be classified (e.g., Black and Young, 1972). Classification may consist of a simple dichotomy as is true of operant and respondent behaviors; or it may emphasize functional aspects and classify behaviors as agonistic, consummatory, and so forth. There is even disagreement on the question of what properties define operants as a class of response (e.g., Schick, 1971; Segal, 1972; Staddon and Simmelhag, 1971). Important as such fundamental problems are, it is obvious that empirical research cannot stop just because they are not resolved. What must be done is to broaden the scope of inquiry into different behaviors, however classified, and in this way reaffirm or limit the generalizations that stem from existing research.

Past Learning, Maturation, and Punishment

A striking feature of animal studies is that they are conducted with naive subjects; that is, organisms that have little or no significant learning history (the minimal learning experience they might have, they have in common). If animals are used that are not naive, their histories are usually known and may be deliberately manipulated as an experimental variable. For example, there have been several studies in which the influence of an organism's history of aversive stimulation on its subsequent reaction to punishment has been investigated (e.g., Abel and G. Walters, 1972; Anderson, Cole, and McVaugh, 1968; Church, 1969; Karsh, 1963; Pearl, G. Walters, and Anderson, 1964; G. Walters, 1963; G. Walters and Rogers, 1963).

The large amount of control that animal researchers can exercise over the lives of their subjects, and the ease with which they can obtain new subjects, is obviously impossible for child-development researchers. Certainly, it is feasible to undertake longitudinal experimental studies in which histories are built into children over several weeks or months, but developmental researchers cannot exercise control over their subjects to the same degree that learning researchers can—a multitude of extraexperimental events happen to a child that do not happen to animals in the laboratory. Research in child socialization, then, unlike that in learning, is made enormously complex by the richness of the past experiences of human subjects. There can be no doubt that previous experiences with discipline, for example, affect a child's reactions in an experimental study of punishment and the nature of such a relationship can only be speculated.

Consider a specific example of how a given "punishing" event can have a different meaning for and therefore a different effect upon the behavior of different children. A spanking is a relatively unpleasant physical experience, but, depending on the context and the events with which it has been paired in the past, it can be much more than that. Suppose that a father who has a warm and loving relationship with his child spanks that child and, at the same time, indicates that he is very disappointed. Future spankings may then be much more than painful stimuli; they may become conditioned stimuli for anxiety in the child, caused by fear of the loss of parental approval and love or by knowing that the parent has been hurt. For other children a spanking may mean that their parents are attempting to use physical coercion to stop their behaving in a given fashion. Instead of having feelings of anxiety and insecurity, such children experience hostility and anger. To still others, a spanking may be humiliating, leading to feelings of shame. Thus the same physical act can have various meanings, which determine the outcome of that act. Anger, shame, and fear of loss of love are emotions that no doubt have quite different effects on response elimination.

The application of a punishing stimulus to a naive organism is much more straightforward. For example, electric shock of a particular intensity and duration does not have most of the meanings that physical punishment can have for human subjects with an extensive history of socialization; there may be variability in reaction because of differences in pain threshold, prenatal environment, and so on, but to a naive organism electric shock is basically a painful stimulus. Not even the dimensions of intensity and duration, however, seem meaningful in talking about children. Parke (1969) found that a loud buzzer produced greater response inhibition in young boys than did a soft buzzer. Accordingly, loud verbal reprimands could be expected to be more effective than soft ones. Yet just the opposite has been reported (O'Leary and Becker 1968; O'Leary et al. 1970): when a teacher loudly reprimanded a child for misbehaving in the classroom, so that the other children in the room could hear the reprimand, misbehavior increased; when the reprimand was given quietly, misbehavior decreased. Obviously, the resolution of the apparent discrepancy in findings lies in the social consequences of the reprimands; it can be assumed that the loud reprimand resulted in attention and approval from the child's peers, which offset any negative consequences of the teacher's disapproval.

In spite of these differences in meaning, it must be granted that there are enough uniformities within a given culture to insure that a particular punishment has approximately the same impact on all children in that culture. In middle-class Toronto, New York, or Boston, a spanking is a spanking, a verbal reprimand a verbal reprimand. But this common cultural heritage is not the same as that of, say, Chinese children in Vancouver or black children in Birmingham, Alabama, so that what is being studied is not general principles of human development but general principles of development in a given culture. Moreover, as child-rearing fashions change, the meaning of a given event changes: for example, a spanking given in 1977 is probably something quite different from one given in 1927.

What does all this mean for research in punishment? First, a given punishing stimulus is more difficult to describe in terms of what it means to a child than to a rat. Part of its meaning for the child, however, can be teased out of studies of animals. Suppose that a relationship that has been fairly well documented in learning studies, such as the positive correlation between the intensity of punishment and the degree to which a response is suppressed, were not found to be true for children. It would then be necessary to look for variables whose effects might override the expected effects, such as the social reinforcement by peers for eliciting a loud reprimand from a teacher. Inconsistencies between the results obtained from child-development research and those from learning studies, then, enhance our understanding of the effects of past experience. Second, in doing observational studies of parent-child interactions, researchers must consider the variables that can alter the expected outcome of a given disciplinary act. Sears, Maccoby, and Levin (1957), for example, point out that, to a child whose parents are normally unaffectionate, a spanking may simply be more evidence of their lack of affection. But, to a child accustomed to being treated with warmth and affection, a spanking may indicate that their feelings have changed and perhaps is more painful than are a dozen blows to an unloved child, requiring that behavior be altered not only to avoid pain, but to regain parental approval. Sears and his colleagues, on the basis of interviews with 379 mothers about their child-rearing practices, report that physical punishment was found to be effective by 66% of the affectionate mothers who used it, whereas only 43% of the unaffectionate mothers who used it found it effective.

Finally, the problem of meaning poses some difficulty for researchers in terms of their methodology. The laboratory experiment, particularly in recent years, has played a large role in the acquisition of information about child discipline. It has been criticized for the reason that any attempt to simulate a single aspect of a naturalistic setting is certain to fail, because such a simulation gives no clues to the complicated interactions that take place in reality. Yet the precision and control afforded in an experimental setting are attractive indeed. To resolve the problem requires the use of a variety of methods of study. If naturalistic and experimental observations tally, researchers begin to feel that the conclusions they are drawing are correct. If these conclusions are confirmed by cross-cultural studies, their confidence in the correctness of their beliefs increases.

In studying punishment, researchers must take into account not only the previous experience of their subjects, but also their level of maturation: the degree to which human subjects have developed intellectually affects the way in which they respond to disciplinary action. For example, as children grow older and are capable of greater independence, they may become more resentful of parental power. Thus punishment may lose its effectiveness, and other, more subtle disciplinary techniques, such as reasoning, must be employed. The maturational level of an animal, on the other hand, probably does not have such a dramatic effect on the behaviors studied in the learning laboratory. Nevertheless, researchers tend to circumvent the problem by using mature animals as experimental subjects. Thus this problem, like that of an animal's past experience, is usually dealt with in the animal laboratory simply by eliminating it.

Just as the predominant use of a single experimental paradigm—that of building in an arbitrary operant response and then attempting to suppress it—restricts our ability to generalize from results obtained in the animal laboratory, so too does the animal researcher's lack of concern with learning history and maturational level limit what can be extrapolated. Little can be said on the basis of research about immature organisms or about those with a long history of learning. The reader should keep this limitation in mind in considering the discussions of some of the major findings in the study of punishment presented in subsequent chapters.

3

THE EFFECTS OF PUNISHMENT

In their review of punishment research in 1966, Azrin and Holz described a variety of circumstances determining the effectiveness of punishment.

> Let us summarize briefly some of the circumstances which have been found to maximize its effectiveness: (1) The punishing stimulus should be arranged in such a manner that no unauthorized escape is possible. (2) The punishing stimulus should be as intense as possible. (3) The frequency of punishment should be as high as possible. (4) The punishing stimulus should be delivered immediately after the response. (5) The punishing stimulus should not be increased gradually but introduced at maximum intensity. (6) Extended periods of punishment should be avoided, especially where low intensities of punishment are concerned, since the recovery effect may thereby occur. Where mild intensities of punishment are used, it is best to use them for only a brief period of time. (7) Great care should be taken to see that the delivery of the punishing stimulus is not differentially associated with the delivery of reinforcement. Otherwise, the punishing stimulus may acquire conditioned reinforcing properties. (8) The delivery

of the punishing stimulus should be made a signal or discriminative stimulus that a period of extinction is in progress. (9) The degree of motivation to emit the punished response should be reduced. (10) The frequency of positive reinforcement for the punished response should similarly be reduced. (11) An alternative response should be available which will produce the same or greater reinforcement as the punished response. For example, punishment of criminal behavior can be expected to be more effective if non-criminal behavior which will result in the same advantages as the behavior is available. (12) If no alternative response is available, the subject should have access to a different situation in which he obtains the same reinforcement without being punished. (13) If it is not possible to deliver the punishing stimulus itself after a response, then an effective method of punishment is still available. A conditioned stimulus may be associated with the aversive stimulus, and this conditioned stimulus may be delivered following a response to achieve conditioned punishment. (14) A reduction of positive reinforcement may be used as punishment when the use of physical punishment is not possible for practical, legal, or moral reasons. Punishment by withdrawal of positive reinforcement may be accomplished in such situations by arranging a period of reduced reinforcement frequency (time-out) or by arranging a decrease of conditioned reinforcement (response cost). Both methods require that the subject have a high level of reinforcement to begin with; otherwise, no withdrawal of reinforcement is possible. If non-physical punishment is to be used, it appears desirable to provide the subject with a substantial history of reinforcement in order to provide the opportunity for withdrawing the reinforcement as punishment for the undesired responses.*

---

*N. H. Azrin and W. C. Holz, "Punishment," in *Operant Behavior: Areas of Research and Application,* Werner K. Honig, Ed., © 1966, pp. 426–427. Reprinted by permission of Prentice-Hall, Inc., Englewood Cliffs, New Jersey.

These statements were derived primarily from empirical studies in which the effectiveness of punishment was assessed by its ability to suppress ongoing operant behavior that had been built into an organism's response repertoire by means of positive reinforcement. However, this does not mean that the circumstances listed by Azrin and Holz are necessarily restricted to such behaviors. The question of the importance of the nature of the punished behavior as a determinant of punishment effectiveness will be discussed later in this chapter. For now, these statements point to a set of conditions that, if they obtain, indicate that punishment can be a very effective response-suppression technique. This is a point of view very different from that held by many psychologists a few years ago—that is, that punishment is ineffective in altering behavior. The curious belief that reinforcement produces permanent alterations in behavior, whereas punishment results in only temporary suppressive effects—a belief that dominated the thinking of psychologists for a long time—is most likely wrong. It is true that in most instances in which the punished organism has no alternative way of achieving reinforcement but to engage in the punished behavior, recovery from punishment (i.e., resumption of the punished behavior) does occur upon removal of the punishing stimulus. However, it is also true that when reinforcement is terminated, responding diminishes—the process of experimental extinction. Thus, both reinforcement and punishment are transient in their effects. This does not mean that they cannot be used to bring about long-lasting behavioral changes—under the right circumstances, they can do just that.

Parameters of the Punishing Stimulus

We shall begin our survey of punishment research by looking at the effects of variables associated with the presentation of the punishing stimulus. These variables include severity, schedule of presentation, contingency, delay of presentation, and the nature of the punishing agent.

Severity of Punishment

Intensity: Learning Studies. The punishment of positively reinforced behavior yields a degree of response suppression directly related to the intensity of the punishing stimulus (e.g., Appel, 1963; Azrin, 1960; Camp, Raymond, and Church, 1967; Karsh, 1962). An example of the suppressive effects of a wide range of shock intensities on the key-pecking of individual pigeons for intermittent food reinforcement is shown in Figure 3-1 on page 62 (Azrin 1960); the degree to which responding is suppressed ranges from little suppression at a low intensity (60 volts) to virtually complete suppression at higher intensities (110 and 130 volts).[1] Very severe punishment has often been shown to result in the complete suppression of responding, which is not resumed for long periods and then only after the punishment contingency has not been present for several days (see Azrin and Holz, 1966). However, if the punishing stimulus is low-intensity shock, there is usually some recovery over a prolonged series of punishment sessions. Indeed, recovery during punishment may be complete if shock of very low intensity is employed and positive reinforcement of punished behavior is continued (e.g., Appel and Peterson, 1965; Azrin and Holz, 1966; G. Walters and Rogers, 1963).

Given that severe punishment is capable of producing long-term suppression of the punished response, what happens when the punishment is terminated? If the organism does not have an alternative (unpunished) means of obtaining reinforcement, the typical outcome of terminating punishment is a relatively rapid return to the prepunishment baseline of responding. In some

---

[1]Boe (1971) has reported that varying the intensity of a punishing stimulus between 50 and 110 volts produces more suppression of lever-pressing in rats than does a fixed intensity of 80 volts.

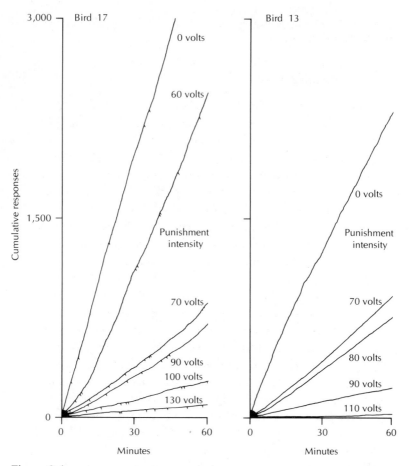

Figure 3-1
Rate of response as a function of the intensity of the punishment administered to two subjects. Each curve is a record of cumulative responses in a one-hour period of concurrent delivery of reinforcement, in the form of food, and punishment. The delivery of reinforcement is indicated by short oblique lines on the record for Bird 17 but not for Bird 13. [From N. H. Azrin, Effects of punishment intensity during variable interval reinforcement. *Journal of the Experimental Analysis of Behavior* 3(1960): 123–142. Copyright 1960 by the Society for the Experimental Analysis of Behavior, Inc.]

cases, however, when the punished response has been completely suppressed, recovery may be greatly delayed. Appel (1961), for example, found that very intense shocks produced an immediate and total suppression of responding in monkeys from which recovery took as long as 400 test hours to occur. It would seem that, after responding has been reduced to zero, the animal does not have occasion to learn that the punishment contingency is no longer in effect, and, until it takes the opportunity to test for the presence of punishment, responding will remain suppressed. However, after responding has been resumed, it generally returns to its prepunishment rate very quickly, if positive reinforcement is still available. Another example demonstrates that, even though the suppression of responding has been virtually complete, responding may return to its original strength within a single postpunishment test session (Appel and Peterson 1965). Figure 3-2 (on page 64) illustrates this general point: punishment greatly reduced the rate of responding for both rat and pigeon subjects, and yet the prepunishment rate was resumed as soon as punishment was stopped. In fact, the rate of the pigeon's postpunishment responding was higher than its prepunishment baseline. This is called *punishment contrast* (Azrin 1960; Holz and Azrin 1962).[2]

Intensity: Child-Development Studies. The assumption could be made on the basis of animal studies that the degree to which children's responses are suppressed is greater as the inten-

---

[2]The reason for the occurrence of punishment contrast is not completely clear. Probably any transition from a high punishment frequency to a lower one can produce punishment contrast, even though it is not always produced if the transition is from punishment to no punishment. Thus, such a transition is a necessary but not a sufficient condition for punishment contrast to occur. Punishment contrast is important because it demonstrates that punishment may result in a temporary *increase* in the output of the punished behavior once punishment is no longer in force (see Azrin and Holz, 1966, for a discussion of this topic).

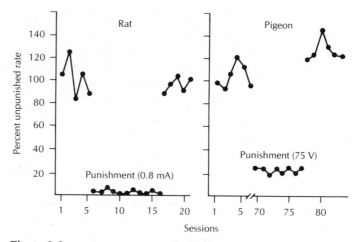

Figure 3-2
Average performance of rats and pigeons before, during, and after
relatively severe punishment. The pigeon data are from Azrin and
Holz (1961) and the rat data are unpublished. [Reprinted with
permission of authors and publisher from J. B. Appel and N. J.
Peterson, Punishment: Effects of shock intensity on response suppression. *Psychological Reports* 16(1965):721–730, Figure 5.]

sity of the punishment administered is increased. The situation is
not as straightforward as this, however. In our very first attempt
to compare findings from the two lines of current inquiry it will
become clear that the picture is complicated by at least two
factors. First, the paradigm used by child-development researchers to study the effects of such parameters as intensity has differed from that employed by researchers in the operant laboratory, and results have differed accordingly. Second, as soon as
some sort of cognitive structuring (e.g., a statement that tells the
child which behavior is prohibited) is introduced, the effects of
intensity differ from what they would be in its absence.

Although correlational studies have been made of the child-
rearing practices of parents in an attempt to assess the effects of
the intensity of punishment on suppression of responding, a de-

scription of their findings would not be very helpful for this discussion because intensity ratings have been confounded with such things as duration and consistency. A number of studies have been conducted within the laboratory, however, and their results are somewhat easier to evaluate. The general format of these studies has been to arrange a series of trials in which a child is punished for selecting one of a pair of toys by being subjected to noise (ranging over subjects from approximately 52 to 96 decibels), sometimes with the addition of verbal rebuke and/or the loss of a candy. The child is then left alone with toys that are identical with or similar to the prohibited one and, sometimes, with the one that is not prohibited as well. The latency of punished behavior (i.e., how much time elapses before the child touches the prohibited toy), the number of times the child plays with it, and the amount of time the child plays with it are then assessed. Such a format is more complex than the free operant one that has so far formed the basis for our statements about punishment intensity. Moreover, in child-development studies, unlike animal studies, testing for response suppression is carried out in the experimenter's absence; thus the testing conditions are very different from those in which training was done. In some studies, data are collected on speed of learning during training, but, in most studies, the emphasis is on whether the child resists playing with the prohibited toy during the experimenter's absence.

Data on the intensity of punishment and on the speed with which the subject learns to discriminate during training do not always indicate a relationship between the two (e.g., Aronfreed and Leff, 1963; Leff, 1969), although this may reflect a lack of sensitivity of the response measure to punishment parameters because learning occurs so quickly. Response suppression in the absence of the person who punishes the child is greater if the intensity of the punishment is high than if it is low, a finding reported by Aronfreed and Leff (1963) for a simple discrimination task and by Cheyne, Goyeche, and R. Walters (1969) and Parke and R. Walters (1967). However, Aronfreed and Leff report that, if the task is a difficult one, response suppression in the experimenter's absence is greater if the intensity of the punishment is low rather than high. They suggest that subjects are so anxious if the intensity is high that punishment takes on the quality of reinforcement as an event that terminates this anxiety.

The introduction of cognitive structuring—telling the subject immediately after punishment that a particular toy should not be played with—also seems to modify the relationship between intensity of punishment and response suppression. Independent of intensity, in fact, cognitive structuring, or supplying rules, has an overall suppressive effect on responding simply by making the relationship between punishment and responding clearer. But the inclusion of cognitive structuring in a punishment procedure seems to make punishment of moderate intensity more effective than punishment of high or low intensity (Cheyne, Goyeche, and R. Walters 1969). Cheyne and his colleagues suggest that intense punishment produces a defensive reaction that prevents the utilization of information contained in the experimenter's instructions.

In a different experimental paradigm, J. Freedman (1965) threatened one group of children with mild disapproval and another with severe disapproval for touching an attractive toy. Both groups complied with the experimenter's prohibition in a test given immediately, whether or not they were under surveillance. One month later, however, children for whom the punishment had been mild touched the prohibited toy *less,* in the absence of surveillance, than did those for whom the punishment had been severe. Freedman suggested that the children who were threatened only mildly had insufficient justification for their immediate compliance and so were placed in a state of cognitive dissonance, which they resolved by subsequently becoming less interested in engaging in the forbidden activity. Recently, Ebbesen, Bowers, Phillips, and Snyder (1975) have suggested that Freedman's results may not be due to a reduction in dissonance; rather they may be a reflection of attempts to cope with the frustration of temptation. In their view, severe disapproval keeps children from thinking about the forbidden toy, whereas mild disapproval does not. In an attempt to reduce the frustration engendered by the latter, the toy is subjectively devalued and hence played with less. Their data, however, indicate that other mechanisms may contribute to the results they obtained as well.

Whatever the explanation, it is clear that with the use of the paradigm employed by Freedman researchers are entering an area of child behavior for which there is no apparent animal analogue. They are faced with the task of finding a more complex explanation of the role of cognitive processes than the mere provision of information about relationships between punishment and responding. We shall have a great deal more to say about the problem in Chapters 5 and 6. For now, we shall merely make a few observations about Freedman's study. First, it should be noted that there was no immediate transgression in either group. This suggests that the prohibited activity may not have aroused the children's interest very much and, had the temptation to deviate been greater, the results may not have been the same. Second, the nature of the punishment, involving as it did personal displeasure on the part of the experimenter, was quite different from the use of a tone or a buzzer. Freedman looked at the long-term effects of punishment as well. Perhaps similar findings would have emerged in the kind of paradigm employed by Aronfreed and Walters and their associates. Whatever the outcome, it is evident that the relationship between intensity of punishment and response suppression so well documented in the learning laboratory may hold up less well in child-development studies.

Duration of Punishment. The effects of duration of the punishing stimulus on response suppression are more straightforward than those of intensity, perhaps only because there are fewer data with which to deal. It should be noted that there are punishing stimuli, such as the withdrawal of a privilege or a verbal rebuke, for which duration cannot be manipulated.

A good example of how duration affects the results obtained in the animal laboratory can be seen in a study by Church, Raymond, and Beauchamp (1967), whose data are shown in Figure 3-3. In this study, rats were trained to lever-press for food reinforcement and then punished with shock of low intensity delivered on an intermittent punishment schedule. The degree of suppression resulting from punishment was directly related to the duration of the punishment. Similarly, White, Nielsen, and Johnson (1972) found that time-out lasting 15 or 30 minutes was more effective in the suppression of aggression, tantrums, and self-destructive behavior in institutionalized retarded children than was time-out lasting one minute, although punishment of one minute's duration was very effective if the subjects were being exposed to the punishing stimulus for the first time.

If the punishing stimuli being used are not physical, such as the withdrawal of love, duration may consist of minutes, hours, or even days. There are no data with which to assess the effectiveness of punishment of very long duration or to determine how such punishment affects an organism's attempt to so respond as to terminate it. In addition, during prolonged periods of punishment, responses that would ordinarily be reinforced would be made while punishment was being administered. Such considerations add to the complexity of the problem.

Some investigators have used the term severity to refer to the interaction of the intensity and duration of the punishing

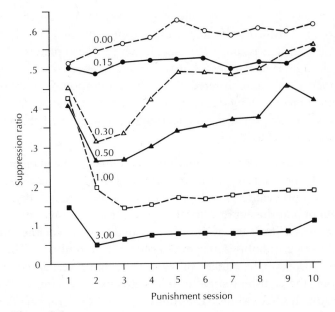

Figure 3-3
Mean suppression ratio as a function of duration of punishment in seconds. [From R. M. Church, G. A. Raymond, and R. D. Beauchamp, Response suppression as a function of intensity and duration of punishment. *Journal of Comparative and Physiological Psychology* 63(1967):39–44. Copyright 1967 by the American Psychological Association. Reprinted by permission.]

stimulus (see Church, 1969; Hull and Klugh, 1973). However, even when the suppressive effects of these variables are similar, it does not necessarily follow that the similarity is produced by the same behavioral mechanisms. For example, it is well known that a motor response produced by a brief intense shock is quite different from that produced by a longer shock of moderate intensity. Thus, different motor responses elicited by shocks of differing intensities and duration could be a factor in modulating the effects of these two punishment variables (see, for example, Goodman, Dyal, Zinser, and Golub, 1966). Furthermore, the termination of a shock of long duration is likely to coincide with the completion of a well-organized response, but this is less likely to occur if the shock being administered is of short duration. Therefore, punishment of long duration can be expected to suppress responding by promoting the learning of new escape behavior, which it usually does.

Introduction of the Punishing Stimulus. The manner in which the punishing stimulus is introduced into the experimental procedure must be taken into account in any discussion of punishment severity. The absolute suppressive effect of any given intensity of punishment depends on whether the punishing stimulus is introduced suddenly or gradually. There are, for example, studies showing that, under certain conditions, the punishing stimulus is less effective if it is introduced gradually. N.E. Miller (1960) has reported that, for rats that have been exposed to a series of shocks that gradually increase in intensity, the effectiveness of subsequent intense punishment of approach behavior in an alleyway is decreased. However, this result seems to hold only if the series of shocks to which the rats are exposed have been given in the goalbox in which the hungry animals received food (see also Feirstein and N.E. Miller, 1963; Karsh, 1963; Masserman, 1946).[3]

---

[3]Miller argued that these results could be explained by counterconditioning; that is, rewarding the animal in the presence of the fear-eliciting shocks. However, there also is evidence that, in classical conditioning, previous exposure to gradually increasing shocks reduces the magnitude of the unconditioned cardiac response to a shock of high intensity presented as an unconditioned stimulus (Church et al. 1966). Church and his colleagues suggest that the previous exposure alone functions to reduce the *subjective severity* of later intense shocks, thus accounting for Miller's results. Yet, in his study, Miller did include a group of animals that had been subjected to shocks of gradually increasing intensity outside of the goalbox in which reward was received. The effectiveness of intense shocks administered to these animals later was not diminished.

Schedules of Presentation of the Punishing Stimulus

As noted earlier, schedules for the delivery of punishment, like those of reinforcement, vary, and the schedule of punishment, like the schedule of positive reinforcement, is an important determinant of the amount or kind of response suppression produced. A schedule of punishment is simply a rule that describes the way in which the delivery of the punishing stimulus is related to an organism's responses. A schedule in which punishment follows a fixed number of responses is known as a fixed-ratio (FR) schedule. The simplest schedule is one in which the punishing stimulus is delivered for each response—called an FR 1 schedule. The general conclusion to be drawn about fixed-ratio punishment is that the more frequently the punishing stimulus is presented, the greater is the degree of response suppression. This is illustrated in a study by Azrin, Holz, and Hake (1963) in which responding was maintained by a variable-interval schedule of food reinforcement and subsequently punished according to schedules ranging from FR 1 to FR 1,000. Figure 3-4 (on page 72) shows the orderly relationship between responding and the density of punishment, *density* being the number of shocks presented per unit of time. Note also the uniformity of the rate of response for each FR schedule—overall response rate is affected without changing the basic pattern of responding maintained by the reinforcement schedule. Other research has supported this general conclusion, including work done with human subjects on the punishment of the spontaneous electrodermal response (Crider, Schwartz, and Shapiro 1970). Further, studies in which pigeons are subjected to time-out punishment (Zimmerman and Ferster 1963) and others in which human subjects are punished by means of time-out (Zimmerman and Baydan 1963) also have demonstrated that continuous punishment is more effective than intermittent punishment.

Another way of scheduling punishment is to present the punishing stimulus contingent upon a response but after a given

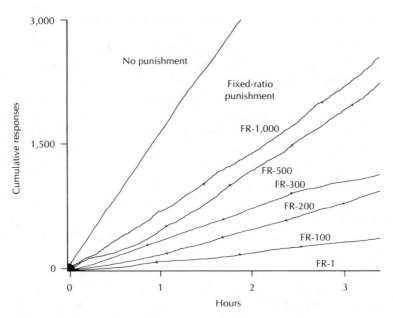

Figure 3-4
Rates of responding maintained by a 3-minute variable-interval schedule of food reinforcement while punishment is delivered according to the FR schedules indicated. Short oblique lines indicate delivery of punishment (240 volts). [From N. H. Azrin, W. C. Holz, and D. F. Hake, Fixed-ratio punishment. *Journal for the Experimental Analysis of Behavior* 6(1963):141–148. Copyright 1963 by the Society for the Experimental Analysis of Behavior, Inc.]

amount of time (which is constant for the entire experiment) has elapsed since the last punished response—a schedule known as a fixed-interval (FI) schedule. The characteristic effect of FI punishment is the development of *anticipatory* suppression (Azrin 1956); that is, after a few punishment sessions, rate of responding is most affected about the time the punishing stimulus is scheduled to occur. In this way FI punishment produces a characteristic pattern of responding within any given punishment session.

If the presentation of the punishing stimulus is less predictable, such as on a variable-interval (VI) schedule, the rate of responding is generally unaffected by differences in absolute frequency of presentation unless the punishing stimulus is shock of high intensity, in which case the response is completely suppressed (Filbey and Appel 1966).

Although relatively little work has been done on schedules of punishment in the learning laboratory, that which has been done indicates that scheduling can be a major determinant of its effectiveness. Clearly, the effects of schedules of punishment on response suppression are open to the same kind of precise investigation that has been undertaken on the effects of schedules of reinforcement on response maintenance.

There have been few studies of the effects of intermittent punishment reported by child-development researchers, and none in which different types of schedules have been compared, as has been done by learning researchers. Moreover, the results of one of the few studies of intermittent punishment were confounded by the fact that reinforcement for responding was discontinued at the same time that punishment was introduced. In this study, Parke and Deur (1972) trained boys to punch a Bobo doll by giving them marbles as reinforcement. They found that those who were then punished by being subjected to the sound of a loud buzzer *after they were no longer receiving reinforcement* stopped their aggressive behavior sooner than those who heard the buzzer on half the trials and received marbles on half the trials. In another study, in which the results were not confounded, Leff (1969) reported that children who received continuous punishment learned to choose an unattractive over an attractive toy faster than those who were punished on only half the trials, although there was no difference between the two groups in the degree of transgression when left alone.

An interesting extension of the aforementioned work on consistency of punishment deals with the effects of intermittent punishment and reinforcement on subsequent persistence of responding under conditions of continuous punishment and extinction combined. Banks (1966), for example, found that rats who had received intermittent punishment while being reinforced for lever-pressing continued to press for a longer time when they were continuously punished than did rats who had not been punished occasionally during acquisition. Similarly, boys who were being punished for hitting a Bobo doll took longer to stop hitting the doll if they had previously been both reinforced and punished for the response than if they had received only reinforcement for it (Deur and Parke 1970). This phenomenon has been explained by an extension of Amsel's (1958) theory of frustrative nonreward; that is, that anticipatory punishment becomes conditioned to stimuli preceding reward and thus eventually becomes a cue for approach. Another explanation for the finding is that organisms that are punished while receiving reinforcement take longer to discriminate that the reinforcement contingencies have changed than do organisms that are not subjected to punishment until the extinction procedure is introduced.

In summary, primarily on the basis of data from studies of animals, it can probably be concluded that continuous punishment more effectively suppresses responding than does intermittent punishment. The application of this conclusion to child-rearing is self-evident: parents who have decided to punish a child for behaving in a specific way should be consistent in their practices. Correlational studies support this conclusion, although the definitions of inconsistency employed are vague and subject to change. Glueck and Glueck (1950) and McCord, McCord, and Zola (1959), for example, have reported that erratic discipline and a mixture of punitiveness and permissiveness seem to be more characteristic of the parents of delinquent boys than of the parents of boys who are not delinquent.

Punishment Compared with the Noncontingent Delivery of an Aversive Stimulus

Implicit in any definition of punishment is the assumption that there is a direct relationship between the occurrence of a response and the presentation of an aversive stimulus. But must the presentation of that stimulus necessarily be contingent on the occurrence of the behavior to be punished in order to suppress it? Or could its presentation be random? Further, which of the two procedures produces the greater amount of response suppression and which the most enduring?

Animal Studies. There is evidence from the early work of Estes (1944, Experiment 1) that noncontingent shock superimposed on a food-reinforced lever-pressing response produces a greater decrease in responding than that produced if no shock is used. Church (1969) compared the effects of five different intensities of noncontingent shock on lever-pressing for food reinforcement and reported that response suppression increases with increasing intensity. Clearly, noncontingent shock does lead to suppression of behavior, but comparisons of the effects of contingent and noncontingent shock support the conclusion that, at least for responding supported by positive reinforcement, suppression is greater with punishment than with a noncontingent-shock procedure (e.g., Azrin, 1956; Camp, Raymond, and Church, 1967; Church, 1969; Church, Wooton, and Matthews, 1970; Frankel, 1975; Quinsey, 1972).

More recently, Kadden (1973) trained monkeys to perform a shock-avoidance task. After the animals had learned the task, their performance of it resulted in the delivery of shocks. Individual animals were successively exposed to shock ranging on a contingency continuum from completely noncontingent to punishment. Response suppression increased as shock delivery became increasingly more response-dependent; that is, approximating a punishment procedure. An interesting sidelight of Kadden's study is that, before the shock-avoidance behavior showed signs of suppression, it was facilitated by all shocks presented, with the greatest facilitation occurring when their presensation was totally contingent on responding. Since such results are not obtained in studies of behavior maintained by positive reinforcement, this work suggests that the nature of the punished response itself is an important determinant of the effects of aversive stimuli.

Schuster and Rachlin (1968) have demonstrated that under certain conditions animals may prefer contingent to noncontingent shock, even though the former produces greater response suppression. In their study, a pigeon was trained to peck two keys for which it received identical variable-interval reinforcement. The procedure (a concurrent-chain schedule) was such that, although both keys were simultaneously available at the beginning of a trial, a peck on one key deactivated the second key so that the bird would have to continue pecking the first key in order to obtain reinforcement. After a key had been chosen, the reinforcement schedule remained in effect, but either punishment or a series of noncontingent shocks was added to the program, depending on the key chosen. After a five-minute interval of reinforcement and shocks, the procedure was started over again, with the bird given the opportunity to choose one of the two keys. In this manner Schuster and Rachlin were able not only to assess whether contingent or noncontingent shock led to greater suppression, but to determine the effects of the two conditions on the choice that the bird made. The results clearly showed that punishment caused much greater suppression than noncontingent shock, as would be expected. However, which key was chosen in any given trial, was determined on the basis of the density of the shock programmed for a given key. In other words, when shocks of differing densities were tested the pigeons preferred the key for which the rate at which the shock was presented was lower regardless of whether the shock was dependent on responding. Thus, even though the suppression of responding was greater if the bird pecked the key for which punishment had been programmed, that key would be chosen if the response-contingent schedule consisted of fewer shocks than did the noncontingent key.

Child-Development Studies. There has been no direct assessment of the effects of noncontingent aversive stimulation on response suppression in children. A study by Morris, Marshall, and R. Miller (1973), however, supplies material for speculation about them. In this study, six- and seven-year-old girls watched movies of peers who refused to share. In one movie, the peer model was punished for this refusal by being reprimanded and told to leave the room; in another movie, there was no punishment. Girls who had seen the model punished shared more than those who had observed the unpunished model. The amount of sharing also increased among girls who saw a model receive the same punishment as that administered in one of the movies but were given no indication of the reason for the punishment, which might be considered an example of noncontingent aversive stimulation. The many differences between this study and the animal studies discussed in the preceding section are very apparent. First, the aversive stimulation in this study was vicarious rather than direct (i.e., punishment was delivered to someone other than the subject). Second, the aversive stimulation was much less intense—a mild verbal rebuke and a request to leave the room—and was presented once rather than repeatedly. In learning studies, it is generally assumed that animals that receive intense noncontingent aversive stimulation are emotionally aroused and that this arousal disrupts behavior and is therefore responsible for whatever suppression of responding does occur. However, this was probably not what was happening in the study by Morris, Marshall, and R. Miller, who suggest that the children observed the model so as to find out how they themselves should behave. Those who saw a model being punished for not sharing learned that they were expected to share; however, for those who watched a model receiving noncontingent aversive stimulation, the information was much less specific, and so they may have decided to avoid engaging in any behavior that was likely to be punished. And refusing to share would obviously be such a behavior. In a second experiment, girls who saw a model receive noncontingent aversive stimulation were more willing to help the experimenter than were those who had seen the model receive no consequences for refusing to share, probably presuming that a refusal to help also might lead to punishment. In keeping with their explanation, Morris and his colleagues found that subjects were not more willing to help after watching a model being punished for not sharing. These children knew why the model had been punished, and so it was not necessary for them to take the precaution of engaging in all manner of prosocial behaviors.

There is a difference, however, between not knowing why a model has been punished—presumably the case in the study by Morris and his colleagues—and knowing that a model has received a series of punishments for no reason. The latter situation comes closer to what is generally involved in the noncontingent presentaton of aversive stimulation. It may be that similar results are obtained under both sets of circumstances; that is, children increasingly engage in prosocial behavior in the hope of avoiding punishment. But suppose that prosocial behavior was occasionally followed by negative consequences, which would have to happen if delivery of the aversive stimulus were truly random. Perhaps suppression of all behavior would be the eventual outcome, but at present there is no evidence to substantiate this. Nor is it known whether there would be any difference in the effects of noncontingent aversive stimuli if applied directly to the child rather than to a model. This is a subject to which developmental researchers have not yet addressed themselves. Although children in real life are not frequently exposed to noncontingent aversive stimulation, a knowledge of its effects should aid in understanding the mechanisms of punishment.

The Conditioned Emotional Response. Suppose that a rat were placed in a chamber and, independent of its engaging in any specific behavior and without warning, a few intense electric shocks were delivered. At first the rat would make a few attempts to escape from the chamber, but then its behavior between shock presentations would consist largely of immobility—crouching, or "freezing"—one of the typical responses of laboratory rats to the presentation of aversive stimuli in inescapable environments. If the animal were then removed from the chamber and returned to it later without the presentation of shock, it would behave in a similar way. This would indicate that the static cues of the chamber—its physical characteristics—had become conditioned stimuli for the elicitation of such behaviors, which have been referred to as emotional or fear-produced. If each presentation of shock were then preceded by a three-minute tone, this "emotional display" would soon be seen mainly for the duration of the tone—a very specific pattern in which a conditioned emotional response is tied to a specific stimulus administered in the chamber. Many investigators have studied this situation—a special case of noncontingent aversive stimulation—in a standardized experimental setting called the conditioned emotional response (CER) paradigm. This paradigm is of interest to psychologists studying the effects of punishment because it shows that ongoing behavior can be suppressed in the presence of certain stimuli that have been associated with aversiveness when these stimuli are applied in a noncontingent manner.

The study of the conditioned emotional response has its origin in the work of Estes and Skinner (1941). It is often considered a way of isolating the emotional, rather than instrumental or cue, components in response suppression. A number of tones, each followed by an electric shock, is presented to an animal. Subsequently, when the animal is lever-pressing for reinforcement, the tone is sounded and the lever-pressing response is suppressed for the duration of the tone and is resumed with the cessation of the tone. Such selective elimination of responding is termed *conditioned suppression.*

As would be expected, the response-independent CER procedure is not as effective as punishment (Hulse, Deese, and Egeth 1975; Myer 1971). Church (1969), however, has indicated that the amount of suppression produced by a CER procedure is no different from that produced by a discriminative punishment procedure—that is, one in which an experimenter-controlled signal such as a light or tone "sets up" the occasion for a response to be followed by punishment.

Conclusion. Studies of noncontingent aversive stimulation, including those of the conditioned emotional response, show that there is a strong case to be made for the superiority of punishment over noncontingent aversive stimulation as a response-suppression technique.[4] Behavior suppression is most successful in cases in which the punishing stimulus serves as an unambiguous cue signalling that a specific response is being isolated as the one that "produced" the punishment. The value of the punishing stimulus as a carrier

---

[4]However, these studies are hampered by methodological problems that make their comparison somewhat forbidding (e.g., see Church, 1969, and Myer, 1971, for a discussion of the problems in the often used yoked-control technique for studying contingency effects).

of information is undoubtedly of great importance in determining the effectiveness of punishment. Its importance will become evident in a later discussion of response facilitation by punishment.

Delay of Punishment

Does the interval between the occurrence of the to-be-punished response and the presentation of the punishing stimulus affect the outcome of a punishment procedure? In other words, is the contiguity of response and punishment an important variable?

Although punishment can always immediately follow a given response in the laboratory, the natural environment of an organism is not so arranged that punishment always automatically follows a response. Thus, it is reasonable to inquire into the effects of a simple delay procedure. Theories of learning that emphasize the acquisition of associative relationships as fundamental to the learning process have traditionally required close temporal contiguity of response and reinforcer for learning to occur. According to such theories, learning becomes degraded as the amount of time between a given response and reinforcement increases. There is support for the similar contention that the effectiveness of punishment decreases as the time between a response and the presentation of the punishing stimulus increases. For example, Baron (1965) trained thirsty rats to run an alleyway for water reinforcement. After the behavior had become established, the rats were divided into groups and punished for entering the goalbox; the delivery of shock ranged from 0 to 30 seconds after entry and each group was punished at one of five different intervals of delay. Although the performance of all the animals was disrupted to a degree, the effectiveness of punishment was found to decrease as a monotonic function of the interval of delay (see also Camp, Raymond, and Church, 1967; Myer and Ricci, 1968). Similar results were obtained in several other studies in which subjects were working for positive reinforcement. In one study, in which the subjects were human adults, punishment delays ranged from 30 to 120 seconds (Banks and Vogel-Sprott 1965); in another, in which the subjects were college students, punishment delays ranged from 10 to 40 seconds (Trenholme and Baron 1975); and, in yet another, in which the subjects were children, punishment was presented 0, 10, or 30 seconds after responding (R. Walters 1964).

When negative reinforcement has been used to acquire and maintain the subsequently punished response, such as in studies of avoidance learning, delay gradients similar to those found for positively reinforced behaviors are also obtained (Baron, Kaufman, and Fazzini 1969; Kamin 1959; Misanin, Campbell, and Smith 1966).

The results of studies in which the presentation of the stimulus is delayed have frequently been accepted as support for the proposition that the effects of the delay of punishment, along with those of a variety of other independent variables such as intensity and contingency, on punished behavior are analogous but opposite to the effects of such variables on positively reinforced behavior. As will be apparent in a discussion of theories of punishment later in this chapter, this presumed equivalence is considered by some to offer strong support for the return of a form of the negative law of effect, which would mean that we have come full circle to a modified version of Thorndike's original law of effect.

It should be noted that Myer (1971), in reviewing the literature on the delay of punishment, has listed exceptions to the typical effect of delay. He argued that there are some behaviors (e.g., consummatory responses), which he terms "continuing" behaviors, for which the response is not as discrete as such operant behaviors as a lever-press or key-peck. The delayed punishment of a continuing behavior may mean that part of the designated response is still being emitted when punishment is finally administered. One would expect that in such cases short delays would be as effective as immediate punishment. Myer cites work by Solomon, Turner, and Lessac (1968), in which dogs were punished for consummatory behavior, and his own work dealing with the punishment of rats for mouse-attack behavior as support for this argument. Certainly this work emphasizes the importance of knowing what kind of behavior is being punished in any given experimental situation.

Delay of Punishment and the Solomon Paradigm. The work of Solomon, Turner, and Lessac serves as an introduction to a series of studies that constitutes most of the work done on delay by child-development researchers. In the study by Solomon and his colleagues, food-deprived puppies were swatted either as they approached a bowl of forbidden horsemeat or several seconds after they had begun to eat it. There was no difference in the rate at which the dogs learned not to eat the horsemeat in the presence of the experimenter. However, for puppies punished early in the eating sequence, the suppression of eating when they were alone later was greater than for those punished late in the eating sequence. (Interestingly enough, parallel results have been obtained in studies of operant lever-pressing. Dardano and Sauerbrunn [1964] have reported that the punishment of responses in the early part of an FR chain is more effective than that in the middle or end of the chain [see also Church, 1969; Dardano, 1970, 1972a, 1972b].)

Early reports of the Solomon work inspired a number of attempts by child-development researchers to replicate his findings. The basic procedure used in these studies was to punish a child for choosing one of a pair of toys, either in reaching for it or after picking it up. The effects of delaying punishment on the rate at which the children learned to discriminate varied. Aronfreed and Reber (1965) reported faster learning when punishment was delivered immediately than when it was delayed, whereas Parke and R. Walters (1967) and R. Walters, Parke, and Cane (1965) reported no effect of delay on learning—a replication of the findings in the studies in which dogs were the subjects. In the absence of the experimenter, however, suppression of the responses of children who were punished early was greater than for those who were punished late. Moreover, as in the study by Solomon and his colleagues, amount of deviation seemed to correlate with the length of delay (Aronfreed 1968).

Similar explanations of the effect of timing have been given for both the animal and the child-development studies. It has been suggested that anxiety becomes classically conditioned to the proprioceptive stimuli produced by the response that is punished, and, in children, to its cognitive representations as well. When punishment is delivered early, anxiety is produced as soon as the organism begins to deviate, and this anxiety is reduced by response suppression; when it is delivered late, anxiety is not produced until the punished behavior is well under way, and so there is less likelihood that responding will be suppressed because anxiety has not been paired with the initiation of responding.

There may well be other, better explanations for the finding. Note, for example, that subjects for whom punishment was delivered late received reinforcement for the deviant response—the puppies ate some of the horsemeat and the children played briefly with the toy—before they were punished. Thus it could be expected that there would be less suppression of responding than would be obtained if the subjects had not received reinforcement. Bandura (1969) has pointed out that a person who reprimands a child as the child starts to engage in deviant behavior may be considered by that child to be more forbidding, punitive, and consistent than someone who does not indicate disapproval until the behavior has been going on for some time. This may well cause the child to decide that it might be wise to avoid future deviation. Cheyne (1971) recorded the heart rate of his subjects during punishment and found cardiac acceleration to be greater when the delivery of punishment was early than when its delivery was late. He suggested that early punishment may be more startling and disruptive, and therefore more anxiety-inducing, because children are interrupted before the completion of a response. Mandler (1964) has argued that interruption of an ongoing response can induce anxiety.

The effects of the timing of punishment also depend on the intensity of punishment. Cheyne and R. Walters (1969) and Parke (1969) found that timing affected response suppression if the intensity of punishment was low, but not if it was high. Their suggestion is that anxiety aroused by high intensities of punishment is great enough to extend the generalization gradient of suppression to response-produced stimuli that accompany the initiation of transgression.

The effects of delaying punishment are negated by the introduction of cognitive structuring: for example, after they have been punished, subjects are told not to touch or play with certain toys because the experimenter does not have any more like them and is afraid they might become worn out or broken (Cheyne and R. Walters 1969; Parke 1969). The fact that cognitive structuring can alter the effects of both intensity and delay of punishment has led to the hypothesis that a child's self-control has two sources: it is generated by internal responses (conditioned anxiety) to anticipated deviation and it is based on the knowledge that anticipated acts are instances of socially disapproved behavior (e.g., Cheyne and R. Walters, 1970). When children are told, for example, that certain toys are not to be played with because they cannot be replaced, they are given a general principle on which to base their behavior, and so the effects of such variables as timing and intensity can be overridden or modified.[5] When no cognitive structuring is provided, subjects learn only

---

[5]We suggest that behavior can be suppressed by the statement of a general principle if the child has previously been punished for failing to obey general principles. The ways in which reasons or rules can govern behavior will be discussed at some length in Chapter 5.

that if they attempt to play with certain toys they will be punished. In this case, the specific relationships between timing, intensity, and anxiety play a more important role in suppression of responding. The distinction between suppression based on conditioned anxiety and that based on adherence to general principles allows the prediction that response suppression produced by cognitive structuring will be more stable over time. In the absence of cognitive structuring, deviations after the punishing agent is no longer present to administer punishment should eventually lead to a reduction in anxiety. Accordingly, the incidence of deviation should increase over time. On the other hand, the omission of punishment for a deviation that has been classified as belonging to a forbidden class should not change a child's knowledge that the behavior is prohibited, and so suppression should be more stable. Figure 3-5 demonstrates this relationship. Under conditions in which the degree of cognitive structure is low, deviation generally increases during each 5-minute period, whereas, under conditions in which it is high, deviation tends not to increase.

Delay of Punishment after Completion of Transgression. Situations in which punishment is delivered either early or late in the performance of a deviant act no doubt occur naturally. But it is not evident that this kind of delay is the most important or frequent one encountered by children. For that reason it is somewhat remarkable that so little attention has been paid by child-development researchers to the problem of punishment delays after the deviation has been completed. It does not seem particularly difficult for organisms to learn the relationship between a response and punishment if punishment is delivered in the course of the deviant behavior. But an interval between the completion of an act and its negative consequences—a matter of hours would not be unusual—may well be detrimental to the learning of some relationships. Obvi-

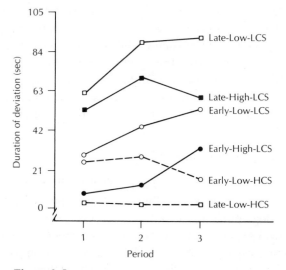

Figure 3-5
Change in duration of deviation over three 5-minute periods, as determined by timing of delivery of punishment (late or early), its intensity (high or low), and degree of cognitive structuring (high, HCS; low, LCS). [From J. A. Cheyne and R. H. Walters, Intensity of punishment, timing of punishment, and cognitive structure as determinants of response inhibition. *Journal of Experimental Child Psychology* 7(1969):231–244. Copyright 1969 by Academic Press.]

ously, such a gap can be bridged by children by means of a symbolic reinstatement of transgression (e.g., by hearing the misdeed described or by thinking about the misdeed).

In a study by Andres (1967), children were punished by being subjected to the sound of a loud buzzer in the same place where they had broken a toy four hours earlier. Children who saw a videotape of themselves breaking the toy or who heard the experimenter describe the incident subsequently played less with a toy similar to the broken one than did those who were merely subjected to the sound of the buzzer. Unfortunately, this study did not include a group that was punished immediately after breaking the toy. Interestingly, children who were told to re-break the repaired toy subsequently deviated somewhat more than did those who saw the videotape and had been subjected to the sound of the buzzer, perhaps because being told to recreate the act led them to perceive it as a less serious one.

The Nature of the Punishing Agent

In studies in which rats are the subjects, the delivery of a punishing stimulus is impersonal. However, if the subjects are children or even dogs, punishment, with very few exceptions, is obviously mediated by someone. Overeating and its consequent discomfort and being careless and falling downstairs are examples of an activity that has nonmediated consequences. But most of the consequences of a child's misbehavior require that a socializing agent administer the punishment, and the relationship between the socializing agent and the recipient of punishment has a marked influence on the effectiveness of punishment.

Two studies demonstrate the importance of this relationship. Parke and R. Walters (1967) studied a group of children who had spent a 10-minute period on each of two consecutive days interacting with a friendly adult. Compared with another group of children who had not had such an interaction, the first group was better able to resist temptation after having been punished by being subjected to the harsh tone of a buzzer. (This effect is attenuated, as is that of other variables such as intensity and timing, under conditions in which there is a high degree of cognitive structure [Parke 1969].) Presumably, a friendly socializing agent can use punishment effectively because the punishment increases in subjective intensity for the child who is accustomed to a generally positive interaction. It might be expected that someone who is generally punitive would be less effective in producing resistance to deviation, though G. Patterson (1965) reported the opposite: in a seminaturalistic setting, boys whose parents were punitive and restrictive changed their responding on a simple motor task more readily when they received disapproval from their parents than did boys whose parents were not punitive.

Carlsmith, Lepper, and Landauer (1974) have shown that children are more likely to comply with a request from a rewarding experimenter than from a punitive one; this holds, however, only when the children are relaxed, and not when they are anxious. If they are anxious, children are more compliant with punitive experimenters. Although reactions to requests for compliance and reactions to punishment may differ, these findings suggest that the state of the child be considered in attempting to assess the effects of the characteristics of the punishing agent on punishment effectiveness. Such a consideration may help to account for the apparently discrepant finding of Patterson noted above. He found that parents rated the boys who responded well to social disapproval as more ineffective and immature than those who responded less well. To the extent that these characteristics correlate with a negative emotional state, then, Patterson's finding is more easily understood.

It is evident from our survey of the effects of various parameters of the punishing stimulus on response suppression that the approaches and interests of investigators conducting studies in learning and child development differ enough to limit any attempt to integrate their findings. The difference in interest will become even more apparent in the next four sections of this chapter. The first section deals with the question of how punishment interacts with variables that support the maintenance of the punished behavior; the second with how punishment can facilitate behavior; the third with how the nature of the punished response affects punishment; and the fourth with whether learning is facilitated by the punishment of incorrect behavior or by the reinforcement of correct behavior. With few exceptions, material covered in the first three sections comes from animal studies; investigations pertinent to the fourth section have all been conducted with children.

Positive Reinforcement Variables and Punishment

Given that most of the research on punishment has concentrated on the study of behaviors established by positive reinforcement, it is not surprising that many investigators have been concerned with the question of how punishment interacts with variables supporting the maintenance of the punished behavior. In this section, we shall explore the relationship between the effectiveness of punishment and (1) the schedule of reinforcement; (2) the frequency of reinforcement, particularly the extreme case in which reinforcement maintaining the punished behavior is removed, as in experimental extinction; (3) the strength of the punished response; (4) the organism's motivation to respond; and (5) the availability of an alternative unpunished response, which also leads to reinforcement.

Punishment and Positive Reinforcement Schedules

In most experimental work, punishment is used to counter the response-maintaining properties of concurrent reinforcement, the outcome usually being response suppression. However, as indicated by Azrin and Holz (1966), the effect of punishment, except that which is very severe, on the number of reinforcements obtained depends on the schedule of reinforcement employed, and it is the number of reinforcements obtained that affects the eventual strength of the punished response. If interval schedules are used, especially the variable-interval schedule, the number of responses greatly exceeds that needed to obtain the maximum number of programmed reinforcements. Thus, although punishment does reduce the rate of responding maintained by such schedules, the number of reinforcements obtained is usually unchanged or is affected only a little.

This is not true if ratio schedules are used, in which case the number of reinforcements is linked closely to the number of responses. In a fixed-ratio schedule of reinforcement, there is a characteristic pause in responding after each reinforcement, and one effect of punishment is to increase the duration of the pause. Thus, the overall effect of punishment is to decrease the frequency of reinforcement, the amount of decrease being directly related to the intensity of the punishing stimulus (Azrin 1959).

If responding is maintained on a schedule in which there is differential reinforcement of low rates of responding (DRL), punishment in the form of either shock (Holz, Azrin, and Ulrich 1963) or time-out (Kramer and Rilling 1969) may increase the number of reinforcements obtained relative to prepunishment conditions. This happens because, under a DRL schedule, the organism is required to withhold responding for a fixed period—say, 30 seconds. The first response emitted after this period produces reinforcement. However, any responses emitted before the 30-second period has elapsed function to reset the clock programming the delivery of reinforcement and the organism has to wait for an additional 30 seconds before responding will produce reinforcement. By reducing the overall rate of responding, punishment works in favor of the organism in this case, because a reduction in the rate of responding makes it more likely that the minimum 30-second period of nonresponding will be achieved.

The rate of responding during punishment is also affected by variations in density of the reinforcement schedule supporting the behavior. For pigeons, punishment produced a lower rate of responding under a 6-minute variable-interval schedule of positive reinforcement than it did under a 1-minute variable-interval schedule (Appel and Peterson 1965). Similar results were obtained for rats in a study by Church and Raymond (1967). Further, the relationship between rate of responding and density of reinforcement in both the presence and absence of punishment is linear (Tullis and G. Walters 1968).

What all of the foregoing examples illustrate is that the punishment of responding on any given schedule of positive reinforcement may result in no change in the absolute number of reinforcers obtained under punishment or in a decrease or even an increase in rate of reinforcement. And, because the maintenance of the behavior being punished is intimately linked to the reinforcement of that behavior, a knowledge of how punishment interacts with various schedules of reinforcement is important in understanding punishment outcomes.

Punishment and Extinction

Given the proposition that it is desirable to reduce the frequency and density of reinforcement in order to maximize the effectiveness of punishment, what happens if the experimenter is able to eliminate reinforcement completely at the time that punishment is introduced; that is, what happens during extinction? Since both punishment and extinction are response-weakening procedures, an intuitive approach would suggest that their combined use might lead to a more rapid and more enduring suppression of behavior. In their early work, Skinner (1938) and Estes (1944) investigated this very question. They found that, although punishment administered during extinction did decrease the rate at which animals responded while it was in force, upon termination of punishment the rate of responding increased relative to that of unpunished controls. Thus, punishment had no overall effect. Because punishment did not decrease the resistance to extinction of the punished behavior, they concluded that punishment did not have permanent effects on behavior.

However, as both Azrin and Holz (1966) and Fantino (1973) have argued, the effect of punishment in the Estes and Skinner procedures was apparently confounded with the discriminative, or signalling, properties of the punishing stimulus, making interpretation of their data ambiguous. Consider what happens in a typical extinction procedure. An organism is trained to press a lever for food reinforcement. After the response is well established, reinforcement is terminated and pressing the lever no longer produces the food, nor any of its accompanying stimuli such as the click of the food magazine as it delivers the reinforcer. It is well known that stimuli associated with primary reinforcement themselves take on reinforcing properties (e.g., Bugelski, 1938). According to one analysis of the extinction process, an organism must learn not only that food is no longer produced by an emitted response, but that the cues associated with its delivery, such as the noise produced by the operation of the empty food magazine, are predictive of nonreinforcement. Indeed, extinction of positively reinforced behaviors can be a prolonged affair because the organism will continue to respond until it learns that all the stimuli formerly associated with food reinforcement have become signals for nonreinforcement.

In view of the preceding discussion, it is worthwhile reexamining the Skinner and Estes studies to see what may have accounted for their results. In both studies the punishing stimulus was delivered during extinction so that, along with whatever aversive properties it had, it functioned as a discriminative stimulus for the absence of reinforcement. Furthermore, not only did the punishing stimulus signal nonreinforcement, but its removal recreated the conditions under which the punished behavior had been acquired; one could argue, as Fantino (1973) has, that under this condition extinction as such was just beginning.

Azrin and Holz (1966) have supplied empirical support for this analysis by duplicating the essentials of Estes' study except that, whereas Estes used rats and gave his animals only a few hours of acquisition training, Azrin and Holz used pigeons, which were trained for many hours. After the pigeons had completed their prepunishment training, a distinctive stimulus, a "neutral" flash of light, was substituted for the punishing shock used in the Estes procedure. The combination of the "pseudopunishing stimulus" (the light) and extinction produced rapid response suppression, but when pseudo-punishment was stopped—extinction still being in force—a rapid increase in responding was found to occur.

It is not surprising that the presentation of any stimulus, even a so-called neutral one, can result in temporary response reduction. This transient effect presumably results from the distracting properties of any newly introduced stimulus. In this respect, all aversive stimuli can be placed on a continuum in terms of their disruptive properties, with neutral stimuli at one end of the continuum and severe punishing stimuli, such as intense electric shock, at the other. If punishing stimuli are intense enough, their effects may be long term, a point illustrated in a study by Boe and Church (1967). In this study, the procedure employed by Estes (1944, Experiment A) was basically replicated, using several different intensities of electric shock as punishing stimuli. In accord with Estes' procedure, Boe and Church's prepunishment training consisted of three hours of acquisition training in which rats pressed a lever for food reinforcement delivered on a 3-minute fixed-interval schedule. Nine one-hour extinction sessions followed during which separate groups of animals received electric shock varying in intensity from 35 to 220 volts. As in the Estes procedure, intermittent punishment was given only during a single 15-minute period of the initial extinction session; there was no further punishment in the remainder of that session nor in any of the remaining eight extinction sessions. As shown in Figure 3-6, resistance to extinction was an orderly function of the intensity of the punishing stimulus, with responding reduced to zero in all groups. More important, however, is that recovery from the punishing stimulus was never complete, with responding never as high as in a control group that had received only extinction. In the two groups for which the intensity of shock was the highest, 120 and 220 volts, very little recovery took place at all. Boe and Church refer to these

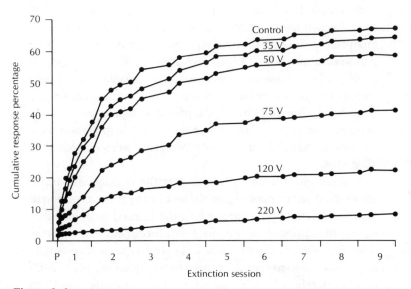

Figure 3-6
Cumulative median response percentage during extinction. (Punishment, P, was contingent upon lever pressing during Minutes 5–20 of the first extinction session.) [From E. E. Boe and R. M. Church, Permanent effects of punishment during extinction. *Journal of Comparative and Physiological Psychology* 63(1967):486–492. Copyright 1967 by the American Psychological Association. Reprinted by permission.]

effects as "permanent," and indicate that, had Estes used intense shocks, he too would have found such an effect. Thus it would seem that there are conditions under which punishment can be shown to reduce substantially the persistence of responding undergoing extinction.

Amount of Prepunishment Training

Even a cursory review of the literature reveals that there are wide variations in the amount of positive-reinforcement training given to subjects before punishment is introduced. Researchers working in the operant tradition typically train their subjects until performance has become asymptotic, or has reached a steady state. Such training usually takes many hours, and it is commonplace to see experimental reports such as Azrin's (1960) on punishment intensity in which each subject received a minimum of fifty 1-hour sessions of training on a variable-interval reinforcement schedule before punishment was introduced. On the other hand, Church (1969) has reported a comprehensive series of experiments in which only five 30-minute prepunishment sessions of variable-interval reinforcement were employed in all studies.

Is there any reason to believe that the conclusions drawn about the effectiveness of punishment in any given experiment may be affected by the strength of the learned response; that is, by the amount of previous reinforcement training the punished response has received? There has been surprisingly little work done to find an answer to this question. N. E. Miller (1960) referred to a "paradoxical overtraining effect" in one of his studies investigating the punishment (in the form of shock) of rats trained to traverse an alleyway and enter a goalbox for food reinforcement. He noted that rats who had been *overtrained*—defined as having undergone a number of additional discrete trials after achieving asymptotic performance as measured by alleyway running speeds—were less resistant to the disruptive effects of punishment than were rats in the control group, which were punished as soon as performance had become stable. Karsh (1962), using similar performance measures, also found an indication of this overtraining effect, although she noted that it was not a robust phenomenon. Both investigations were discrete-trial studies that employed continuous rather than intermittent reinforcement of the to-be-punished response. More representative of the bulk of contemporary research on punishment, in which free-operant, intermittent reinforcement is used, is the study by Estes (1944, Experiment F). He reported that, during extinction, punished animals that had been trained for five hours by means of intermittent reinforcement resisted the suppressive effects of punishment more than a group of animals that had been trained for only one hour—a finding that is opposite those of Miller and Karsh. One of us (Walters) has recently completed a study, moreover, in which the results indicate that there are conditions under which the amount of prepunishment training has no effect at all on the subsequent suppressive effects of punishment. In this study, different groups of rats were trained by means of variable-interval reinforcement for varying lengths of time ranging from 7 to 63 hours. With reinforcement still in effect (recall that Estes discontinued reinforcement), punishment was introduced. The number of hours of prior training did not modify the effects of punishment; the responding of animals that had received 63 hours of training was suppressed to the same degree, both initially and asymptotically, as that of animals trained for as few as 7 hours. Nor was there any difference in rate of recovery upon removal of the punishment contingency.

Certainly, a great deal more empirical investigation is required in order to determine the role of prepunishment training in studies on punishment. Obvious problems such as determining what constitutes both asymptotic behavior and overtraining will have to be solved, and variables known to influence the effectiveness of reinforcement, such as frequency and density, will have to be taken into account. Further, the nature of the interaction, if any, between amount of training and those variables known to have specific effects on the outcome of punishment, such as intensity and duration, need to be examined. All these problems can be studied easily enough in the learning laboratory where the subjects are trained to respond through positive reinforcement. But their study becomes considerably more complicated when the responses under observation are already existing behaviors—such as playing with toys and aggressiveness—which figure so prominently in child-development studies.

Motivation to Respond

Is an organism's motivation to engage in behavior for which it is being punished a factor in determining the effectiveness of the punishment? Intuitively, it would seem that the greater the motivation for the prohibited response the less effective punishment or, for that matter, any other response-reduction technique would be. Considering the importance of this question it is rather surprising to find that very few attempts have been made to answer it. Azrin, Holz, and Hake (1963) compared the effects of five different degrees of food deprivation on the reinforced responding of a pigeon. As shown in Figure 3-7, when deprivation was "standard"—that is, the amount most frequently used in studies of food deprivation for both pigeons and rats, or 85% of the organism's free-feeding body weight—responding was almost completely suppressed. However, as the degree of deprivation was increased, punishment had less effect. Azrin and Holz (1966) have suggested that when punishment decreases responding completely when motivation is low, attempts to restore responding by increasing motivation are unsuccessful (see Boroczi, Storms, and Broen, 1964; Masserman, 1946; Storms, Boroczi, and Broen, 1962). If this is accepted as a general rule, then it

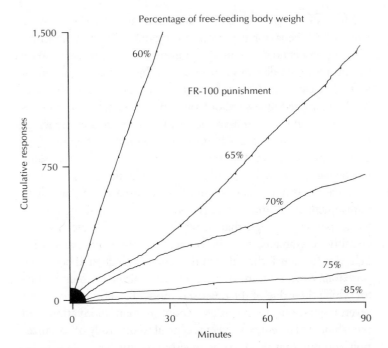

Figure 3-7
Effect of food deprivation during fixed-ratio punishment of a pigeon for responses reinforced by food. Every hundredth response is being punished (160 volts) at the moment indicated by the short oblique lines on the response curves. Food reinforcement (not shown) is being delivered on a 3-minute variable-interval schedule. [From N. H. Azrin, W. C. Holz, and D. F. Hake, Fixed-ratio punishment. *Journal for the Experimental Analysis of Behavior* 6(1963):141–148. Copyright 1963 by the Society for the Experimental Analysis of Behavior, Inc.]

may be important to distinguish between prepunishment and postpunishment motivational effects; perhaps motivational manipulations that precede the introduction of punishment are influential in determining its outcome, whereas those done after responding has been suppressed by means of intense punishment are ineffective.

Motivation can also be considered in terms of the reward value of the behavior for which an organism is being punished. This concept is no doubt more common among those who study the problems of deviation in human subjects than it is among animal researchers. Certainly, a person cannot be considered to be truly tempted unless the outcome of a given behavior supplies a strong incentive. And it would seem that the greater the temptation the less likely a given amount of punishment would suppress that behavior. On the other hand, perhaps the same mechanisms that make punishment of moderate intensities more effective than that of severe intensities cause a given amount of punishment to be more effective when the value of the reward for responding is high than when it is only moderate. Greater cognitive dissonance may be induced by the suppression of a behavior for which the value of the reward is high, and hence the probability of its future occurrence reduced more, than for one for which the value of the reward is moderate. This is but one of several questions to be asked about human motivation and punishment. The entire subject is central to the study of socialization and one that needs to be investigated further.

Availability of Alternative Responses

If an organism is punished for a given response but receives reinforcement for another, alternative response, it will quickly cease the responding for which it is being punished and will begin to emit the alternative response. Giving an organism an opportunity to gain reinforcement in another way is one of the most powerful means of suppressing ongoing behavior, even when the punishment being administered is moderate. Evidence for its effectiveness comes from studies in which a variety of punishing stimuli—such as loud noise or time-out—have been used to punish human subjects for behavior that was also being reinforced (Herman and Azrin 1964; Azrin and Holz 1966) and from a study in which boys were punished for playing with certain toys but were given other toys to play with as well during a test for resistance to deviation (Perry and Parke 1975). An example of the use of the alternative-response procedure is taken from Herman and Azrin (1964). Male adults were trained to operate two levers, each of which delivered a cigarette on a 60-second variable-interval schedule of reinforcement. After rates of responding had become stable on both levers, punishment in the form of a loud noise was delivered for operating one of them. The rate of the punished response was then virtually reduced to zero immediately, and responding shifted almost entirely to the unpunished lever. In a later phase of this study, punishment was terminated, one lever was removed, and the subjects were reinforced for operating the remaining lever. When punishment was then reintroduced, there was a decrease in responding, but it was nothing like the total suppression found when an alternative response was available.

The use of an alternative response has a marked effect on the punished behavior, but is this an unexpected result? It is hardly surprising that any organism would switch to an unpunished alternative response for which it received the same reinforcement. Several questions are raised by such results, however. First, would these same findings obtain if the alternative response was performed at some cost to the organism, such as the loss of some of the reinforcement that could be obtained by continuing to operate the punished lever? A study by Fantino (1973) supplies evidence that they would. In this study, switching to an alternative unpunished lever during punishment cost a subject about one-half the reinforcement it had formerly received. Even so, when pigeons were punished with shock for pecking one of two keys, there was suppression of the punished response and an increase in the unpunished one, but the increase was not as great as that found in the experiments previously cited.

Another question to be asked concerning the alternative-response findings is how they might be applied in a naturalistic setting. It is one thing to arrange for either the reinforcement or the nonreinforcement of a response in an experimental situation and quite another to do this outside the controlled laboratory setting. In using the alternative-response method to suppress a child's behavior, the parent or other socializing agent must find an acceptable alternative behavior and arrange for its reinforcement. Consider, for example, a child who misbehaves by engaging in temper tantrums in order to gain parental attention. The child may simply be punished for such behavior, but suppression of that behavior is greater if the child can engage in an alternative behavior for which it receives the reinforcement sought by means of the temper tantrums. This seems relatively simple. However, consider another example from the behavior-modification literature. In assessing the efficacy of aversion therapy in the treatment of homosexual behavior, Rachman and Teasdale (1969) concluded that a necessary condition for change was the existence of some heterosexual behavior in the repertoire of the patient that could be built up in the course of the therapeutic regimen. In other words, unless there was some kind of acceptable alternative behavior to work with that allowed the patient's sexual behaviors to be reinforced, aversion therapy by itself was not successful.

Given that the availability of an alternative response does facilitate the elimination of the punished response, how durable is this suppression? What would happen if the newly established reinforced alternative response were extinguished? Rawson and Leitenberg (1973) report that, when this happens, there is a rapid recovery of the punished response. It is still unknown, however, whether recovery is a function of the length of time for which the alternative response is reinforced. And what would happen if the alternative response were different from the one being punished?

The use of an alternative reinforced response seems to be an extremely promising technique in producing response suppression. There are many questions about its use, however, that, although easily studied in the animal laboratory, are still unanswered. Moreover, it is apparent that it becomes more difficult to employ as control over the organism's sources of reinforcement decreases.

Facilitation of Behavior by Punishment

Although punishing stimuli have their own specific properties that account for their most typical behavioral effect, response suppression, they also are stimuli in the most general sense of the term. As such they have the capacity to serve as discriminative cues or as information-producing signals. In the latter capacity stimuli employed as punishing stimuli can, under certain conditions, produce a so-called paradoxical effect upon behavior in that their application results in response facilitation rather than suppression. Such an outcome, however, is a paradox only in the sense that it does not fit into our presupposition about punishment as a response-reductive procedure. Punishment does have a variety of effects upon behavior and, under the appropriate circumstances, can result in an increase in the vigor or frequency of the behavior upon which it is contingent. The task of the punishment researcher is to identify the circumstances under which suppression or facilitation is likely to occur.

It is not at all surprising to find that a signal that predicts the availability of reinforcement will trigger behavior that produces the reinforcer. In stimulus-response terms, the organism has learned to associate the signal with the outcome—the signal has acquired discriminative properties such that the behavior tends to occur in its presence and not in its absence. A standard procedure for the establishment of a discrimination is to reinforce all responses in the presence of the stimulus predicting the availability of reinforcement and extinguish all responses in the absence of the signal. This is precisely what Holz and Azrin (1961) did, using a response-produced electric shock (i.e., punishment) as a signal for the availability of reinforcement. Pigeons were first trained to key-peck for food on an intermittent schedule of reinforcement. After steady rates of responding had been achieved, punishment consisting of shock was administered for each response. The shock was adjusted until the response rate of each of the pigeons was reduced to 50% of its nonpunished rate. At this point a discrimination procedure was introduced such that periods of shocks paired with intermittent reinforcement were interspersed with extinction periods—no punishment or reinforcement. After a few weeks, a reliable pattern of responding became apparent. During those periods in which each response produced punishment while intermittent reinforcement was being delivered, the pigeons' rates of responding were considerably higher than they were when responding produced neither punishment nor reinforcement. The higher rates of responding were maintained when reinforcement was removed and only the cue (shock) that had previously signalled reinforcement remained. The facilitating effects of punishment have also been demonstrated with children. Katz (1971) found that a hitting response of boys for whom punishment (subjection to a loud noise) and reinforcement had been paired during acquisition of the response took longer to extinguish when hitting was followed by punishment alone than it did for boys who had not been subjected to the noise until the extinction procedure was introduced.

Azrin (1960) has pointed out that the facilitation effect, not unexpectedly, depends on such experimental parameters as the intensity of the punishment. Severe punishment seems to suppress responding whether or not it predicts reinforcement. Thus, merely establishing a set of conditions under which a punishing stimulus can serve as a signal for reinforcement is not sufficient for facilitating the punished behavior—the effect may be overridden by those of other variables that support response reduction.

Another example of how the signalling function of punishing stimuli can play an important role in the outcome of a punishment procedure is illustrated in a series of studies dealing with the punishment of correct responses in discrimination learning. This work dates back to the early studies of Muenzinger (1934) who reported that rats performing a discrimination task learned faster if they were shocked for correct choices than they did if no shocks were given. Why should punishment for responding correctly in a discrimination-learning task facilitate learning? The answer is found in a series of studies by Fowler and Wischner (1969) and Fowler (1971) in which the conditions under which the effect occurs are spelled out. Their findings emphasize the cue, or signalling, function of punishing stimuli in discrimination learning. For example, shock delivered for correct choices is effective in facilitating the acquisition of difficult tasks but not simple ones. The function of the punishing stimuli is to assist the animal in discriminating between difficult alternative responses. And, not unexpectedly, when the intensity of the shock is increased, learning is less likely to be facilitated by shock delivered for correct choices. As noted earlier in discussing the Holz and Azrin (1961) study, punishing stimuli up to a certain intensity serve important signalling functions that can result in outcomes other than response suppression. When they produce this effect, it is not a paradoxical one; rather it is an effect resulting from one of their many, varied functions.

The Nature of the Punished Response

We know that a wide variety of variables influence the outcome of any given punishment procedure. So far, however, our review of the learning literature has centered on the effects of these variables on one general class of responses—learned operant behaviors established by positive reinforcement. In Chapter 2, we indicated that this reliance upon a single class of responses raises the question of how representative such findings may be in predicting the effects of punishment on other behaviors. Is it correct to assume that generalizations made about one class will be valid in all cases? Or should there be a concern about the extent to which current generalizations about the effects of punishment will remain adequate as research continues?

Unfortunately, compared with the large number of studies dealing with the punishment of learned operant responses established by positive reinforcement, little work has been done in the learning laboratory on the punishment of other behaviors. And there are only a few studies in which an investigator has actually directly compared the effects of punishment within a single experiment on more than one class of response. We believe that in the past there have been reasons, both practical and theoretical, for this emphasis, but an overall understanding of punishment is threatened by the limitations placed on it because of a failure to investigate a wider variety of behaviors. This is especially important in a line of research in which theorists are beginning to integrate existing data (e.g., Bolles, 1975a and b; Estes, 1969; Mackintosh, 1974; Rachlin and Herrnstein, 1969), as well as questioning some of the theoretical assumptions extant (Dunham 1971).

In this section we shall present examples from the literature dealing with punishment of other classes of responses. Although we are not proposing a set of specific response classes to categorize behaviors, we shall use terms such as instinctive and consummatory for convenience in identifying the behaviors studied in any given experiment (see Solomon, 1964). Thus, for the present purpose, the term consummatory simply identifies such behaviors as eating and drinking. Similarly, the term instinctive refers to those behaviors that an organism brings to an experimental situation as a result of its being a member of a particular species having a distinct genetic history. To go beyond this labelling convenience raises many problems concerning the taxonomy of behavior and is beyond the scope of this book.

There are a variety of demonstrations that punishment can function to suppress behaviors other than learned operants. For example, Myer and his colleagues have demonstrated in a series of elegant studies that the aggressive behavior of rats against mice can be suppressed by means of electric shock. Rats that consistently killed mice were punished each time they began to attack. Suppression of this response was both rapid and enduring, although it was always eventually resumed upon termination of punishment (Myer 1966; Myer and Baenninger 1966). Only punishment of the rats while they were engaging in attack behavior resulted in its modification, whereas punishment simply in the presence of the mouse or for post-attack consummatory behavior did not. Suppression was also obtained when secondary punishing stimuli were employed (Baenninger 1967). In other studies, punishment suppressed aggression that had been elicited in pairs of rats by the random presentation of intense electric shocks (Azrin 1970), by mechanically pinching the tails of the rats and causing them pain (Baenninger and Grossman 1969), and by electrical stimulation of the hypothalamus (Stockman and Glusman 1969). Furthermore, the degree to which shock-elicited aggression is suppressed has been shown to be a direct function of the intensity of the punishing stimulus (Roberts and Blase 1971) and an inverse function of the delay of punishment (Wetzel 1972), findings that parallel those that are obtained in studies in which appetitively motivated operant behaviors are punished.

Punishment also suppresses a variety of other behaviors, examples of which are: the gill membrane display of Siamese fighting fish (Adler and Hogan 1963; Grabowski and

Thompson 1969; Melvin and Ervey 1973); the following behavior of imprinted ducklings (Barrett et al. 1971); the eating behavior of dogs (Lichtenstein 1950), cats (Masserman 1943), chickadees (Alcock 1970a), and sparrows (Alcock 1970b); the vomiting behavior of humans (Kohlenberg 1970); the toe-sucking behavior of a young rhesus monkey (Tolman and Mueller 1964); the drinking behavior of thirsty rats (Hunt and Schlosberg 1950); and the sexual behavior of male rats (Beach et al. 1956). With respect to the last finding, however, Rouda (1968) has noted that a punishment procedure that causes rapid and complete suppression of lever-pressing maintained by food reinforcement has little effect on the sexual behavior of the male rat. It may be argued that the difference between the findings of Beach and his colleagues and those of Rouda are due to procedural variations, but the fact that Rouda found strong suppressive effects on instrumental behavior relative to those found on sexual behavior is impressive.

The fact that punishment can suppress a variety of responses is of little use in evaluating the relative degree to which punishment is effective for all classes of responding and in determining whether the variables influencing its effectiveness in suppressing one behavior will necessarily act in the same way for another. To do this requires comparing the behaviors in question within the same punishment paradigm while not confounding variables, such as effort and proximity to the reinforcer, associated with the different responses studied (see deCosta and Ayres, 1971; Dunham and Klips, 1969).

Punishment of the Dominant Response to Aversiveness

What evidence is there that punishment may have different effects on different responses? In one study, G. Walters and Glazer (1971) punished Mongolian gerbils with a secondary punishing stimulus, a tone that had previously been paired with shock, either for digging in sand covering the floor of a large experimental chamber or for assuming an alert posturing position. Punishment for digging resulted in immediate and virtually complete suppression during several days of punishment, whereas there were no signs that posturing was being suppressed; rather it increased in frequency during the punishment phase of the experiment. Later work by Weber (1974) indicates that the increase in posturing found in the Walters and Glazer study cannot be attributed solely to the generalized aversiveness of the environment in which tone-shock pairings took place—that is, posturing did not increase in frequency in the absence of tone presentations. Rather, posturing was facilitated only when it was followed by punishment. In separate studies Weber also found that posturing was quickly learned as an avoidance response, and that the frequency of both digging and posturing was increased by positive reinforcement. Thus, it seems that only when punishment was used was posturing not subject to control by means of an operant contingency.

Why are some behaviors difficult to suppress by means of punishment, whereas others are readily changed? In the studies just mentioned, it is not because posturing is an innate behavior. Other innate behaviors, such as the digging behavior of the gerbil, the gill display of Siamese fighting fish, and the aggressive behavior of rats, are easily suppressed by punishment. What makes posturing different from those innate behaviors? One possible explanation is that posturing is a defensive response; it is one of the gerbil's dominant responses to aversiveness (Milne-Edwards 1867; Eisenberg 1967). Therefore, it is not altogether surprising that the potential response-reductive properties of the punishing stimulus were overridden by the facilitative effects of aversiveness on posturing. It may be, as Mackintosh (1974) has suggested, that such facilitation depends on the use of punishing stimuli of low intensity. Indeed, although there is no empirical evidence to support this claim, we would expect very severe punishment to suppress posturing. However, the fact remains that the same punishing stimulus that increased the posturing behavior of the gerbil also produced a dramatic suppression of the digging behavior of the same animal.

Admittedly, this general interpretation is speculative. However, it is interesting to compare these findings with those of the early studies of traumatic avoidance conditioning undertaken by Solomon and his associates. In 1953, Solomon, Kamin, and Wynne trained dogs to jump over a hurdle in a shuttlebox to avoid an extremely intense electric shock—one so strong that it was just below the intensity at which the animals' muscles would go into tetany. After responding a few times to escape the painful shock, all the animals learned to avoid it by jumping over the hurdle when given a warning signal that preceded each shock by 10 seconds. That this behavior was very well learned is indicated by the fact that it was virtually nonextinguishable. Thus the dominant response to aversiveness became jumping.[6] Under these conditions, a punishment contingency was introduced in such a way that the dogs were subjected to shock each time they completed an avoidance response: punishment did not suppress the avoidance response. Further, not only did most of the dogs keep jumping the barrier, but they began jumping faster and more vigorously than before. Is this similar to the effects of punishment on the gerbil's posturing response? Certainly there is an empirical parallel between the effects of punishment on the posturing response of the gerbil and the traumati-

---

[6]Solomon (personal communication) has pointed out that the barrier-jumping of a shocked dog is a nondominant response to shock—a low-probability response for which the mean latency of escaping is from 10 to 30 seconds during early shock-avoidance training. It is only after escape latencies have shortened that avoidance responding becomes a high-probability response. We use the term dominant here in the sense of the learned barrier-jumping becoming, through training, a high-probability response to aversiveness.

cally induced jumping response of the dog, even though the former is an innate response to aversiveness, whereas the latter became a high-probability response to aversiveness through learning.

It is clear from other work, especially studies of so-called self-punitive behavior, that there are many circumstances under which the punishment of learned escape or avoidance behavior may actually facilitate the punished response (e.g., Brown, 1969; Gwinn, 1949; Melvin, 1971; Mowrer, 1947). Self-punitive behavior has been demonstrated in the laboratory in the following way. Animals are trained to escape into a safe goalbox by being shocked in the startbox and along the length of the alley leading to the goalbox. After learning to escape, some animals no longer receive shock, whereas others do not receive shock in the startbox but do receive it in various parts of the alley. Which animals stop running first? Because those running from a safe startbox into shock are being punished for running, they might be expected to quickly learn to stay in the startbox. However, what has been found to happen in many studies is that, although the animals given extinction training slow down and eventually stop, the punished animals continue to leave the safety of the startbox and run into shock. Although punishment of escape and avoidance behavior does not always produce such facilitatory effects (Black and Morse 1961; Kintz and Bruning 1967; Riccio and Marrazo 1972; Seligman and Campbell 1965; Seward et al. 1965), there clearly are conditions under which these effects are produced.

In the three examples considered, the punishing stimulus seemed to "elicit" a dominant response to aversiveness; it energized posturing, jumping, and running, each of which was a high-probability response to aversiveness at the time punishment was introduced. In barrier-jumping and alley-running the dominance was achieved through training, whereas in the posturing response it was due to the innate characteristics of the behavior. Thus we conclude that this elicitation may account for the failure of punishing stimuli to suppress behavior in these situations.

Punishment and Consummatory Behavior

There is additional research that suggests that the punishment of different classes of responses produces different outcomes. Some time ago, Solomon (1964) suggested that the data available then indicated that consummatory behaviors were very easily disrupted by punishment. Solomon's conclusion seems to have been based primarily on several early studies such as Lichtenstein's (1950). He reported that shock punishment given to dogs at the initiation of eating produced a marked and enduring suppression of eating, whereas punishment that accompanied the presentation of food had little suppressive effect on eating (see also Masserman, 1943; Masserman and Pechtel, 1953). Seward (1969) has questioned Solomon's assertion, pointing out that there are very few studies directly comparing the effects of punishment on different types of responses. And in those studies in which an attempt has been made, it is not clear whether consummatory behavior itself has been punished or some operant behavior leading to the consummatory behavior (e.g., Church, 1969). However, Bertsch (1972) has reported that the water-licking of rats is suppressed more if the rats are punished while engaging in the consummatory behavior than is their lever-pressing if they are punished for pressing the lever that produces the water reinforcer. This clearly offers support for Solomon's contention. A major problem with such studies is that it is difficult to compare operant and consummatory responses directly because of the difficulty of equating the amount of reinforcement obtained by the animal. In a consummatory response the reinforcer is necessarily ingested, whereas in operant responding it does not have to be consumed. A series of studies was conducted in one of our laboratories (Walters) in an effort to solve this problem.

In one study, an attempt was made to separate the consummatory from the operant response, using a "dry lick" tube, or lickometer; that is, a glass-insulated tungsten rod that is similar in shape to the licking tube in an animal's cage but that does not deliver water (Wall, G. Walters, and England 1972). It does register all licks to the electrically sensitive underside of the tip. Thus operant dry-licking can be recorded independently of any reinforcement that is presented in another part of the test chamber. And, because the lickometer is electrically isolated from all parts of the testing chamber, including the grids, electric shocks can be confined to the grid floor and will not pass through the animal's tongue. This allows a comparison of the effects of punishment for different responses, while relatively similar conditions for delivering the punishing stimulus are maintained. The study was designed to compare the effects of punishment for a seemingly arbitrary operant, lever-pressing, with those for an operant that may be considered to have consummatory components, dry-licking. The initial question was simple—would there be greater suppression of dry-licking than of lever-pressing? If so, then this would demonstrate that not all operants are affected equally by punishment and it would imply that the functional similarity of dry-licking to the rat's water-consummatory behavior may be an important variable in determining differential sensitivity to punishment.

In this study thirteen rats were trained to dry-lick in one chamber and to lever-press in another. Both chambers were identical except for the presence of either a lickometer or a lever, which, in each case, was located so that the animals had to make similar gross body movements to gain access to it. Each rat was trained on alternate days to dry-lick or lever-press for water reinforcement, which was presented in a different part of the chamber and delivered on a variable-interval schedule, six rats being started first on lever-pressing and seven on dry-licking. This, then, was a within-subjects study, with all animals learning to both lever-press and dry-lick. After 62 days of training, the responses of all animals had become stable (see Figures 3-8 and 3-9, pages 116–119, left-hand column) and punishment was introduced in the form of a 0.25-mA electric shock delivered for 200 msec on a 30-second variable-interval schedule. The results for each animal are shown in the second column from the left in Figures 3-8 and 3-9. Dry-licking was more suppressed than lever-pressing.

There are two features of these data worth noting. First, differential sensitivity to punishment was uniform in spite of differences in stable response rates at the prepunishment baseline: for some rats, the rate of dry-licking had been higher than that of lever-pressing and, for others, the opposite was true. However, the differential suppression was unaffected by this. Second, while the punishment contingency remained in effect there was no sign of recovery of dry-licking, although lever-pressing recovered in virtually every case; for many rats, lever-pressing recovered to its prepunishment rate. After the punishment contingency was removed, the rate of responding of most animals eventually returned to its prepunishment baseline (Figures 3-8 and 3-9, third column from the left). When responding resumed its stable state, punishment was again introduced, this time at a higher intensity of 0.40 mA. Again, suppression of dry-licking was greater than that of lever-pressing, as it was when punishment consisted of 0.25-mA shock (Figures 3-8 and 3-9, middle column). After termination of punishment (third column from right) the same pattern of punishment (0.40 mA, third column from right) and no punishment (right-hand column) was repeated, producing basically the same results. Bertsch (1972) has reported similar results, using a slightly different experimental situation. He trained groups of rats to lick from a dry tube or to press a lever for water. In his study, however, the water rein-forcer was delivered through the same tube that served as the operant manipulandum. In spite of this and other procedural differences, he found that the suppression of dry-licking by means of shock punishment was greater than that of lever-pressing.

Conclusions

Are there any general conclusions to be drawn from what is known about the effects of punishment on different types of responses? Unfortunately, too little information is available at present to allow the formulation of a comprehensive set of rules about interactions between punishment and various classes of responses. But that which is available serves as a reminder of the fact that the punished response itself is a variable that *must* be taken into account in considering the effects of punishment on behavior.

Should We Punish for Incorrect Behavior or Reward for Correct?

To those concerned with the practical problems of socialization one obvious question is whether it is better to punish for bad behavior or reward for good behavior. A large body of research, all of it carried out with children, suggests that punishment for incorrect behavior leads to faster learning than does reinforce-ment for correct behavior, and a combination of reinforcement and punishment is no better than punishment alone (e.g., Hamil-ton, 1969b; Meyer and Offenbach, 1962; Paris and Cairns, 1972; Penney, 1967; Spence, 1966; Witte and Grossman, 1971). Attempts to understand this seemingly counter-intuitive finding, which holds for both normal and mentally retarded children,

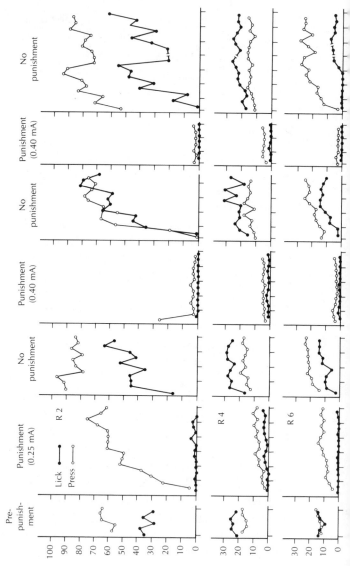

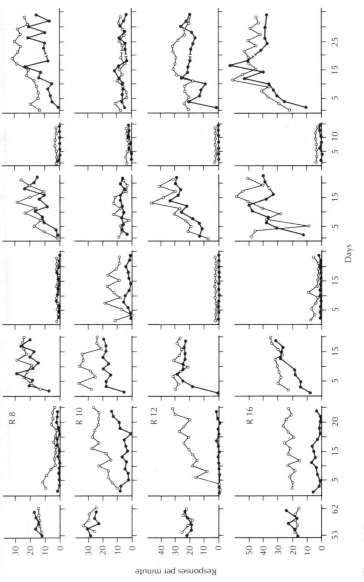

Figure 3-8
Response rates for individual animals (identified by R2, R4, etc.) trained to dry-lick and lever-press on alternate days, starting with dry-licking. Rates shown are for responses during prepunishment, punishment, and subsequent phases of the experiment as indicated at the top of each column. Note that rates for both dry-licking and lever-pressing are given for each animal during each phase.

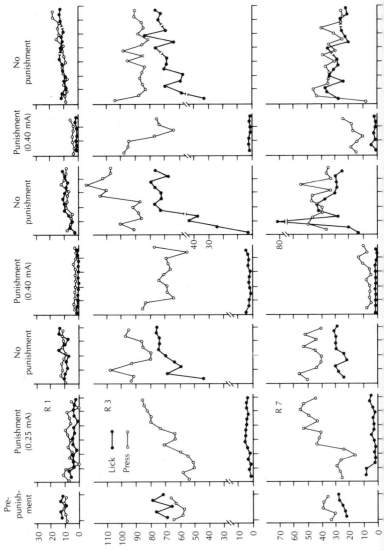

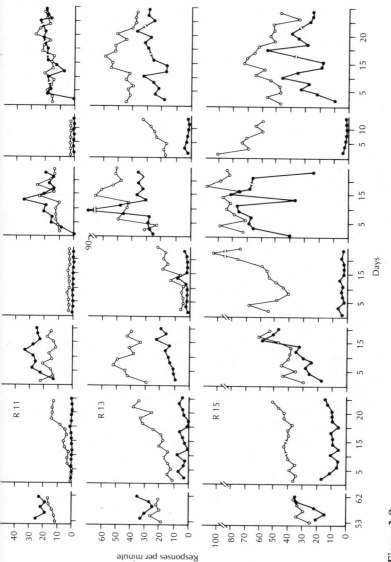

Figure 3-9
Response rates for individual animals trained to dry-lick and lever-press on alternate days, starting with lever-pressing. See legend for Figure 3-8 for details.

reveal certain shortcomings in the use of social and material rewards, which are not apparent in the use of punishment.

By far the greatest number of studies dealing with this problem have employed discrimination learning tasks and have used verbal statements of "right" as reinforcement and "wrong" as punishment. A number of researchers have suggested that the effects obtained can be accounted for by the possibility that children interpret silence after a response as an indication that they have performed correctly. Thus children who are told "wrong" after one response and hear nothing after another response assume that no reaction from the experimenter means that they have performed correctly; those who hear nothing after an incorrect response and "right" after a correct response also assume that no reaction means they have responded correctly. If such is the case, children who are punished receive more information about the correct way to behave than do children who are only reinforced. Indeed, when they are told what no reaction means, the differences between punishment and reinforcement disappear (Hamilton 1969a; Spence 1966), although not for those who are mentally retarded (Paris and Cairns 1972).

A somewhat different explanation of the phenomenon is offered by Paris and Cairns who suggest that so-called social reinforcement is a relatively ambiguous event for a child because it is used frequently and indiscriminately in everyday interactions, whereas a negative social evaluation tends to be used in referring to a particular act. A child who hears the comment "right," or "good," after a particular response, then, would not be sure whether it was because the response was a correct one, whether it was for behaving well generally, or whether the experimenter was simply being pleasant. The word "wrong," however, would inform the child that an incorrect choice had just been made.

The explanation of Paris and Cairns is enhanced by the fact that they conducted a study in which they looked at the ways in which reinforcement and punishment are typically used in the classroom. Often those who perform experiments with children are forced to make suggestions about what events that take place in the laboratory mean to their subjects as a result of the kinds of experiences they have outside the laboratory. Although many of these suggestions sound plausible, they are rarely checked to see if, in fact, they bear some correspondence to what occurs in real life. Paris and Cairns did this, however, and report that, in special-education classes for mentally retarded children, positive evaluations occur more frequently, serve more diverse functions, and are less contingent on specific behaviors than are negative evaluations. Although it is possible, of course, that normal children receive much less nonspecific positive evaluation, it seems likely that the adults with whom they are in contact are more inclined to be generally pleasant and rewarding, independent of specific behaviors they observe, than they are to be generally unpleasant and negative. It is easier to say, "You are doing well," without accompanying justification than it is to say, "You are doing badly," in the absence of justification. Such a contention, of course, needs to be subjected to further examination in a naturalistic situation.

So-called social reinforcement, then, seems to have its limitations in terms of how effective it is in promoting learning. So, too, does material reinforcement, which often is found to distract from the learning task. Penney (1967) and Witte and Grossman (1971) report that children who received either a candy or a token for correct responding oriented themselves toward or touched stimuli less often than those who heard the sound of a loud buzzer after responding incorrectly. Their assumption is that learning was retarded in the children receiving reinforcement because they paid less attention to those stimuli relevant to learning the discrimination. Grusec (1966) punished children for deviation by turning off a chip-dispensing machine and attempted to reinforce them for self-criticism by turning the machine back on. The children did not learn that they should be self-critical, however, presumably because they were distracted during the time the machine was turned off by looking at and counting the chips they had just received. Indeed, in a later study (Grusec and Ezrin 1972) in which a large number of chips were given to subjects at the beginning of the experiment rather than as it progressed—a procedure designed to lessen the distraction of a continuous increase in winnings—self-criticism *was* learned. Spence (1970) has also commented on the distracting influence of material reward.

So far we have focused on the informational properties of reinforcement and punishment in situations in which subjects are asked to discover and give the right answer and there is no reason for them not to. It is assumed that most children in an experiment are motivated to do what the experimenter wants them to—it makes little difference to them whether that consists of putting a marble in one hole rather than another, or choosing a triangular rather than circular object. And, for one of a number of reasons, the use of verbal or material punishments seems to convey the correct answer more easily to them than does the use of verbal or material reinforcement. Merely showing a subject the "correct" answer after each response is apparently sufficient to facilitate learning under these conditions, with the addition of reinforcements and punishments being superfluous (Spence 1972). But what happens when a child knows what appropriate behavior is but receives reinforcement for engaging in inappropriate behavior? This is more like the typical resistance-to-temptation situation that has been discussed so far in this chapter and is a major problem for agents of socialization. Given that information about how to behave is available, do reinforcement and punishment differ in their abilities to suppress responses when there may be a reason for continuing to respond "incorrectly"? Is it better to punish children for engaging in forbidden behavior or to reward them for not doing so? (Note that this is a rather different question from one that asks whether it is useful to punish children for a response for which they are receiving reinforcement and, at the same time, to give them an opportunity to make an alternative response for which they receive the same reinforcement. As was seen earlier, this is quite an effective technique for producing response suppression.)

Little research has been done on this particular aspect of the problem except for a study conducted by Costantini and Hoving (1973). They instructed children to walk as slowly as possible along a six-foot-by-six-inch board and to wait as long as possible after having decided on the correct answer to a simple problem before telling it to the experimenter. Both these tasks tap a child's ability to withhold responding. Some children were reinforced for not responding, winning one marble (exchangeable for prizes) for each ten seconds they delayed, up to a total of 120 seconds. Other children were punished for responding, losing one marble for each ten seconds of the 120 seconds that remained after they had responded. Even though all the children were aware of the task required of them, those who were punished delayed responding more in a series of trials than did those who were reinforced for not responding. The authors concluded that the motivational effect of losing marbles was greater than that of receiving them, even when the number of marbles that the subjects retained or acquired was the same. Why might this be so? Perhaps the effect of punishment is greater because of its novelty; children are more accustomed to receiving material rewards than to losing them, just as they may be more used to receiving praise than criticism. If this is so—and it is a hypothesis that merits investigation—then a case could be made for the greater effectiveness of punishment for incorrect behavior over reinforcement for correct behavior even when the amount of information given is constant. If socializing agents use punishment less often than reinforcement, the former has the advantage of being a more novel stimulus, and the introduction of novel stimuli, of course, will suppress responding. Aside from any ethical reason for the minimal use of punishment, then, there is also the likelihood of its decreasing effectiveness with increasing use. Indeed, we have good reason to suspect that agents of socialization may well have diminished the effectiveness of social and material reinforcement by being much too prodigal in its use, or at least by often administering it independent of the behavior engaged in.

Theories of Punishment

It is perhaps not too great an oversimplification to state that theories of how punishment works begin and end with Thorndike. Recall that Thorndike's original position was that the function of punishment was opposite that of reinforcement. Reinforcement caused learned associations to be stamped in and punishment functioned to eradicate them. Later, after he rejected the negative law of effect, punishment was relegated to a secondary or derivative process. Its function was merely to compete with ongoing learned behaviors, not to have a primary effect upon learned associations. Since Thorndike's time, psychologists have come full circle in their thinking. Several versions of competing-response theory have been offered to explain punishment, but the most recent suggestions are that Thorndike's original version of the law of effect, which considered reinforcement and punishment to be opposite sides of the same coin, was basically correct. The main difference between the latest formulations and Thorndike's original one is that they exclude the theoretical notion that learning is simply a matter of the forming and undoing of hypothetical stimulus-response associations. We shall present only the highlights of various theoretical positions; there have been several good reviews of punishment theory to which we refer the reader who wishes to pursue this subject further (e.g., Azrin and Holz, 1966; Bolles, 1975b; Church, 1963; Estes, 1969; Fantino, 1973; Mackintosh, 1974). We shall conclude this discussion of theories with our own view of how punishment works.

Competing-Response Theories

By far the most popular forms of punishment theory invoke the idea of competing responses to explain punishment's suppressive effects; that is, punishment causes an organism to engage in behavior that is incompatible with the behavior for which it is being punished. Sometimes the competing behaviors suggested have simply been skeletal responses, as in Guthrie's (1935) explanation of how punishment works. According to the theory of learning advocated by Guthrie, stimulus-response bonding occurs through simple contiguity of events. During punishment the punishing stimulus automatically elicits freezing, jumping, and other skeletal responses from an organism such as the rat. According to the principle of contiguity, those responses become attached to the stimuli in the experimental situation and, from then on, compete and interfere with the emission of the punished response.

Not all competition theorists have suggested that the competition is at the response level. Estes (1969) has argued that, when punishment is effective, it is because it affects an organism's motivational system. Instead of producing responses that conflict with the behavior for which the organism is being punished, punishment undercuts the organism's motivation to engage in that behavior. For example, a hungry rat responding for food reinforcement loses its appetite when punished, because it is frightened; thus fear competes with hunger and the result is a reduction of the punished behavior.

Traditional competing-response theories have relied upon "two process" explanations of punishment. First, the punishing stimulus is said to elicit an emotional response, such as fear, which then becomes conditioned to environmental stimuli, in accord with Pavlovian principles. Second, avoidance is assumed to take place. The avoidance response can be any response that terminates the presentation of stimuli that elicit the emotional response or enables the organism to escape from them. The organism is reinforced for the avoidance response by a reduction in the emotion elicited by those stimuli that have been terminated. The instrumental avoidance response thus established is then in direct competition with the punished response and the result is response suppression. Variations of this two-process explanation are found in the theories of Mowrer (1960a) and Rescorla and Solomon (1967), among others. And Dinsmoor (1954; 1955) has offered a Skinnerian translation of a two-factor avoidance theory of punishment. Behavior that leads to punishment produces aversive stimuli (rather than fear-producing stimuli) whose reduction is reinforcing.

The primary merit of the two-process explanation would seem to be that it can account for response suppression by using known learning principles—those of respondent and instrumental conditioning. In addition to being favored by many learning researchers, the two-process explanation has been accepted by a great number of investigators whose primary interest is child development. In part this may be a legacy from the psychoanalytic theory of moral development, which is centered on notions of avoidance. Freud suggested that children who adopt the standards of their parents—a process fostered by punishment—eventually punish themselves for misbehavior. The self-punishment takes the form of guilt, an unpleasant emotional state that resembles early anxieties about punishment and abandonment and is avoided by acting in accord with parental prohibitions. There is a great similarity between the psychoanalytic notion of guilt and anxiety and the concept of conditioned fear (see Mowrer, 1960b).

Almost since Thorndike's original formulation of it, the negative law of effect has been rejected in favor of some type of avoidance hypothesis to explain punishment (see Solomon, 1964); presumably this has been done for the sake of parsimony. Because avoidance learning invokes the positive law of effect, it was considered desirable to account for suppression by means of punishment using the same law. However, Rachlin and Herrnstein (1969) maintained that, for all avoidance theories of punishment, it has been assumed that the unobservable "nonresponses" characteristic of punishment-produced suppression are dependent upon experimental manipulations in exactly the way that observable responses are. They argued that this may be an incorrect assumption and offered experimental evidence to support their contention. When a pigeon was punished for pecking a key, this response decreased; however, under comparable conditions, punishment for not pecking a key (nonresponding) did *not* lead to a decrement in nonresponding. Rachlin and Herrnstein argued that this demonstrates that nonresponding is not manipulable in the same way as responding and that it calls into question one of the fundamental assumptions of avoidance theories of punishment.

If Rachlin and Herrnstein are correct, the competing response referred to in avoidance theories must be something other than nonresponding. But that makes such theories subject to the kind of criticism that can be made about other competing-response theories, namely, that, although competing responses involved in response suppression can be easily identified after they have occurred, it is not so easy to predict which ones will occur and when. In a sense, all competing-response notions are simply expressions of the fact that response suppression—that is, nonresponding—is a result of the punishment procedure. To make competing-response theories credible it would seem necessary to have some way of predicting which competing responses will occur for a given response in a particular situation. This would require an understanding of the functional behavior patterns of any given organism, which could be obtained through observation of the organism's activities in their natural context. Bolles's (1970) conceptualization of the role of species-specific defense mechanisms, which has been influential in reshaping thinking about avoidance learning, is representative of this approach. A complementary approach to the study of punishment, suggested by Dunham (1971), is to describe and measure the behavior of an organism in the experimental environment before, during, and after punishment. This enables the investigator to determine just what behaviors constitute "nonresponding" and how the punished organism's behavioral profile differs from that before punishment was introduced. In other words, it can be known whether new behaviors are introduced into the organism's behavioral repertoire by punishment or whether already existing responses are simply arranged differently in terms of their probability of occurrence from what they were before punishment. Most likely both things occur together.

The Negative Law of Effect

The other major approach to dealing with the data of punishment is decidedly atheoretical. When the negative law of effect is invoked, "explanation" becomes the identification of independent variables that affect punishment outcomes. This is a descriptive approach and because it requires that punishment be viewed as a primary process, analogous to reinforcement in its effects on behavior but opposite in the direction of behavior change, it preserves a symmetry that many workers find appealing (e.g., Azrin and Holz, 1966; Fantino, 1973; Mackintosh, 1974; Rachlin and Herrnstein, 1969).

Fantino (1973) recently summarized several of the major studies that are considered to support a return to the negative law of effect. The basic argument is that, just as reinforcement is effective in strengthening behavior, punishment is instrumental in its suppression. Further, the empirical symmetry between their properties indicates a corresponding conceptual symmetry. Thus a positive law of effect accounts for increased responding and a negative law for decreased responding. Evidence in support of this view, and the logic behind it, may be seen in the following statement from Fantino:

> We now turn to some of the evidence which affords further tests of the proposition that punishment affects behavior in a way that is analogous, but opposite in sign, to the effects of reinforcement. Rachlin (1966) examined one of the supposed differences between the consequences of reward and punishment, namely, that the high rate of responding generated by primary reinforcement is likely to be permanent, while the low rate of responding generated by introducing punishment may not be permanent. This fact has been taken as support for the asymmetrical law of effect that we have identified with the later Thorndike and with Skinner, Estes, and Bolles. Rachlin (1966) notes that their "theory implies that the sudden suppression of responses caused by punishment is an elicited emotional disturbance which disappears as the organism becomes accustomed to the stimulus" (p. 251). Such recovery of punished responding is hard to reconcile with the symmetrical law of effect view that we have identified with the early Thorndike . . . . Rachlin conducted an extensive investigation of recovery in which pigeons were studied on a multiple schedule of food reinforcement. Two distinctive stimuli (green and orange key lights) alternated throughout one session; each was associated with a VI 1-minute schedule of food reinforcement. The pigeons were then punished with mild electrical shock for pecking during one of the two components of the multiple schedule . . . [and they]

eventually recovered so that they responded at the same rate during both components of the multiple schedule. Rachlin next introduced shocks during the other component of the multiple schedule: The subjects were shocked for responding during the green period as well as during the orange period. Since responding during the orange period had recovered from the effects of punishment, if behavior during the two components of the multiple schedule were truly independent, there should now be a selective suppression during the green period which had not been previously punished and therefore could not have "recovered." Instead, the rates of responding in the two components were about equal. This leads us to an important conclusion: The recovery generalized from the orange component to the green. Next, Rachlin removed punishment during the orange period. Responding in the orange component rose well above the rate of responding in the green component, as was expected, . . . what was not expected, however, was that the relative rate of responding during the orange component did not return to 50 per cent; the rise following suppression appeared to be more permanent than expected on the basis of previous work. Rachlin then repeated the same cycle of events (i.e., shock in neither stimulus, shock in orange only, shock in both, shock in green only) a second and third time. The hint of a more enduring effect of punishment with more experience in the situation emerged much more clearly in the successive cycles of the experiment.*

What this description of Rachlin's work indicates is that, even if a very mild punishing stimulus is used, the punishment procedure is capable of producing a rather permanent effect upon behavior. In discussing his own results, Rachlin (1966)

---

*From *The Study of Behavior,* edited by John A. Nevin. Copyright © 1973 by Scott, Foresman and Company, p. 258. Reprinted by permission.

emphasized that a punishing stimulus has two major effects on behavior, one a transient emotional effect, the other a long-term instrumental effect. The emotional effect is traceable to the fact that the punishing stimulus, like any other stimulus, is at first a novel stimulus. But, after the effects of the novel stimulus wear off, the primary effects of punishment remain; that is, the instrumental suppression of the punished behavior.

How is this approach to a study of punishment to be evaluated? For those who accept the negative law of effect, understanding requires the identification of variables influencing the effectiveness of punishment. Although this may be a useful approach, it does not lead to identification of the mechanisms by which response suppression is produced by punishment. At some point, then, it is necessary to go beyond the descriptive stage.

A Motivational Theory of Punishment

Earlier in this chapter, evidence was presented that punishment produces, in the rat, greater suppression of a dry-licking response than of a lever-pressing response. Recently, G. Walters and Herring (1976) reported the results of a series of studies aimed at explaining this differential effect of punishment. They argue that, although both of these responses were supported by the same reinforcement contingency (water given to thirsty rats following the response), dry-licking, unlike lever-pressing, is intimately linked to that part of the rat's motivational system involving thirst. They make the assumption that punishment of an organism's internal stimuli associated with a given motivational system will result in a decrease in the organism's tendency to engage in behaviors supported by that system. Dry-licking has stimuli more directly associated with thirst than has lever-pressing. Therefore, punishment of stimuli associated with the dry-licking response would undermine the thirsty rat's motivation to continue responding to a greater extent than would punishment of stimuli associated with the more arbitrary response of lever-pressing. If this analysis is correct, it should be possible to demonstrate that the differential effect of punishment is under the control of motivational conditions supporting the two responses of dry-licking and lever-pressing. In one study, Walters and Herring found this differential effect when rats were deprived of water and reinforced by water, but not when they were deprived of food and were given food reinforcement. In another study, rats were deprived of food and water simultaneously; differential suppression *did* occur regardless of whether food or water was the reinforcer. Thus the nature of the reinforcer does not seem to be important in producing the effect. Finally, in an experiment in which all animals were reinforced with a sucrose solution, only for those rats that were deprived of water was differential suppression of dry-licking obtained; for other rats, which were deprived of food to varying degrees, the effect did not occur. A single conclusion can be drawn from the results of these studies: differential suppression occurs only when rats are dry-licking while deprived of water. Evidently, the effect cannot be predicted by knowing only the type of response being punished or only the deprivation. Both must be known.

What does this imply for a general theory of punishment? It indicates that Estes's (1969) formulation of a motivationally based theory of punishment is a useful one. We suggest that one of the major functions of punishment is to undercut an organism's motivational system by interfering with stimuli that lead to behaviors associated with that system (e.g., licking and chewing). The more closely linked the punished response and its accompanying stimuli are to behaviors supported by the motivational system, the greater is the effectiveness of punishment. To the extent that any response is suppressed by punishment, it is because the response and its stimulus elements are associated with the motivational system that is functioning when it is made. Some responses and their motivational systems have innate connections. For others, the association must be learned, possibly through simple contiguity of the response with the motivational system. For example, a rat learns to press a lever for food when it is hungry; in this way lever-pressing and hunger become associated. Or a child who seeks peer approval engages in disruptive classroom behavior; in this way deviant behavior in the classroom becomes associated with the desire for peer approval. Punishment would then work not by suppressing the response (classroom disruption) directly, but by undermining the child's interest in behaviors involved in the seeking of peer approval.

All of the foregoing is speculative, but it does follow from the data on differential suppression of licking and pressing, data that are not accounted for by other approaches. Thus the negative law of effect argues that *any* response followed by a punishing stimulus will be reduced in strength, and so this law has no way of accounting for the fact of differential suppression. Nor does a standard model of response competition seem helpful for it must be asked why punishment of one behavior (dry-licking) yields more response competition than that of another (lever-pressing). The answer is not obvious. The data seem to be accounted for best by a theory emphasizing events at the motivational level. (A similar point of view has been expressed by Hogan and Roper [1977] with respect to understanding the effects of positive reinforcers. They conclude that each reinforcer has unique effects that are determined by the structure of the behavior system with which the reinforcer is associated.)

To the extent that a theory of this kind proves useful, however, it will tell only part of the story in dealing with the punishment of human beings. Punishment may well exert its influence at the motivational level in such a way as to produce response suppression. It is clear, however, that, after responding has been suppressed, children and adults engage in cognitive activities that have an effect on subsequent response suppression. People evaluate their behavior (in this case, their lack of behavior) in a way that animals such as rats and pigeons (and, no doubt, young children) probably do not. Recall some of the suggestions that researchers have made about the nature of these evaluations. J. Freedman (1965) proposed that children who are mildly threatened and resist temptation reduce dissonance by devaluing the forbidden activity, whereas Ebbessen, Bowers, Phillips, and Snyder (1975) have suggested that the frustration induced by thinking about a toy for which they have been punished for touching may lead children to subjectively devalue the toy. Such cognitive activities have important implications for continued response suppression, particularly that which occurs in the absence of surveillance and hence in the absence of the possibility of continued punishment. And any theory of punishment that attempts to include human behavior in its domain must take them into account. Therefore, although a motivational theory of the sort that has been outlined here may mark the beginning of an understanding of the way in which punishment functions, extension of the theory is necessary, particularly when the concern is with internalization of prohibitions. This extension will constitute much of the material in Chapter 5.

4

SIDE EFFECTS OF PUNISHMENT

Many people believe that the use of punishment as a technique for eliminating responses is abhorrent: not only do they consider it a brutalizing and dehumanizing procedure, as noted in Chapter 1, but they maintain that it is not effective. However, the material presented in Chapter 3 indicates that an argument against the use of punishment because of its ineffectiveness is erroneous; there are many conditions under which punishment is a very effective technique for changing behavior. Another concern that those who oppose the use of punishment have is that it can produce deleterious side effects. It is the problem of side effects that will be addressed in this chapter. It will become clear that punishment, even when carefully and efficiently employed, can have undesirable and unintended consequences, although perhaps not as many as is commonly believed.

Discussions of the side effects of punishment can generally be classified into one of four categories. First, punishment has been said to lead to a subsequent increase in aggressive behavior; that is, the organism being punished behaves in a way that is intended to injure, with this aggression directed toward the punishing agent or displaced toward another person or object. Those who hold this view maintain that the price of eliminating a particular behavior is heightened aggression. Second, punishment is supposed to lead to physical or psychological avoidance of the punishing agent or to escape from that person. By "leaving the field," recipients of punishment thereby remove themselves from the controller's influence. Third, punishment may be capable of producing severe and chronic emotional disturbance. And, fourth, the effects of punishment on a specific response are assumed to generalize to other, similar responses whose suppression or elimination is not wanted. We shall examine the validity of each of these four claims.

Before we begin this examination, however, a word of caution must be given about the blanket use of the term punishment. Just as different punishing stimuli can have different effects on response suppression, so, too, can they have dissimilar side effects. Leitenberg (1965), for example, found that stimuli signalling the onset of electric shock produced short-term emotional effects in pigeons that disrupted responding, whereas those signalling the onset of time-out did not. Physical punishment supplies children with a model for aggressive behavior, whereas punishment in the form of the withdrawal of material rewards or love does not. In the following discussion, then, we shall specify the particular kind of punishment with which we are dealing.

Punishment and Aggression

Judging from the available evidence, the question whether there are conditions under which punishment leads to either direct or displaced aggression has been of more concern to child-development investigators than to learning researchers. The most straightforward answer to this question, at least in the learning laboratory, requires an experiment in which a punished organism has an opportunity to display aggression in a measurable way. This has not been done. Although there is substantial information about aggression in the ethological literature and some interesting work done in the learning laboratory on variables that affect aggression, including its punishment (e.g., Myer, 1971), learning researchers have not attempted to determine the conditions under which punishment may *lead* to aggressive behavior.

It is not uncommon in the animal laboratory to observe rats and dogs that are receiving electric shock suddenly "attack" the grid floor and lever through which the shock is being administered by vigorously biting them. This type of behavior has been labelled *elicited aggression* by Ulrich and Azrin (1962) and is attributed to the delivery of painful stimuli of any kind. The original demonstration of this phenomenon by O'Kelly and Steckel (1939) did not employ a punishment paradigm in that delivery of aversive stimulation was not contingent on the performance of a specified behavior. Rather, two rats were placed together in an experimental chamber containing a grid floor through which shock could be administered. Although the animals did not exhibit aggression before the administration of foot-shock, as soon as shock was delivered they quickly assumed a stereotyped fighting posture and continued to attack one another as long as the painful shock was continued. More recently, the characteristics of elicited aggression and some of the variables influencing its occurrence have been extensively studied by Azrin and his colleagues (e.g., Azrin and Holz, 1966). In addition to demonstrating that such aggression may be elicited by specific stimuli, their studies have shown that the opportunity to engage in aggressive behavior has reinforcing properties in that animals will learn to perform an operant response to gain access to an object against which they can aggress; thus, laboratory-produced aggression can be brought under instrumental control as well as being elicited reflexively (e.g., Azrin, Hutchinson, and McLaughlin, 1965; Myer and White, 1965).

Several researchers have questioned whether the behavior studied in these experiments can really be considered aggression. Johnson (1972), for example, has argued that the natural fighting response of a rat is not a single, stereotyped response such as is seen in elicited-aggression studies. Rather, a much more complicated sequence of behaviors is observed, including many different types of attack and defense. The important point, for the present purpose, is that the elicited aggression studied in the laboratory may bear little relation to the natural aggression of a rat. However, even if this were not a problem in the study of laboratory-induced aggression, it would still be necessary to specifically demonstrate that such behavior would occur in the context of a punishment paradigm; that is, one in which presentation of the aversive stimulus is contingent on the performance of a particular behavior. For such a demonstration to force the conclusion that aggression is an inevitable side effect of punishment procedures, the conditions under which aggression did and did not occur as a result of punishment would have to be determined. For example, if aggression did occur, what were the intensity and the duration of the punishing stimulus? It could be expected that a punishment procedure employing brief shocks of low intensity would be less likely to result in the display of aggressive behavior than one using prolonged, intense shocks. Did the aggressive behavior consist of an unlearned response, or was the response one that had been reinforced by successfully removing the punishing stimulus? Was an unpunished alternative response available to the organism being punished? It would seem that, if one were available, it would minimize the likelihood of aggression.

Even though aggression did occur under some conditions of punishment, it is becoming evident that aggression is also a consequence of techniques of intervention other than, and supposedly more benign than, punishment. Recent work, for example, has been done on schedule-induced aggression— aggressive behavior resulting from schedules of positive reinforcement (e.g., Azrin, Hutchinson, and Hake, 1966; Dove, Rashotte, and Katz, 1974; Looney and Cohen, 1974; Rashotte, Dove, and Looney, 1974). But this, of course, begs the question. That aggression will become part of a punished organism's behavioral repertoire as a direct result of punishment remains to be demonstrated, at least in the animal laboratory. Research in child development, on the other hand, has yielded more information on the topic and will be reviewed in the next section.

Punishment, Frustration, and Aggression

The origin of the notion that punishment increases the incidence of aggression can be traced to the writings of Freud. He referred to a relationship between frustration (i.e., the blocking of pleasure-seeking or pain-avoidance) and aggression. Punishment, however, has been considered by most developmental psychologists to be a source of frustration (Feshbach 1970). Thus Freud's ideas about frustration and aggression are most pertinent to those of punishment and aggression and, for the present purpose, the reader can substitute "punishment" for "frustration" in the following discussion.

Although Freud's statements about aggression changed through time, one of the earlier and more influential ones was that frustration leads to aggression, even when that aggression is not instrumental in removing the source of frustration. What frustration does is to induce an aggressive drive, which, in turn, motivates behavior that is intended to injure the person or thing toward which it is directed. It is assumed that inflicting the injury reduces the aggressive drive, whether or not the aggression is effective in reducing the frustration. According to this analysis, children who are excessively punished can be expected to display a great deal of hostility and anger, even though such displays do not help them to avoid future punishment. The form of this hostility need not be overt; it can be repressed completely or it can be turned inward against the self. But it is there.

A more formalized statement of the frustration-aggression hypothesis was made in 1939 when Dollard, Doob, N. E. Miller, Mowrer, and Sears said that the existence of frustration *always* leads to a form of aggression. This position was soon modified (e.g., N. E. Miller, 1941) to state that frustration increases the probability of occurrence of many different responses, including dependency, withdrawal, regression, and problem-solving, but that aggression is always among them, and, moreover, is the naturally dominant response.

Several studies have been reported that apparently support the frustration-aggression hypothesis. N. E. Miller and Bugelski (1948), for example, prevented boys at a work camp from attending an eagerly awaited "bank night" at the local movie theater by giving them a series of difficult and boring tasks. They found that, after this manipulation, attitudes toward two minority groups became much less favorable. Others, however, have failed to replicate this finding. Stagner and Condon (1955), for example, frustrated college students by having them fail a number of performance tests, but did not find any change in attitude toward minority groups. Moreover, the frustration-aggression hypothesis has been criticized for, among other things, a failure to define just which set of frustrating events is linked to increases in aggression. Thus it has been suggested that arbitrary frustrations elicit hostility more than accidental ones (Pastore 1952). Maslow (1941) suggests that frustrations caused by threats to basic security are much more likely to evoke hostility than are those caused by physiological deprivation; others (e.g., Berkowitz, 1962) have argued that differences in aggression produced by qualitatively different types of frustration may be due to differences in the quantity of goal-blocking that produces each kind of frustration. About all we can conclude is that the relationship between various kinds of frustrations and the subsequent aggression of human beings is as yet unclear.

Nor are animal studies particularly illuminating in this regard. It is interesting to note, however, that the introduction of an extinction procedure following operant training can lead to attack behavior. Azrin, Hutchinson, and Hake (1966) have demonstrated that a hungry pigeon trained to key-peck for food reinforcement will, upon the initiation of extinction, attack another pigeon in the experimental chamber. If frustration can be assumed to result from extinction, then frustration can be linked to the extinction-produced aggression observed. The interpretation of these findings, however, is complicated by the fact that such attacks do not take place if the trained animal can see but not obtain the food reinforcer. A further difficulty results from the general topographical similarity between the key-peck operant, the consummatory, and the attack behaviors: all three include pecking movements. Although there are both specific topographical and functional differences between these behaviors, it must be asked whether the attack behavior would still be found if markedly dissimilar operants and consummatory responses had been studied.

One explanation for the apparent increased aggression that follows frustration has as its basis research done largely in the learning laboratory. This explanation has the virtue of being simpler and more explicit than the frustration-aggression hypothesis, as well as being consistent with a substantial body of research. Several investigators (e.g., Amsel, 1958; Brown and Farber, 1951) have suggested that when an organism is frustrated (i.e., when it is prevented from responding in a way that theretofore had reliably produced satisfaction) motivation is increased. This increase is added to whatever amount of drive already exists in the organism, thereby increasing the vigor with which it responds. Bandura and R. Walters (1963) have suggested that frustration produces a temporary increase in motivation and, consequently, more vigorous responding, which can be interpreted as aggressive behavior. Although the usual response to a stimulus is not considered aggressive if it is mild, it is considered aggressive by most people if it is vigorous. No one thinks that a child who politely requests an object and tugs gently at its mother's hand is aggressive, but a child who does not succeed in getting that object and who then screams the request and yanks hard at its mother's hand is likely to be thought of as aggressive and to be reprimanded for being overly assertive.

Most of the research carried out within the framework of frustration or arousal theory has nonreward as the frustrating event. Although we are, in effect, extrapolating information on nonreward to punishment situations, such extrapolation seems to be justified. Wagner (1966), for example, argued on the basis of a number of studies employing electric shock that punishment and nonreward are similar in that both produce primary emotional responses that have behavior-energizing properties. We are suggesting, then, that some punishing stimuli lead to arousal and invigoration of subsequent responding and that, depending on the nature of that responding, it might be termed aggressive even though it was not intended to cause harm. Some highly vigorous responses are, of course, more likely to be labelled aggressive than are others. Davitz (1952), for example, rewarded some children for being competitive and aggressive and others for being cooperative and constructive. He then frustrated both groups by interrupting a movie they were watching at a crucial point and taking away the candy bars he had given them earlier.

Children reacted to this frustration either aggressively or constructively, depending on the nature of their training. Similarly, Christy, Gelfand, and Hartmann (1971) had young boys observe either an aggressive model or a very active but nonaggressive one. Some of the boys then played a competitive game (presumably an arousing experience). After playing the game, they imitated the model they had seen—either the aggressive or the active one—more than did a group of boys who had seen either the aggressive or the active model but had not played the competitive game. This occurred even though the opportunity to engage in nonmodeled behaviors was also provided.

Proponents of the frustration-aggression hypothesis cite as support for their position the examples from real life of the punished child who hits a younger sibling when no one is looking, or the man who has just had an altercation with his boss and then picks an argument with his best friend. Those who maintain that frustration-producing events lead not directly to aggression, but simply to increases in arousal, however, would argue that the child and the man in these examples are aroused because of the aversive experiences they have just undergone, and that responses they might not even make under ordinary circumstances increase in strength. The child who is slightly annoyed by a sibling and who might normally do nothing about it is aroused to a degree that activates an aggressive response. Similarly, the man who is frustrated because he has been criticized by his boss may be slightly disgruntled when his friend makes an error while they are playing bridge. Ordinarily, he would say nothing, but under the circumstances he reacts in a stronger and more audible way.

There are other ways of conceptualizing what happens in situations of this sort. A somewhat more cognitive approach, for example, in line with the work of Schachter and Singer

(1962), might be to suggest that a punished child who retaliates against a sibling is aroused because of having just been punished. The child believes that it feels as it does not because of having been punished but because of having been wronged by that sibling. Thus the punished child's actions are consistent with the way it feels. This way of describing the situation, however, still depends on the element of arousal.

A final note about the arousal function of punishment, and one that does not fit in with the classic frustration-aggression hypothesis, is that the effects of frustration are temporary (Amsel 1971). If an organism is prevented from acting in response to frustration, its level of arousal will return to normal in time. Proponents of the frustration-aggression hypothesis, however, do not acknowledge the existence of such a mechanism for reducing arousal. The effects of frustration are presumed by them to accumulate if they cannot be released in the form of aggression, often with quite devastating results. They believe that children who are severely punished and are not allowed to express their aggressive feelings will eventually have so much hostility within them that it will be forced to express itself in some way.

In spite of the fact that there are data indicating that arousal dissipates with time, however, other data suggest that punishment also has the kind of long-term effects in its capacity to produce aggression that are predicted by the frustration-aggression hypothesis. This evidence has come from studies such as those by Sears, Whiting, Nowlis, and Sears (1953), Sears, Maccoby, and Levin (1957), Bandura and R. Walters (1959), and Eron, Walder, Toigo, and Lefkowitz (1963). They are consistent in reporting that the children of parents who rely on physical punishment tend to be more aggressive than are those of parents who use other disciplinary techniques. Similar findings have been obtained by animal researchers. In a study of the relationship between maternal punishment and the aggressive behavior of monkeys, Mitchell, Arling, and Moller (1967) found that adolescent monkeys that had been physically punished by their mothers for the first three months of life displayed more aggression and less social exploration than those that had not been so treated. Rather than supplying clear-cut support, however, these findings in fact cast more doubt on the usefulness of the traditional frustration-aggression hypothesis. Why should only physical punishment lead to aggression? Would not withdrawal of love also lead to an increase in aggression? Being subjected to physical or psychological isolation is surely as much a block to the attainment of satisfaction as is a spanking, and constitutes the threat to basic security that Maslow suggested will produce frustration that evokes hostility, as mentioned earlier. Nor does the frustration-arousal hypothesis supply an adequate way of conceptualizing these data. As indicated earlier, the effects of arousal last for only a short time; therefore they cannot account for anything more than temporary effects of short duration. Some other explanation of these longer-lasting effects of punishment on aggression is certainly in order.

The Imitation of Aggression

Since 1961, extensive and rather compelling evidence has accumulated suggesting that children who observe others engaging in aggressive behavior will imitate that behavior. A parent who is yelling at or slapping a child is certainly supplying that child with a model for aggression and, in light of the findings of innumerable laboratory studies, it should not be surprising to find the child behaving in the same way. Certainly this idea is supported by the naturalistic studies that link physical punishment and aggression. We shall now briefly survey some of the literature in order to document this rather important point.

In early studies on the imitation of aggression (e.g., Bandura and Huston, 1961; Bandura, Ross, and Ross, 1963a), children of preschool age watched adults or the characters in filmed cartoons assaulting an inflated plastic clown (a Bobo doll). Compared with children who had viewed more passive behavior, these children subsequently engaged in more hostile behavior toward the Bobo doll, whether they were frustrated or not. A large number of subsequent studies, employing variations on this basic theme, have greatly strengthened the contention that observation of aggression leads to hostility: not only do subjects copy the behavior they have observed, but they become generally more aggressive. Steuer, Applefield, and Smith (1971), for example, report that children who viewed aggressive cartoons subsequently were more aggressive toward other children; their aggression took the form of hitting, pushing, kicking, squeezing, or choking them, holding them down, or throwing things at them. Hanratty, Liebert, Morris, and Fernandez (1969) found that young boys, after watching an aggressive model, were aggressive even toward an adult dressed as a clown. Children who have observed adults tear pages out of books and break balloons have also copied these behaviors (Grusec 1972). The evidence seems strongly to favor the contention, then, that children imitate aggression whether they are frustrated or not and that their aggression can be directed toward both people and inanimate objects.

There is a major difference between the experimental format used in the studies that have just been described and a naturalistic situation in which parental aggression is expressed in the form of physical discipline. In the laboratory, the child observes aggressive behavior that is being directed toward an object or someone else; in other words, the aggression is not being aimed at the child. If the contention is made that children whose parents punish them physically will be more aggressive because they will imitate their parents' behavior, it must be noted that the children are not only observers but recipients of that behavior. It might be expected that undergoing the unpleasant physical and psychological experience of punishment could be a deterrent to imitating the behavior of the punishing agent. However, this does not seem to be the case. Gelfand, Hartmann, Lamb, Smith, Mahan, and Paul (1974) report that children who were trained to play a game by being fined for incorrect responses employed a similar training technique when they later taught another child to play the game. Mischel and Grusec (1966) found that preschool children who were criticized and denied immediate gratification reproduced that behavior when they subsequently interacted with an experimental confederate. Even though they themselves had been forced to wait before they could play a game and verbally punished or deprived of rewards for their actions, these children were willing to impose these aversive experiences on someone else.

It may be that people are more willing to imitate some forms of aggression and punishment to which they have been subjected than others. Perhaps intensity is a variable that influences imitation: mild forms of punishment may be more likely to be imitated than severe forms. There is no evidence from laboratory studies that bears on this question, but findings from naturalistic studies suggest this may not be the case. In recent years there has been a great deal of interest in the widespread and serious problem of child-battering. Extensive investigations have been undertaken in an effort to find an answer to the perplexing question of what kind of people can beat, maim, and even kill their own children. Different characteristics of parents who batter their children have been noted by different researchers, and several explanations for this behavior have been offered. But the one finding that consistently emerges is that parents who abuse their children were themselves abused or neglected, physically or emotionally, as children (Spinetta and Rigler 1972). The data are correlational, but they do support the suggestion that the child-rearing practices employed by parents are imitated, even when they include extreme and severe forms of punishment.

Conclusion

There is an abundance of evidence that children imitate what they observe and that this imitation includes behavior that causes them to undergo unpleasant experiences (Gelfand et al., 1974; Mischel and Grusec, 1966). The obvious extrapolation is that if parents employ physical punishment their children will become physically aggressive, whereas if they rely on other forms of punishment (such as withdrawal of approval and privileges or social isolation) their children are less likely to become aggressive. It could be argued that, because of the lack of sufficient evidence, it is premature at this point to maintain that physical punishment leads to aggression. However, because an experiment in which children are physically assaulted can never be carried out, it will never be possible to assess the effects of such treatment on subsequent behavior in the laboratory. And not all naturalistic studies of child-rearing have shown a positive correlation between physical punishment and aggression (see Yarrow, Campbell, and Burton, 1968). Moreover, an interpretation of those in which the correlation is positive must be tempered by the possibility that the relationship is reversed and that aggressive children require aggressive treatment in order to keep them under control. But the data certainly suggest to us that there is a strong possibility that physical punishment—and physical punishment alone—leads to an increase in aggressive behavior and that the mechanism for this increase is imitation.

To summarize our position on punishment and aggression, it can be said that punishment of *any* kind elevates arousal and, hence, increases the vigor of responding. However, if responses of a nonaggressive nature are prepotent, this elevated arousal does not result in aggressiveness. Moreover, the effects of punishment-produced arousal dissipate with time: even if an organism is prevented from responding, there will soon be no evidence that it is in an aroused state. However, physical punishment—administered by a socializing agent—can have an undesirable, long-term side effect in the form of increased aggression produced by imitation of the socializing agent.

Escape from Punishment

Does punishment promote escape behavior and, if so, under what conditions? The answer to this question is of interest to people trying to modify behavior because, if they lose contact with those whom they are attempting to control, the opportunity to influence them is also lost. Consider, for example, therapist-patient and parent-child interactions: a therapist will not be successful in modifying the behavior of a patient who elects to avoid contact because of a perceived punitive relationship, nor will a parent succeed in disciplining a child if the child leaves the environment either physically or psychologically (e.g., by daydreaming or being inattentive). Thus it is important to determine whether punishment disrupts the social relationship between the punisher and the recipient of punishment. Certainly, the general assertion is not new: Woodworth and Schlosberg (1954) summarized their review of the then available punishment literature by stating that "the typical response to punishment is escape." At the time, little research had been done on which to base such a conclusion, but recent work supports the notion that escape can be a side effect of punishment.

Evidence from the learning laboratory indicates that cues associated with escape from punishment take on reinforcing properties (Buchanan 1958). In addition, Hearst and Sidman (1961) have demonstrated that the removal of a punishment contingency has reinforcing properties—it can be used to support escape behavior. In their study, rats learned to lever-press for food reinforcement delivered on a variable-interval schedule in the presence of a discriminative stimulus. When this response was subsequently punished by shock delivered on a fixed-ratio schedule, a second lever was made available that, when pressed, always produced a temporary time-out during which the discriminative stimulus was turned off and both reinforcement and punishment were interrupted. Some, but not all, of the rats learned to escape with great regularity by pressing the time-out lever. This only occurred, however, when both shock punishment *and* reinforcement were programmed simultaneously. When either the reinforcement or the punishment contingency was removed, these escape responses seldom occurred. These results have suggested to some psychologists (e.g., Seward, 1969) that the simultaneous presence of conflicting events—that is, both reinforcement and punishment—is an important factor in generating escape behavior.

Although the Hearst and Sidman study gives evidence that punishment may generate escape behavior under certain conditions, it does not allow the conclusion that punishment alone tends to promote escape behavior. An attempt to demonstrate this is found in the work of Azrin, Hake, Holz, and Hutchinson (1965). These investigators trained a pigeon to key-peck for food delivered on a fixed-ratio schedule. Then they introduced electric shock, which accompanied each key-peck. During the punishment period, a second key was made available, which functioned to permit an "escape" response: that is, a peck on this key produced a different stimulus, which signalled an opportunity to respond on the original reinforcement-punishment key *without the punish-*

ment contingency being in force. The reinforcement remained in effect on the original key until it had been operated, after which the pigeon had to peck the escape key in order to set up the next reinforcement. There were several interesting findings: although few escape responses were made under mild punishment, the number of such responses increased as the intensity of the punishment increased, until the pigeon spent virtually the entire experimental session responding in order to escape punishment. Furthermore, Azrin and his colleagues were able to demonstrate that escape responding was high when the intensity of punishment was such that it would cause little or no suppression of responding in a standard punishment procedure in which there was no means of escape. In discussing these findings, they suggest that

> the advantages gained by the high degree of effectiveness of punishment on the specific punished response may be outweighed by the escape tendency . . . punishing a child for undesired responses might succeed in reducing the frequency of the undesired responses; but, in addition, reinforcement might be expected for any behavior that resulted in escape from the situation in which the punishment took place. . . . This tendency of the organism to escape from a situation involving punishment, and not any inherent ineffectiveness of punishment, may constitute one of the major disadvantages in the use of punishment for the practical control of behavior. [p. 43]

These findings raise a number of questions. The results obtained by Azrin and his colleagues differ from those obtained by Hearst and Sidman primarily because their subjects were able to obtain reinforcement by operating a separate manipulandum during the time-out period and to set up reinforcement repeatedly without undergoing punishment. Although escape behavior was maintained under these conditions, it had nevertheless been originally established in the context of simultaneous reinforcement and punishment. The question remains, then, whether escape behavior would have necessarily occurred had reinforcement and punishment not been presented simultaneously. It would also be helpful to know whether the tendency to escape would have been as strong if escape had led to a loss of reinforcement. Given that a punishment-free environment is no doubt preferable to one in which an organism is subjected to punishment, would the organism nevertheless learn to tolerate punishment and remain in the environment in which it is subjected to punishment if that were the only place that it could obtain reinforcement? In most child-rearing situations, the punishing agents are also sources of reward: parents who withdraw love must have given it in the first place; those who punish by withholding privileges and material rewards had to have granted them initially. To find answers to the questions raised requires a long-term investigation, perhaps one in which an organism is studied in an environment in which observations of escape behavior and its interaction with reinforcement and punishment can be made around-the-clock.[1]

---

[1]An alternative way of determining whether the interaction between reinforcement and punishment is a necessary condition for producing escape behavior would be to select a response for which an organism is to be punished that does not depend on reinforcement for its establishment or maintenance. Although an experiment of this kind has not been done, Leitenberg (1967) has reported on the effects of making the termination of punishment for the performance of a nonreinforced operant contingent on the performance of a second, dissimilar operant. The punished operant was depression of a floor-level platform, which resulted in the presentation of the punishing stimulus—a bright light. The punishing stimulus remained on until another operant, lever-pressing, was performed. Leitenberg was specifically concerned with whether the presence of an escape contingency would diminish the suppressive effects of punishment, which indeed it did. Unfortunately, although the punished operant in this study was not linked to any explicit reinforcement contingency, the fact that the punishing stimulus remained on until an escape respose was performed makes it difficult to compare Leitenberg's results with those of Hearst and Sidman and of Azrin and his colleagues, whose studies included a discrete punishing stimulus and

Child-development studies have not shed a great deal more light on the problem of escape from punishment. Although there are suggestions that punishment will lead to escape, which removes a child from the socializing agent's sphere of influence, support for this statement supposedly derives from learning studies. And, as revealed in the studies just examined, this evidence is not totally compelling. In fact, in the literature on behavior modification, there is little indication of support for the escape hypothesis. Risley (1968) reports that an autistic child's eye contact with a therapist, reinforced with food, continued to increase even though the therapist was also punishing the child with electric shock for undesirable behavior during the same session. Similarly, Lovaas and Simmons (1969) found that avoidance by retarded children of a therapist who punished them physically decreased; moreover, no fear of the therapist appeared to develop. Others (e.g., Bucher and Lovaas, 1968) have indicated that the suppression of undesirable social behaviors by means of punishment has led to a general improvement in social functioning.

So long as its parent is the major source of reward as well as punishment, a child is forced to stay within the range of influence of that parent in order to obtain rewards. Although animal studies suggest that it is just this combination of reward and punishment that leads to escape, we have already questioned whether this escape would occur if no other source of reinforcement were available. Should the parent become a source of punishment only, escape seems more likely. But no caretaking agent *could* become a source of punishment

---

"escape" responses that were not motivated by the explicit termination of the punishing stimulus. Thus, although Leitenberg has demonstrated that the degree of control exerted by an organism over the punishment contingency can be an important variable in determining the amount of suppression produced by punishment, the escape behavior generated by his procedure cannot be compared with that studied by means of the other two paradigms.

only—children must be fed and sheltered, or they will die. Others who administer punishment but who are not responsible for the child's basic welfare might come to be avoided, as illustrated in a study by Redd, Morris, and Martin (1975). Five-year-old children performed a task in the presence of a pleasant person who made positive comments and in the presence of an unpleasant one who made negative comments (e.g., "Stop throwing the tokens around" or "Don't play with the chair"). Although the unpleasant person was more effective in keeping the children working at the task, they preferred working with the pleasant one. Again, we must keep in mind the kind of punishment being used. People who make negative comments could hardly be effective as punishing agents if they had not established themselves as a valuable source of approval in the first place. The point to be made is simply this: if the concern is that punishment will lead to avoidance of the punishing agent, it seems reasonable to determine what the ratio of rewards to punishment delivered by that agent is; if a child is rewarded more than punished by that agent, attempts to escape would no doubt be minimal.

Punishment and Identification

An important mechanism of personality development is imitation, or identification—the process by which children take on the personality characteristics of those who socialize them. Obviously, this cannot happen if a child is attempting to escape from such people. And, interestingly enough, a number of theories emphasize that the punitive aspects of the caretaker are of primary importance in the development of identification. Freud, for example, suggested that boys identify with, or become like, their fathers as a way of reducing anxiety about being punished by them. Mowrer (1950) has suggested that the development of character (i.e., the adoption of the values and standards of conduct of the parents) is a product of defensive identification, resulting from conflict generated during socialization between strong feelings of love for the parents and equally strong feelings of fear of them. Other theories of identification (e.g., Maccoby, 1959) stress the importance of parental control of resources, both rewarding and punitive, as a factor in a child's becoming like, or imitating, a parental figure. Recently, Chartier and Weiss (1974), using socially disadvantaged children as subjects, have demonstrated that imitation of an adult model who administers punishment does occur. Although they report that, overall, punishment is less likely than reward to facilitate imitation of an adult model, any interaction between that adult and the child—even if it happens to be giving and receiving punishment—seems to enhance identification more than no interaction at all. A female model in fact was imitated as much when she punished children as when she rewarded them. She was initially viewed as a source of possible reward, having been introduced as the owner of candies and pennies to be dispensed during a game, but she subsequently became totally negative, punishing the children by criticizing them and refusing to dispense either candies or pennies.

Although an agent who administers punishment but does not deliver reward is imitated by the recipient, that agent may be less effective in socializing that organism by other means. D. Freedman (1967) reports that puppies that had had only negative interactions with a training agent and had been physically punished for eating a particular kind of food deviated more quickly than puppies that had also had positive interactions with the trainer. An alternative interpretation of these data is that the punished dogs became so adapted to punishment that it ceased to have any effect on their behavior. Data from one of our own laboratories (Grusec and Kuczynski 1975) indicate that punishing agents may be hampered in their efforts to produce conformity. Children who were punished by an experimenter who took pennies away from them were then left alone with attractive toys with which they had been asked not to play. The length of time that children who deviated played with the forbidden toys was greater in this group than in a group in which the children had voluntarily taken pennies away from themselves. Although the results of neither of these studies speak to the question of escape, they do suggest that some kind of hostility, or a reduction in compliance, may be one of the side effects of punishment.

Punishment and Emotional Disturbance

Perhaps one of the most persistent concerns about the side effects of punishment—and one that has achieved the status of legend among laymen as well as psychologists—is the role it may play in the etiology of behavioral disorders. Experts are constantly reminding us of the severe emotional damage that punishment may inflict on the psyches of both children and adults. Maurer (1974), for example, has catalogued a wide range of complaints against the use of punishment, quoting scientists who described it as resulting in social deviance, rigidity, regression, and poor adjustment. Any discussion of punishment must therefore come to grips with the concern that punitive actions have the potential to turn an otherwise warm, friendly, social animal into a neurotic misfit. What is meant specifically by emotional disturbance is seldom made clear.

The only concern that seems to be expressed as often as that of punishment's undesirable emotional consequences is that it is an ineffective technique for controlling behavior. Solomon (1964) has recognized this dualism:

> When punishments are asserted to be ineffective controllers of instrumental behavior, they are, in contrast, often asserted to be devastating controllers of emotional reactions, leading to neurotic and psychotic symptoms, and to general pessimism, depressiveness, constriction of

thinking, horrible psychosomatic diseases and even death. This is somewhat of a paradox, I think. The convincing part of such generalizations is only their face validity.[p. 250]

Although it is possible to argue that punishment can be an ineffective control technique and can produce severe emotional side effects as well, a position that has become very much a part of the punishment mythology, Solomon is correct in pointing out that the belief is an anomalous one. This is not to say that there are not some impressive demonstrations of disruptive emotional effects resulting from techniques in which punishment was employed: there are different conditions that do combine to produce such effects. These demonstrations will be considered here, but it is important to bear in mind that there is a very notable *absence* of reports of emotional side effects in the general punishment literature. Thus, what is necessary for the present purpose is to specify the conditions under which such emotional side effects are likely to occur, and to assess the likelihood of these conditions occurring in real life.

A striking observation to be made about the use of aversive stimuli in the animal laboratory is how unemotional the subjects appear to be when exposed to such stimuli, at least at the intensities employed in most studies on aversive control. In studies on avoidance learning, for example, one is struck by the apparent lack of observable emotional behavior displayed by subjects after the initial period of exposure to the aversive stimulus has passed; animals performing under a punishment contingency display no more emotion than do animals undergoing extinction. This is not to say that casual observations should be given the status of hard evidence, but it should be remembered that there are very few controlled demonstrations of severe and disruptive emotional side effects resulting from the use of even intense punishment. We do not wish to underplay the possibility of emotional side effects but believe it to be important that this possibility be placed in its proper perspective.

What evidence is there for neurotic outcomes of punishment? Not all punishment procedures produce emotional outcomes, and those that have traditionally been cited as evidence for the establishment of neurotic behavior have had to be very extreme to produce such results. Experimental support for the argument that emotional side effects are a result of punishment comes from a series of dramatic demonstrations of so-called experimental neurosis in animals, some of which have included the use of punishment procedures. The question to be answered, however, is not whether bizarre behavioral changes can be produced by a punishment procedure, but whether such changes are a typical outcome of its use. Looking ahead to the discussion that follows, we can say that the answer to this question is clearly "no," although specific circumstances can be contrived to produce such effects.

Experimental Neurosis: The Study of Fixated Behavior

In 1936 Norman R.F. Maier, in competition with investigators representing all divisions of science, received the annual award of the American Association for the Advancement of Science for outstanding research. The award was given to Maier for his studies of experimentally produced neurosis in animals. This work centered on the study of an insoluble problem—any situation in which an animal is forced to choose between several ways of responding and is not consistently rewarded or punished for the choices it makes. Most of Maier's demonstrations utilized a discrimination learning task in which rats were tested on the Lashley jumping stand. To test a rat on this apparatus, the animal is placed on a small platform some distance from a wall on which there are two stimulus cards, each blocking a window leading to a rear platform. On any given trial the rat is made to jump from the front platform at a stimulus card, one of the cards being held firmly in place and the other free to fall away from the opening; the position of the cards is randomly determined. If the rat chooses the correct card, it can jump through the opening to the rear platform where food is waiting. If it chooses the incorrect one, it is prevented from getting to the rear platform by the card that is locked in position and falls into a net below. Thus, the animal is reinforced with food for a correct response and punished by striking the rigid card and falling into the net for an incorrect one. A reluctant animal is encouraged to jump by the presentation of an aversive stimulus such as a blast of air or an electric shock, which remains in effect until the animal executes a response. As might be expected, the rat soon learns to discriminate between simple geometric forms (a triangle and a circle) or between brightness and darkness (white and black). After training the animals on a soluble problem, Maier made the task insoluble by locking the cards into the openings in random order so that there was never a consistently correct stimulus: a rat was punished on half the trials and rewarded on the other half, but never in a predictable manner. With continued exposure, the animals developed perseverative position responses manifest by their constant jumping to the same side throughout hundreds of trials; Maier called these responses "abnormal fixations" and attributed them to frustration arising from an animal's being forced to respond though the problem is insoluble (Maier 1949). Such behavior persisted even after the problem had been made easily soluble by blocking only one of the two openings with a card.

The present purpose, however, is not to detail the presumed course of experimental neurosis, but to determine the specific role that punishment may have played in producing such behavior. Maier asserted that whether punishment produced undesirable side effects such as severe frustration depended on a host of variables such as the organism's frustration threshold, the intensity and duration of punishment, and the organism's perception of the situation. Everything else being equal, punishment, he felt, was less likely to produce frustration, and subsequent neurotic behavior, if it was administered in a situation in which learning could take place. It was in those situations in which problems were insoluble that punishment produced adverse side effects. (It is interesting to note that, in general, Maier thought that punishment procedures in themselves were not very helpful in the direct modification of behavior, but he apparently believed in the efficacy of vicarious punishment: the punishment of another organism served as an example, thereby controlling the behavior of individuals other than those punished.)

Because Maier's experimental procedures were very complicated it is impossible to determine the specific role played by punishment or how punishment may have interacted with other variables such as problem solubility. The animals were subjected to intense and persistent aversive stimulation to make them jump from the platform to a card. When an animal struck an unmovable card and fell into the net, aversive stimuli were operating in two procedurally different ways: one was to force the animal to "escape" and the other was to punish it in an unpredictable way for escaping. Whether punishment played a role in producing fixated behavior in Maier's studies, and exactly what that role was, is not clear: as Maier suggested, such behavior may simply have been a result of the unsolvable nature of the learning task, or of the fact that the animals were forced to respond in such a predicament.

In a more recent study, Karsh (1970) has demonstrated that fixated behavior can be obtained by means of another experimental procedure. She employed a two-choice reversal learning procedure in which rats are trained to press either of two levers: pressing lever A produces food reinforcement and pressing lever B produces both reinforcement and moderate punishment. Confronted with this task, a rat soon learns to choose the lever for which it will not be punished. However, when the results of pressing the two levers are reversed so that lever B produces reinforcement and lever A produces reinforcement and punishment, the rat immediately fixates on one alternative and continues to choose it during further reversals whether or not it is punished for that choice. Other animals that are given a choice between pressing a lever for which they obtain only reinforcement and pressing one for which they receive only punishment or a choice between reinforcement only and neither reinforcement nor punishment do not exhibit fixation. These results are similar to Maier's and yet are produced without the severe frustration of the insoluble problem, which Maier felt was important in the production of fixated behavior, and without continuous exposure to aversive stimulation forcing the animals to respond. Karsh's task was certainly not unsolvable because the rats had ample opportunity to learn to press the reinforcement-only lever during the reversals. Her findings indicate that there is something about the conflict between being both reinforced and punished for an incorrect choice that is responsible for the production of fixated responding. Not surprisingly, when the incorrect choice produces either punishment alone or neither reward nor punishment, animals quite readily choose the reinforced alternative. It is only when punishment is accompanied by reinforcement that fixated behavior occurs. Recall that Hearst and Sidman (1961) also reported that rats will escape from a situation in which they are punished and reinforced simultaneously but not from one in which they are only punished. The phenomenon is puzzling and implies that the presentation of punishment and reinforcement together sets up a conflict that generates undesirable behavior.

Masserman's Studies of Experimental Neurosis. Jules Masserman carried out a series of studies in the 1940s and 1950s in which he attempted to describe animal analogues of human psychiatric problems. Although he studied a variety of animals, Masserman became best known for his demonstrations of so-called experimental neurosis in cats and monkeys (e.g., Masserman, 1943). Such disorders he thought to be rooted in experimentally produced motivational conflicts between consummatory behaviors and fear. In a typical demonstration of the production of such conflict, monkeys were trained to operate a switch in order to obtain food (Masserman and Pechtel 1953). When a monkey accepted the food, a physical punishing stimulus such as a blast of air was delivered to the face, often accompanied by an electric shock delivered through the floor of the cage. Interestingly, in some studies, the punishing stimulus was, to use Masserman's term, "psychological"; that is, an object such as a rubber snake or lizard, which can elicit innate fear in many species of monkey, was placed in the animal's feeding box. After repeated applications of these techniques, Masserman observed a variety of bizarre behaviors that he believed indicated the experimental induction of a neurotic disorder: continual apprehensiveness, feeding disturbances, persistent palpitations, sexual deviations, and severely altered social relations with other members of the monkey colony and with the experimenter.

Although one may question whether these behaviors constitute neurotic behavior, the significance of Masserman's studies is that they demonstrate that dramatic and prolonged changes in behavior can be produced by specific experimental conditions. But was punishment a necessary part of those conditions? Masserman, influenced by Freudian notions of the etiology of neurosis, placed great emphasis on conflict as an inducer of neurotic behaviors. And his punishment procedure was probably sufficient to produce such conflict. However, note that Masserman was dealing with the punishment of consummatory behavior and it may have been that, rather than conflict itself, that produced the deviant behavior. Punishment was always contingent on the acceptance of the food by the animal—a part of its pattern of consummatory behavior—and not on the operant behavior that produced the food. As noted in Chapter 3, the outcome of punishing consummatory behaviors may be different from that obtained by punishing operant behaviors. Unfortunately, too little work has been done on the effects of punishment in relation to class of response to warrant generalizations. It is nevertheless interesting to note that, in discussing Masserman's work, Solomon (1964) suggested that neurotic disturbances of the type described by Masserman seem to arise in those cases in which instinctive or consummatory behaviors are being punished and he speculated that this would happen only when the organism was incapable of learning when a given response would or would not be punished. Whether Solomon is correct is not yet known because no one has put his suggestion to the test using a procedure similar enough to Masserman's.

However, we do know that it is possible to train animals to seek out the traumatic consequences of the kind Masserman used in his studies by having the punishing stimulus signal the availability of food. Masserman and Jacques (1948) trained a kitten to open a box for food in the presence of a light-sound signal. When the kitten was punished for getting the food by being subjected to a blast of air and electric shock, it developed neurotic behaviors that continued outside of the experimental chamber. A second kitten was trained in the same manner except that the punishing stimuli were gradually incorporated into the light-noise signal. The signal was then diminished as the punishing stimuli became more intense. Under these conditions the blast of air and the shock, administered at full strength, eventually replaced the light-noise signal with no adverse reactions noted in the single test animal. Masserman and Jacques were able to train other animals to engage in an operant behavior that produced the intense punishing stimuli, after which the animals were permitted to raise the cover of the box and consume the food. This is not unlike the later work of N. E. Miller (1960) in which he demonstrated that rats would traverse an alleyway to consume food in a goalbox even though its comsumption was accompanied by intense electric shocks if the animals' previous experience in performing this task had included being subjected to gradually increasing intensities of shock in the presence of food in the goalbox.

These studies seem to indicate that it is not merely the use of a punishment procedure, even one employing intense shocks, that experimentally produces neurotic outcomes; something else must contribute to their production in work such as Masserman's. It could be the association of fear with consummatory activity, the artificial restraint, the confinement of an organism under certain laboratory conditions in which aversive contingencies are employed, or the inability of the organism to escape from the cues signalling the threat of punishment. Some of the classic studies of Gantt (1944) and Liddell (1956), both of whom studied with Pavlov and used his conditional-reflex methodology to produce behavioral pathologies in animals, indicate that the tremendously confining restraint imposed on their subjects by these workers could have been influential in producing pathology. Liddell (1956) has commented on this possibility in reporting his work, indicating that neither the shock employed nor the use of difficult discrimination tasks seemed essential in producing pathology in the variety of animals studied in his laboratory. Rather, he felt the unnatural restraint and the monotony of the experimental situation were more important factors. Whether this is true is simply not known.

There is no reason to believe, on the basis of the existing experimental evidence, that punishment is necessarily accompanied by undesirable emotional disturbances. In the studies discussed herein in which fixations and experimental neurosis have been the outcomes, punishment was only one of several variables included and its particular role is difficult to determine. Karsh's data are the least equivocal, but it is not clear how they should be interpreted except that, under certain conditions, punishment paired with reinforcement may lead to maladaptive behavior, just as that combination seems to lead to escape behavior. Anecdotal evidence reported by several contemporary punishment researchers, together with the limitations of the studies of experimental neurosis in animals, leads us to the conclusion that punishment, by itself, does not produce emotional disorder.

A number of child-development researchers have suggested that physical punishment fosters "social deviance" and "poor adjustment" in children, but it is entirely possible that these labels refer to simple increases in aggression as a function of imitation rather than emotional disabilities. Excessive aggression may well give rise to emotional disturbance. Thus children who are aggressive—who are socially deviant or poorly adjusted—might be disliked by their peers. If peer approval is valued, this could produce emotional arousal, depression, regression, or anger, which might well interfere with their effective functioning. Such interference, however, would be an indirect rather than a direct outcome of punishment.

Neurosis and Guilt

A direct outcome of punishment—one that has been investigated and can be construed as an example of emotional disturbance—is excessive guilt. Among the aims of most socializing agents is the production of guilt after deviation, but too much guilt may be maladaptive—a result of punishment that is too effective. Hoffman (1970a) has offered an interesting analysis of the production of guilt during socialization. He suggested that the moral orientation of some children is external (such children are concerned mainly with detection and punishment), whereas that of others is internal. Those in the latter group are either humanistic—caring about the human consequences of behavior and taking into consideration extenuating circumstances—or conventional—rigidly adhering to institutional norms regardless of consequences and circumstances.

The control that conventional children have over their antisocial impulses is excessive, automatic, and influenced more by the subconscious than by higher cognitive processes. The disciplinary technique particularly implicated in the production of a conventional moral orientation is withdrawal of love; control is achieved through anxiety about deviation, generated by fear of losing parental approval. The control exhibited by humanistic children is characterized by empathy and identification with parents who are responsive to extenuating circumstances and who communicate the importance of considering others. In contrast to a conventional internal orientation, a humanistic one invokes higher cognitive processes and requires that impulses be conscious so that they may be dealt with in accord with reality. Parents of humanistic children are flexible in their use of disciplinary tchniques but tend to rely on socializing techniques that call to the attention of their children the harm that their deviations inflict on others. The quantity of guilt produced in children whose moral orientation is internal is the same whether that orientation is humanistic or conventional, but it differs in quality. The guilt experienced by humanistic children tends to be benign, with the potential for having a constructive effect on personality in the sense that it may heighten concern for the condition of others. For those whose orientation is conventional, guilt is less constructive and can even be destructive—it is withdrawal of parental love turned inward, leading to that heightened arousal occasioned by dread of abandonment. Hoffman suggested that this arousal causes a child to avoid any cognitive material relevant to the effects of its deviation on others, and so its empathic sensitivity to the rights of others becomes blunted.

These are provocative ideas and Hoffman, in the same article, has supplied correlational data that support his analysis. Indeed, what may be obtained from that analysis is a useful framework within which to try to understand possible deleterious effects of *one* kind of punishment. When cognitive functioning is introduced into any discussion of punishment and its effects, of course, animal data then prove to be of little use. Fear of abandonment is probably experienced by a number of mammals, but it is difficult to conceive of a rat being motivated to avoid pressing a lever because it fears being abandoned by the experimenter. The question, then, is how to tie together the studies of experimental neurosis in rats and the development of conventional—or ego-alien, to use a psychoanalytic term—guilt. At present, it is clear that the work done by researchers in learning and child development overlaps very little.

Punishment and Generalization of Suppression

The effects of reinforcement and punishment are not limited to those specific responses upon which they have been made contingent. They extend to other behaviors that are similar in nature. The suppressive effects of punishment on one behavior may generalize to other, related behaviors that the socializing agent or experimenter does not wish to suppress. For example, a child severely punished for masturbating might have difficulty participating in socially sanctioned sexual activities as an adult. Or, a child punished for being aggressive—if that punishment is nonaggressive in nature—might have all assertive behavior eliminated.

There are situations in which generalization of suppression is desirable. For example, a parent who punishes a child for being aggressive at home, may want the effects of that punishment to generalize to the child's behavior at school. Similarly, a socializing agent who punishes a child for lying about a specific event undoubtedly wants the result to generalize to other situations in which the child might be tempted to lie. Indeed, such generalization is necessary for successful socialization. A child must internalize prohibitions in the sense that the prohibited behaviors continue to be suppressed not only in the absence of a socializing agent, but also in settings in which the child has never been punished for them.

There have been several animal studies that are relevant to the question of generalization of the effects of punishment. Taken together, these studies indicate that, initially, suppression achieved by the use of punishment generalizes to situations other than the one in which punishment occurs. But this effect gradually disappears: nonresponding becomes restricted to the punishment period and responding in the absence of punishment eventually recovers, often to its prepunishment baseline rate (Azrin 1956; Azrin and Holz 1966; Dinsmoor 1952; Honig and Slivka 1964). More specifically, Honig and Slivka have determined that, for pigeons, punishment-generalization gradients are similar in shape to gradients obtained from studies of positive reinforcement, although the punishment gradients are, of course, inverted. Therefore, the more similar a situation is to that in which punishment occurs, the more likely it is that punishment effects will generalize to that situation.

Varied results have been obtained from studies of generalization in children. LaVoie (1973a; 1974a) found that punishment with a loud buzzer produced generalization of suppression in girls but not boys. Cheyne (1971) reported generalization of suppression when a loud buzzer of high intensity (98 decibels) was administered at the beginning of a response sequence but not when a less-intense (75 decibels) buzzer was used nor when either high- or low-intensity punishment was delivered at the end of the response sequence. It is interesting to note that the occurrence of generalization seems to correlate with greater response suppression in these studies: punishment was more effective for girls than for boys (LaVoie 1973a), and high-intensity punishment at the beginning of a response sequence was more effective than other combinations of intensity and timing (Cheyne 1971). Finally, Aronfreed and Leff (1963) found that generalization of suppression occurred when children were punished with a combination of verbal disapproval, deprivation of candy, and activation of a buzzer and the learning task was a simple one, but not when it was a difficult one. Because the degree of response suppression that was produced in their study was affected by the interaction of punishment intensity and difficulty of the task, the relationship between response suppression and generalization is not as clear as it is in the studies by LaVoie and Cheyne.

Given that the effects of punishment do become generalized, it seems necessary to identify the variables that could minimize the extent of generalized suppression. Intensity, duration, and scheduling of punishment, amount of training, and degree of motivation could certainly be among those variables, and yet little information is available about their effects. A measure of the degree of similarity between the punished response and other responses of both a desirable and an undesirable nature would be useful in assessing the effect that a given form of punishment would have on related responses. A system of discrimination training might be useful in decreasing the amount of generalization. Honig (1966), for example, punished pigeons when they pecked a key in the presence of a vertical line, but not when they responded in the absence of any line. Their rate of responding to lines that were not vertical was subsequently higher than that of pigeons that had not been given an opportunity to engage in nonpunished responding. Generalization gradients for the group that had not been trained to discriminate were flat; the pigeons in that group did not respond differentially to lines having different spatial orientations. Apparently, reinforcement for desired behaviors, coupled with punishment for undesired ones, is an effective procedure for reducing the negative effects of learned suppression.

Although it could be expected that punishment for responding to one stimulus would lead to the suppression of responding to another, similar stimulus, this is not always the case. Under certain conditions, if an organism's response to a given stimulus is suppressed by punishment, responding to a second stimulus is enhanced, even though the consequences for responding to the second stimulus remain unchanged (Brethower and Reynolds 1962). This is the phenomenon of punishment contrast. A more general term, *behavioral contrast,* has been used to designate a change in the rate of responding to a given stimulus that is opposite to the change in rate of responding to another stimulus when the latter change is induced by modifying the consequences for responding. For example, if the rate of responding to the first stimulus increases, the rate of responding to the second stimulus decreases as a function of a change in the consequences of responding to the first stimulus.

The conditions under which behavioral contrast is obtained instead of generalization of suppression are not clear. Amsel (1971) argued that behavioral contrast is a result of short intertrial intervals and massing of trials, although the evidence for his argument is not conclusive. In spite of extensive work by learning researchers on both generalization and behavioral contrast, it is still not easy to predict which of the two phenomena will be obtained in any given situation. There are very few studies of either child development or behavior modification that shed light on the problem. Wahler (1969) did attempt to assess the effects of punishment on behaviors similar to the punished one. A young boy was subjected to brief social isolation contingent on uncooperative behavior at home, and an assessment was made of the effect of this isolation on his behavior both at home and at school. Although uncooperative behavior decreased at home, such behavior at school remained the same. Thus *neither* generalization of suppression nor behavioral contrast was obtained.

Konstantareas (1974) investigated the effects that changing the consequences for responding in one situation might have on responding in another. She had nine-year-old boys and girls press one of two illuminated keys in order to receive marbles. The children were presented with first one illuminated key and then the other, responding alternating between the two throughout the experiment. Reinforcement for responding was the same for both keys: marbles were delivered on a 45-second variable-interval schedule. After a stable, and similar, rate of responding had been established on both keys, response-cost punishment (the loss of a marble) on a 45-second variable-interval schedule was introduced for responding on one of the keys. The schedule of reinforcement remained unchanged for the other key. Punishment was successful in reducing the rate of responding on the key with which it was associated. At the same time, rate of responding increased on the key for which the schedule of reinforcement remained unchanged; that is, on the constant component of the procedure. Thus Konstantareas was able to demonstrate the existence of punishment contrast in children, obtaining no evidence at all for generalization of suppression. Note that she was able to demonstrate its existence by using response-cost punishment rather than electric shock, which has been the stimulus employed in animal studies of contrast.

Konstantareas carried out another experiment designed to more closely approximate the naturalistic situations in which socialization takes place. Eight- and nine-year-old boys and girls were instructed to engage in a series of "aggressive" behaviors that consisted of stepping on a rubber snake, punching an inflated plastic doll, beating a drum, and throwing a dart. The experiment was so designed as to include two different settings in which the children were to respond—first in one and then in the other. In both settings reinforcement in the form of chips, exchangeable for prizes, and social approval was delivered on a 45-second variable-interval schedule. Punishment, in the form of loss of a chip, was then instituted for aggression in one of the settings. This punishment was delivered on a 45-second variable-interval schedule. In the other setting the schedule of reinforcement remained the same. Punishment was effective in reducing the rate of responding in the setting in which it was applied. In the constant setting, in which the schedule of reinforcement was unchanged, punishment contrast was not obtained. Rather, generalization of suppression resulted, as evidenced by a decrease in rate of responding.

In an attempt to explain the discrepancy between the results of the two experiments, Konstantareas called attention to the fact that there was a difference in the amount of time between exposure to the alternating conditions in the two studies. In the first study, in which behavioral contrast was obtained, responding on one key or the other was regularly alternated within each session, with no time elapsing between the alternations. In the second study, in which generalization of suppression was obtained, each setting was presented only once in each session, with approximately two minutes elapsing between them. The arrangement in the second study is more like a naturalistic situation in which children are not constantly being thrust back and forth between different sets of conditions. Amsel (1971) has suggested that, with long intertrial intervals and discrete trials, generalization of suppression, rather than behavioral contrast, is to be expected. According to this analysis, the invigorating effects of punishment are temporarily labile and dissipate with time (recall the discussion of frustration or arousal theory), allowing for the more permanent effects of generalized conditioned suppression to take over. Because of the rapid alternation of settings in the first experiment—exposure to each stimulus lasted 90 seconds and there were, within a session, ten presentations of each of the two stimuli—the children may have been in a state of high arousal and therefore responded more vigorously to the constant stimulus. The time that elapsed between presentation of the two settings in the second experiment may have been sufficient to allow for dissipation of arousal. On the basis of this line of reasoning, it could be assumed that generalization of suppression, rather than punishment contrast, would be more likely to occur in naturalistic socialization situations, because such situations are not likely to be characterized by massed exposure to schedule components and rapid alternation between them. Even in real life, however, a distinction should probably be made between the long- and short-term effects of punishment. Punishment contrast may be found in naturalistic settings, but it will be of short duration. The long-term effects of punishment may well be in the direction of generalization.

Konstantareas also commented on the importance of the history of reinforcement that the subjects in her experiments have had. The response employed in the first experiment was a neutral one in that children are generally neither reinforced nor punished for pressing keys, whereas the responses in the second experiment were not neutral—children are frequently punished for aggressive behavior in real life. After punishment had been instituted in the alternate setting, it may have evoked conditioned anxiety in subjects through generalization from past experience, in addition to being an aversive experience in itself. The anxiety may have served to suppress behavior in the setting for which reinforcement remained unchanged. The children may have brought to the experimental situation the attitude that aggressive behavior is bad. They may have engaged in it initially because they were encouraged by the social and material reinforcement offered by the experimenter. However, after being punished for aggressive behavior in one of the settings, they may have been less able or willing to discriminate between the reinforced response in one of the settings and the punished response in the other than if they had been pressing keys. Being punished by the experimenter may have evoked the anxiety associated with all displays of aggression.

If the nature of the response and its past reinforcement must be taken into account in order to understand the results of Konstantareas's work, then both the length of the intertrial interval and the nature of the responses produced generalization of suppression in the second experiment. Had aggression been the behavior used in the first experiment, it would have counteracted the effect of short intertrial intervals and would have produced either generalization, reduced contrast, or no generalization or contrast at all.

Given the existing evidence, it seems reasonable to suggest that punishment contrast, although obtainable in a laboratory setting under a variety of conditions (but not with all behaviors—see Westbrook, 1973), is less likely to occur in naturalistic situations, except as an immediate response to punishment. A reason for this may be that, in real life, the interval between responding in a situation in which punishment is administered and responding in a related, but different, one in which there is no punishment is generally quite long. After the arousal induced by punishment has had a chance to dissipate—which does not take long—heightened responding in another situation is not likely to occur.

Displacement

Punishment contrast is of particular interest because it ties in with the psychoanalytic notion of displacement, which involves the idea that a child who is punished in one situation for a particular behavior will indeed refrain from that behavior in that situation but will display it in other situations. This phenomenon obviously has more in common with behavioral contrast than with generalization of suppression. A child punished for aggression at home, for example, will not be aggressive at home, but will become more aggressive at school. Against whom or what the child directs the aggression depends on the degree of similarity between the original and the new target, and on the severity of the punishment administered for the aggression directed at the original target (N. E. Miller 1948). A child punished mildly for assaulting a sibling might exhibit aggressive behavior toward a peer in the schoolyard, whereas severe punishment for the same behavior might result only in hostile responses on a projective test.

Other explanations for the suppression of punished behavior in one setting and its appearance in another, though, seem more tenable than that of displacement. The notion of punishment contrast is not helpful because the effects of displacement are long-term rather than short-term; however, the idea of differential reinforcement may be useful in this regard. Bandura and R. Walters (1959), for example, reported that they found that highly aggressive boys had parents who punished them severely for aggression in the home. They also found, however, that these same parents encouraged their children to be aggressive outside the home and rewarded them for it. Therefore, it can be assumed that what apparently reflected a displacement of aggression was, in fact, the result of discrimination training.

Imitation offers another explanation for the display, in a different environment, of behavior for which a child has been punished. A child who is physically punished for aggression at home will no doubt suppress that aggression there for fear of further retaliation but will *imitate* the aggressive behavior of the socializing agent in another environment where its aversive consequences are not feared. There is no reason to restrict the discussion to physical punishment and aggression. Suppose that a parent takes a possession away from a child because that child has taken another child's toy. Taking another's possessions may consequently be suppressed in the presence of the parents, but may occur in their absence in imitation of their disciplinary style.

Summary

We have suggested that punishment contrast is a short-term phenomenon, whereas generalization has long-term effects. However, this is no more than a plausible hypothesis at the moment and requires more research to establish its usefulness. What kind of experience an organism has had with the behavior for which it is being punished, whether the behavior is innate or learned, and what the relationship is between the kind of punishment and the punished behavior are but a few of the factors to be considered in understanding the effects of punishing one response on other, related responses.

Conclusion

It is apparent that, although punishment does have undesirable side effects, they are not as detrimental as some people have suggested. Used judiciously, punishment can be quite effective in suppressing unwanted behavior, without adversely affecting desirable behaviors. This excludes extremely severe punishment, that which is administered randomly so that the contingencies are unclear to the recipient, and that which is administered by a hostile and rejecting caretaker. What we are referring to is punishment used by a responsible and concerned person in teaching acceptable behavior.

This should not be taken as a blanket endorsement for all types of punishment. The side effects of corporal punishment may be different from those of verbal rebuke or deprivation of privileges. Children imitate the disciplinary styles of socializing agents, and so there is a good argument to be made that socially mediated physical punishment, used as the predominant technique of discipline, may lead to physical aggression. If nothing else, it teaches children that the way to gain compliance from others is to impose one's superior physical force on them. Psychologically oriented punishment techniques such as withdrawal of love, which produce feelings of loss of security, may also have undesirable side effects. And it is not unreasonable to suppose that punishment that undermines a child's self-esteem may diminish that child's feelings of self-worth. But even if the use of such techniques were abandoned, there is still a wide variety of punishing stimuli that can be profitably used by socializing agents. Response-cost, time-out, and verbal rebuke, although they may produce short-term arousal and even hostility, are not so harmful in their side effects.

5

OTHER RESPONSE-SUPPRESSION TECHNIQUES

To enhance our understanding of punishment, it is useful to compare its effectiveness and limitations with those of a variety of other techniques that can be employed to suppress responses, such as extinction, omission training, and vicarious punishment. There have been relatively few attempts to compare one technique with another, and we are certainly not in a position to assess their effectiveness individually, using punishment as a standard. In our consideration of the techniques other than punishment that are used to suppress behavior, emphasis will be on such characteristics as immediacy and permanency of effect, capacity to produce complete suppression, undesirable side effects, and practical problems encountered in their employment.

Another problem that will be dealt with extensively is that of internalization. It has been the contention of many psychologists in child development that no punishment technique can successfully change behavior, independent of fear of punishment by an external agent. Were we to rely solely on reward and punishment, we would have no hope of producing "moral" citizens; that is, people who behave responsibly even when it is unlikely that their immoral behavior might be detected. To the extent that standards become internalized, a number of people contend that it is necessary to look to other techniques for controlling and eliminating behavior. A technique that has been singled out as vital in the development of internalization is one that relies on reasoning and appeal to cognitive capacities. To evaluate this view requires a consideration of reasoning as a disciplinary technique. Is it effective for long-term suppression of behavior, independent of external punishment? Can it be used to eliminate undesirable behavior rather than just suppress it under certain circumstances?

Extinction

It is common knowledge that learned responses, no longer reinforced, will usually decrease in strength—that is, extinguish. It does not take very many attempts to learn not to deposit money in a vending machine after the first coin fails to produce the product. Extinction, offset by a reasonable degree of perseverance, is an important part of an organism's survival mechanism; although nonreinforced behavior can persist under certain conditions, emission of a previously reinforced behavior in the absence of reinforcement eventually decreases. Extinction is possible, of course, only when the agent modifying the behavior can identify the reinforcer in question and is capable of manipulating it. This is easy to accomplish in the experimental laboratory, where the reinforcer is under the control of the experimenter; it is more difficult in institutional settings such as classrooms and hospitals; and, in practice, is sometimes impossible in naturalistic settings. Nevertheless, much has been learned about extinction and the variables that affect it. Although it is outside the scope of this book to review the topic thoroughly, it is appropriate to elaborate on several of its characteristics.

One of these characteristics has to do with the immediate result of terminating reinforcement—the beginning of extinction. As soon as an organism is no longer being reinforced for a given response, its rate of responding will usually increase and will be higher than it was during acquisition—the behavior becomes more vigorous. This is a short-term effect, and its magnitude depends on a number of acquisition variables. But the fact that behavior undergoing extinction is likely to first become more vigorous must be taken into account in employing an extinction procedure. There are many situations in which such an increase would be undesirable, as in the extinction of the self-mutilating behavior of autistic children. Such children frequently engage in head-banging, face-scratching, and other potentially harmful behaviors. Although in the long run extinction may be a useful procedure for the reduction of such behaviors, the temporary increase in self-mutilating behavior may be unacceptable to the therapist.

Another characteristic of the extinction process is spontaneous recovery: there is always a degree of recovery of the response undergoing extinction if time elapses between one extinction session and the next. Thus, even though a given criterion of extinction has been met in one session, the strength of the response can be expected to recover to some extent by the next session if the subject has been away from the experimental situation for a time. But with consistent repetition of the sessions, the subject will either stop responding eventually or the rate of responding will stabilize at the level that was observed before the introduction of reinforcement.

Extinction is a relatively slow process and does not produce the sudden suppression of behavior that punishment often does, although it is generally considered to produce an enduring effect. However, Holz and Azrin (1963) have obtained evidence that extinction does not produce suppressive effects that are more permanent than those of punishment. As noted in Chapter 3, a combination of the two techniques can greatly reduce the persistence of responding normally found when extinction is used alone.

Extinction has been used as a standard against which other response-elimination techniques may be measured. It is helpful to keep in mind the characteristics of extinction just mentioned in considering these comparisons.

Omission Training

Omission training, also known as the differential reinforcement of other behavior, or DRO, refers to a procedure in which positive reinforcement is given for withholding a prohibited response. If an organism does not respond in the way that is prohibited during a specified period, it is automatically reinforced *without* having to respond in another specified way. Thus, the experimenter is strengthening whatever other behavior the organism may be engaging in at the moment the response-delay requirement has been completed. In most omission-training procedures, the organism is penalized for performing the prohibited response by having to withhold the response for another period of the same length. Ideally, an experimenter reinforces the organism for making a response that is incompatible with the prohibited one, building in appropriate behaviors while eliminating inappropriate ones through response competition. Typically, in animal studies investigating the usefulness of the response-omission procedure, a response is established and maintained using positive reinforcement. Later, the reinforcer is withheld for a specified period in order to satisfy the requirements of the omission procedure. However, Rachlin and Baum (1972) and Zeiler (1976) have demonstrated that it is not necessary to discontinue the reinforcement schedule supporting the response in order for omission training to suppress behavior. Thus, the original reinforcer continues to be delivered contingent on responding even after the omission training procedure has been instituted. This is worth noting because it indicates that, as with punishment, this technique can be effective even if the reinforcer serving to maintain the response to be omitted cannot be isolated.

As an example of how omission training works, consider the disruptive behavior of a child in an elementary-school classroom. The teacher will reinforce any nondisruptive behavior by withholding reinforcement until no disruption occurs for, say, ten minutes. Any occurrence of the disruptive behavior during the ten-minute interval precludes reinforcement and the child has to wait another ten minutes for it. In practice, the teacher could reinforce any behavior occurring at the end of ten minutes, but it would be better to reinforce one that is preferred, such as studying rather than looking out the window or daydreaming. In practical situations, then, the goal of omission training is the elimination of prohibited behavior and the establishment of reliable, desirable competing behavior. This may not be easy at the beginning of omission training, but as training continues and the time during which inappropriate behavior must be withheld is gradually lengthened, the teacher can be more and more selective in choosing "appropriate" behaviors.

Omission Training Compared with Extinction and Punishment

The effectiveness of omission training is impressive. Zeiler (1971), for example, has compared omission training with an extinction procedure. He trained pigeons to key-peck for food delivered on a fixed-ratio schedule. During training the color of the key alternated between red and blue, and training conditions were manipulated so that the rates of responding in the presence of each color were equal. At this point all responses emitted in the presence of one color were extinguished, and those emitted in the presence of the other color were reinforced only if the organism had waited 30 seconds before responding. Thus, each bird was subjected to both extinction and omission training in this within-subject design. The results are shown in Figure 5-1, which reveals interesting differences between the outcomes of the two response-elimination procedures. First, from the very beginning, omission training reduced the rate at which all three subjects responded more rapidly than did the extinction procedure. Second, the response reduction produced by omission training was longer lasting than that produced by extinction. Note that spontaneous recovery occurred after the two 72-hour intervals between sessions during extinction, but not during omission training. Zeiler noted another difference between the two experimental conditions, which is not shown in Figure 5-1: the birds were observed to stand relatively motionless when the stimulus signalling omission training was present, but their behavior became more agitated in the presence of the stimulus signalling extinction. Therefore, omission training may produce fewer emotional side effects than does an extinction procedure, a possibility that warrants systematic investigation.

Of additional interest are the findings of Uhl and his colleagues, obtained from studies in which the subjects were rats. Omission training was compared with other response elimination techniques. The techniques were used either alone or in combination. In summary, extinction used alone produced a somewhat more rapid suppression of responding than did omission training (a finding contrary to that of Zeiler); omission training, however, resulted in longer-lasting effects (Uhl

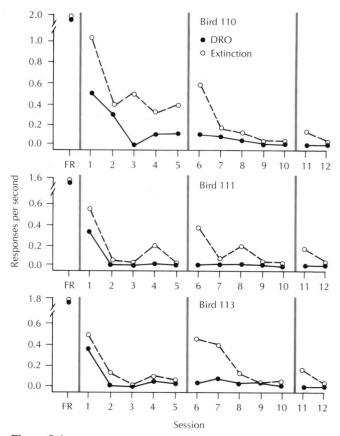

Figure 5-1

Omission training compared with an extinction procedure. Rates of responding are shown for the last day of the fixed-ratio phase (FR) and in each of twelve sessions during which DRO and extinction schedules were employed. Birds had been trained as follows: Bird 110, FR 120; Bird 111, FR 60; Bird 113, FR 30. The vertical gray lines indicate a 72-hour interval between sessions; intervals between other sessions were 24 hours. [From M. D. Zeiler, Eliminating behavior with reinforcement. *Journal of the Experimental Analysis of Behavior* 16(1971):401–405. Copyright 1971 by the Society for the Experimental Analysis of Behavior, Inc.]

and Garcia 1969; Uhl 1973), just as it did in Zeiler's study. The greater durability of suppression produced by omission training relative to that produced by an extinction procedure has also been demonstrated in other investigations (Harman 1973; Topping and Larmi 1973; Topping, Pickering, and Jackson 1971). Combining punishment with omission training increased the rate of response suppression relative to that obtained when omission training was used alone, but reduced the durability of the omission training (Uhl and Sherman 1971). Perhaps the rapid but temporary suppression produced by punishment in combination with omission training prevented the rats from learning what the contingencies were in omission training; that is, that responding postpones reinforcement.

Applications of Omission Training

Omission training is obviously an interesting and promising response-elimination technique, but at present very little is known of its potential. How effective this technique is and how easily it can be put to practical use are just beginning to be determined. As Uhl and Sherman have suggested, omission training tends to be used in rather informal ways to control human behavior, such as allowing a child to engage in free play at school if there has been no misbehavior during formal classtime. There are many other commonplace examples of the delivery of a reinforcer contingent on the withholding of an unwanted behavior, such as giving a child dessert only if the child has not spilled milk during dinner. Indeed, the informal use of omission techniques may be as frequent as is the informal use of reinforcement for a specific behavior such as *drinking* milk in order to get dessert.

In a clinical setting, Corte, Wolf, and Locke (1971) compared the effectiveness of extinction, omission training, and electric-shock punishment in eliminating such self-injurious behavior in retarded children as face-scratching, eye-poking, and head-banging. The extinction procedure, in which social consequences were removed, was found to be ineffective. Omission training, in which food was presented for not engaging in self-injurious behavior, was somewhat effective in eliminating that behavior from one child's repertoire but only under mild food deprivation. Electric shock, which was delivered to a child's arm, was found to be the most effective procedure. Its reductive properties were rapid, complete, and, in some cases, relatively long-lasting. There also was evidence that the effectiveness of punishment generalized from the three adults who administered the punishment to a fourth who had not participated in the punishment procedure.

Conclusions

The question of *how* omission training works has not received much attention. An obvious explanation is that the training procedure leads to the strengthening of responses incompatible with the unwanted behavior; the differential reinforcement of other behavior (DRO) implies that the behavioral mechanism involves the selective strengthening of responses that interfere with the dominant ongoing behavior. It would be useful to observe the behaviors an organism engages in during omission training to determine if they change with changes in response omission. Recently, it has been demonstrated that a procedure in which the original response is no longer reinforced but an alternative response is produces more rapid and complete suppression of the response than does omission training; both procedures result in greater suppression than does extinction alone (Mulick, Leitenberg, and Rawson 1976). However, whether omission training itself works because of the selective reinforcement of responses other than the criterion response remains to be answered.

There is evidence that omission training may have longer-lasting effects than punishment, but, like extinction, it does not have the characteristic of rapid suppression that punishment does. Although there is reason to believe that, early in training, an omission procedure is less effective in reducing responding than is extinction (Uhl 1973), the evidence is not unequivocal (Zeiler 1971). However, after several days of training, the two procedures have been found to produce virtually identical results. There are times when immediacy of effect is more important than durability; in this sense, punishment would seem to be the superior procedure. Because both rapidity and durability are important characteristics of any response-suppression technique, further work is needed to determine the optimal combination of conditions for producing behavioral change.

Vicarious Learning

Although animals imitate (e.g., Myers, 1970), this kind of learning has been most profitably explored with children. It is a well-documented fact that people learn to engage in specific behaviors as a result of watching others engage in them; however, the reasons for this are unclear. In many theories of imitation, or identification, children are assumed to adopt the characteristics of their parents, including their moral standards, for reasons exclusive of hope of reward and/or fear of punishment; they may do so, for example, because imitation enables them to vicariously enjoy gratifications they cannot have, to have a feeling of mastery over the environment, or to allay anxieties about loss of love. Imitation seems to be, then, an excellent device for ensuring internalization of the standards of the parents; the taking over of these standards through identification should make them immune to changes in the likelihood of punishment. Unfortunately, however, most of the data that have been obtained from studies of imitation and resistance to temptation do not form the basis for an explanation involving internalization. An explanation that is easily derived from such data is that models demonstrating resistance to temptation are sources of information about how a subject should behave in an unfamiliar situation. If models of prosocial behavior do indeed supply such information, their influence should be confined to situations in which the subjects believe they will receive positive consequences for appropriate behavior and negative consequences for inappropriate behavior. In that case, the mechanism for internalization no longer exists. This does not detract from the power of modeling as a means of changing behavior. Nor does it mean that, under certain circumstances, children will not adopt the characteristics of models independent of any external consequences they might expect for doing so. Rather, it indicates that modeling, as it has been studied so far in the laboratory, has the same limitation as all other techniques of suppression—it is no longer effective in the absence of an external agent who controls the delivery of reinforcement and punishment.

Observation of Resisting Models

In a typical demonstration of the role of observational learning in the acquisition of self-control, children are instructed not to engage in a particular behavior and then they watch a model who either yields to temptation or resists it. Generally, the yielding model is highly effective; after observing such a model, children deviate much more than they do after having simply been instructed not to deviate. On the other hand, resisting models are either totally ineffective (e.g., Stein, 1967) or only minimally effective (e.g., Rosenkoetter, 1973; Wolf and Cheyne, 1972). The weakness of the resisting model as an agent of behavioral change is not particularly surprising. Such a model always acts in accord with instructions given by the experimenter and hence attracts little of the subject's attention, whereas a yielding model is more noticeable because of behaving in a fashion absolutely contrary to what the subject has been told is appropriate. It seems likely that a child's decision about whether or not to act in accord with an instruction would be less affected by knowing that another person has done so than it would be by the more unexpected observation of failure to do so. Recently, Perry, Bussey, and Perry (1975) reported that boys who observed a resisting peer model were greatly influenced by it. They explained this unexpected outcome by pointing out that their lower-class sample was very deviant in everyday behavior and that, unlike subjects used in other studies, their subjects may have been unaccustomed to conformity; the conforming model attracted more of their attention. Additionally, it should be noted that, if deviation can be assumed to be more attractive than conformity, it is not surprising that it is easier to influence someone to engage in the more attractive behavior.

A study by Grusec and Simutis (1976) suggests that one variable determining the effectiveness of a resisting model may be the nature of the temptation. Children were asked to engage in a card-sorting task and then tempted by "Charlie the talking table." Charlie was covered with interesting toys and periodically spoke, asking the children to come and play with him and repeatedly telling them how much more exciting his toys were than the experimenter's dull task. Under these circumstances, the influence of a resisting model was very strong, as measured by the amount of time the children spent sorting cards and how long it took them to yield to Charlie's temptation (see Figure 5-2). In addition, the effects of the resisting model were still strong after two weeks. This finding contrasts with that of Wolf and Cheyne (1972); using the resistance-to-temptation situation usually employed, they found that resisting models lost their effectiveness after one month.

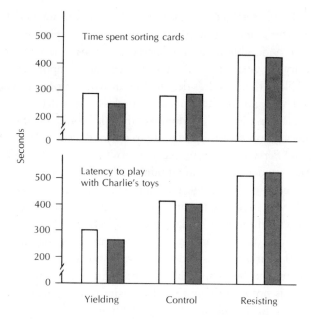

Figure 5-2
Immediate and delayed (two weeks) measures of resistance to temptation in children who had observed either a yielding model or a resisting one. Those in the control group observed neither model. White bar indicates immediate measure and gray bar delayed measure.

Vicarious Punishment

Another way in which responses can be suppressed in observers is by having them watch a model punished for making those responses. Vicarious punishment reduces the amount of antisocial behavior (aggression and yielding to temptation) that observers exhibit relative to that which is engaged in by those who view an antisocial model who receives no consequences for misbehavior. However, children who are simply told not to deviate (in the case of resistance to temptation) or who are told nothing (in the case of aggression) display no more of these behaviors than do children who are given the same instructions and who observe models being punished for their behavior (Bandura 1965; R. Walters and Parke 1964). In this way, vicarious punishment for deviation seems to be as limited in its usefulness for producing response suppression as is the observation of resisting models. The explanation for this may well be similar to that given for the ineffectiveness of resisting models. Children who do not observe a model have the expectation that resistance to temptation or aggression will be punished. For those being tested for resistance to temptation, a particular behavior has been specifically disallowed, whereas those tested for aggression know that adults generally disapprove of violent behavior. Seeing a model being punished for antisocial behavior does not violate this expectation, and so no difference in behavior should be expected. On the other hand, children viewing a model who is not punished for deviant behavior should have their original expectations about appropriate behavior modified and thus be more likely to deviate themselves; hence the difference between their behavior and that of children for whom punishment is vicarious. What this means is that vicarious punishment *should* be an effective technique if the subjects have no expectations about the consequences for a particular act; that is, if they have not been forbidden to do it or previously punished for it.

The Role of Instruction

Given that vicarious punishment is no better than instructing a child not to deviate, what are the implications for socialization? As most parents know, simply telling a child not to do something is generally not very effective. We suggest that a verbal command is powerful only if it is backed up by the expectation that nonconformity will produce punishment, an expectation that the child has learned from direct experience with negative consequences for deviating from verbalized rules. (Justification for this statement is presented in a later section in this chapter on reasoning as a response-suppression technique.) In a laboratory, children are often anxious, unsure of what to do, and worried that an experimenter with whom they are unfamiliar may well be demanding and punitive. Under these circumstances the belief that deviation from stated rules will lead to punishment is no doubt stronger than it would be in the more lenient atmosphere of a home. The increased effectiveness of verbal instructions would thus make vicarious punishment seem weak by comparison, much weaker than it would seem to be under less artificial conditions. Observing a punished model in the home should strengthen a child's belief that the parents are implying that the child will be punished for not complying with their requests for conformity.

Vicarious Learning and Other Response-Suppression Techniques

Several characteristics distinguish vicarious learning from other techniques for suppressing behavior. Unlike extinction and omission training, modelling produces dramatic and sudden suppression of behavior; in this sense it is even more effective than direct punishment, for it requires no overt responding on the part of the observer. In vicarious punishment, the consequences for deviation are never directly experienced by the observer; therefore, some of the emotional side effects of direct punishment should not be experienced either. Finally, it seems logical to conclude (although there are no substantiating data) that a combination of direct punishment and vicarious punishment or of direct punishment and a resisting model may in fact be detrimental, as is a combination of direct punishment and omission training. In such combinations, vicarious processes may lose their effectiveness because they do not violate the expectancies that observers have about the consequences for their own behavior.

Vicarious punishment has the great advantage of enabling socializing agents to anticipate undesirable behavior before it occurs. Theoretically, socializing agents could produce people who *never* steal, cheat, behave aggressively, lie, or yield to temptation, simply by arranging to have them view others who engage in such activities and are punished for them. The problem with this approach, however, is that it may produce the opposite result because the behaviors exhibited by aggressive, cheating, and yielding models might not have occurred to the observers had they been left on their own. And should the chances of punishment for deviation subsequently become fewer, the newly acquired antisocial behaviors might then become manifested. This is a drawback that is not inherent in the use of resisting models for socialization.

Reasoning

Reasoning with a child in an attempt to modify behavior is an important alternative to punishment and is part of the child-rearing practices of most parents. It has been generally assumed to be much more effective than punitive techniques. The argument for efficacy returns us to a discussion of internalization, for theorists have maintained that reasoning does not rely on continued surveillance by socializing agents in order to suppress responding. The idea of dealing with a child on an intellectual level—engaging in rational discussion that excludes an implied or real threat of punishment—is appealing. Whether or not such interactions are ever totally free of threats of punishment, subtle or not, is a question to which we shall return. However, on the surface at least, the use of reasoning seems to be the most "civilized" way of approaching the problem of socialization.

Reasoning as a means of modifying behavior is a technique that is clearly limited to human begins. Yet we shall maintain that the process through which reasoning becomes effective can be understood in terms of principles that are not discrepant with those derived from the animal laboratory.

Reasoning: Correlational Studies

Why should reasoning be superior in its effects to such punitive techniques as withdrawal of love, material rewards, and privileges and as corporal punishment? Hoffman (1970b) and Hoffman and Saltzstein (1967) have dealt extensively with this matter in their consideration of one kind of reasoning, which they call *other-oriented induction.* A child is given a reason for the unacceptability of a given behavior that emphasizes the implications of that behavior for another person. Rather than focusing on the personal consequences of misbehavior, the child's attention is directed to the consequences of that behavior for others. This causes the child to empathize with the suffering of others and to accept the responsibility for their discomfort and pain. The orientation of control is then inward because the child is never able to escape from the consequences of engaging in a given behavior: the knowledge of personal responsibility will always remain with the child. Fear of punishment in the form of loss of love, loss of material goods, and physical pain can never produce this kind of inner control. And thus other-oriented induction affords the ultimate condition for internalization of parental standards; that is, complete absence of external control.

There are additional advantages of other-oriented induction over punitive techniques. Hoffman notes that power assertion (corporal punishment, loss of material rewards and privileges) generates anger in the child, whereas induction does not, and this anger may well lead to noncompliance. Also, fear of punishment, whether the withdrawal of love, the loss of material rewards, or physical, may arouse the child to the extent that the arousal interferes with learning, whereas the degree to which the child is aroused by the implied disapproval that is generated by induction may be more conducive to learning.

Theoretically, then, a disciplinary technique that calls to a child's attention the effect that given behaviors could have on others should have a strong and stable suppressive effect. And there is substantial support for this contention (Hoffman 1970b). Researchers have generally found a positive relationship between the use of induction and degree of development on various moral indices such as intensity of guilt and acceptance of blame. This can be contrasted with a negative relationship between the degree of development as measured by these same indices and the use of power-assertive techniques; there is no relationship at all between degree of development and the use of withdrawal of love. It should be noted that these relationships appear to hold for middle- but not lower-class children and that they have all been derived from correlational studies. The correlational evidence for resistance to temptation—the behavior of primary concern here—is not quite so strong, although it yields the same conclusions.

Given the possibility that a relationship exists between reasoning and response suppression, the problem of causation remains. Is other-oriented induction directly responsible for successful suppression of antisocial behavior? Or is it that parents who are rational in dealing with their children are also likely to have a higher standard of moral conduct, which they directly transmit to their offspring? Are parents who continually point out to their children the consequences their behavior will have for others also the kind of people who try to instill in their children a concern for others and a sense of social responsibility? These are outcomes that would no doubt lead to the suppression of antisocial behavior, but they would not be a direct result of empathizing with the suffering caused others. Rather, they would be a result of imitating parents who showed concern for others and of what those parents had taught their children. Again, other-oriented induction should be more effective than punishment because, in using it, parents are teaching their children the general principle that they should always be considerate of the feelings and needs of others; children motivated by fear of punishment are learning only to suppress behaviors for which they have been specifically punished. There also exists the possibility of a causal relationship between induction and resistance to temptation, but the direction it takes is opposite that originally supposed: children who are generally well behaved (for some as yet unknown reason) elicit calm and rational reactions from their parents on the few occasions on which discipline is needed; children who generally misbehave are more likely to provoke the use of power assertion and the withdrawal of love.

As was mentioned in discussing the side effects of punishment, parents serve as models of behavior for their children in the course of disciplining them. When they use reasoning they are indicating that the way to cope with problems is through the use of a calm, rational approach. Punishment perpetuates the "might is right" philosophy—its use implies that the way to solve problems is in what can be construed as an antisocial way, by using one's superior strength to achieve control without appealing to reason. In this sense, the use of reasoning as a predominant disciplinary technique can be seen as facilitating adoption of standards of socially accepted behavior, although not in a directly causal way.

There are additional difficulties in understanding the relationship between reasoning and response suppression obtained in naturalistic studies. Socialization in real life takes place for a period of years, whereas most studies assess parental discipline at a particular point in the course of socialization. Data that are obtained for only limited periods must be interpreted with caution. Yarrow, Campbell, and Burton (1968) presented a hypothetical example of the development of response suppression that illustrates this point very well:

> Jennifer, at eighteen months, likes to climb up into her mother's new velvet chairs and bounce on the cushions. Her parents may try to "explain" to her at this age that the chairs will be "hurt" and her shoes will make the pretty velvet "ugly." But Jennifer's language development does not allow her to understand these reasons for not bouncing on the chair. Even if she might "understand" that her parents are not pleased when she bounces, it is such great fun that she does not care much about paying attention to what they are saying. But when her mother takes her by the arm and says, "No, no, Jennifer! You have to sit in this chair because that was naughty to bounce on the velvet chair," and physically takes her to a chair that isolates her from the other persons in the home, Jennifer does experience something she does not like and cannot ignore. Most parents will add enough direct physical control of the child with their actions so that the child will find the situation aversive. Sometimes in the months that follow the parent may take Jennifer quite roughly from the velvet chair and place her in the isolation chair, another time she may shake her, the next time she may raise her voice, and another occasion may elicit a spanking from the parent. The parent may also try to anticipate Jennifer's behavior and to stop her from climbing into the chair before she places her foot on the velvet. The parent may also think that Jennifer is about to climb into the velvet chair but then she turns away. The mother may then say, "Good girl, Jennifer, not to climb into the velvet chairs. You know you are not to climb into those chairs." One day the parent may observe Jennifer saying to herself, "No, no, Jennifer, naughty!" when Jennifer has one

knee on the velvet seat and is about to climb into the chair. The mother may then say, "Good girl, Jennifer", and watch her turn to something else. Another time, she may find Jennifer, of her own volition, sitting in the isolated chair and then discover that the spring has come through the cushion of the velvet chair.

As the months go by, Jennifer's linguistic ability increases so that she does comprehend many parental attempts to explain or reason with her about not breaking a rule. The parents also find that the verbal reprimands, which have accompanied the direct techniques and which were originally ineffective because Jennifer ignored them, are eventually sufficient to terminate or to prevent her undesired behavior. Even certain facial expressions from the parent now seem effective as punishment. Increasingly the parents rely on these less direct forms of control since they can be applied at a distance and with greater immediacy than the direct physical types of control. Occasionally it may be necessary for the mother to employ some direct control when it seems Jennifer does not react to the indirect forms. Gradually, such occasions diminish in frequency. [p. 120–121]

Although Jennifer at the end of this process would be rated high on conscience development, as measured by response suppression, it would be wrong to suggest that this is solely a reflection of her parents' current use of reasoning and some withdrawal of love. Had these been the *only* techniques employed from the beginning, the chances are they would not have been very successful.

Finally, it should be noted that disciplinary techniques may tend to differ in the way they are used: some may be made to last longer than others; some may be stopped when a child attempts to make reparation, whereas others may not; some may be used while parents are visibly angry, whereas others may be used only when they are calm; and some may be more likely to be accompanied by a statement of what is wrong. The differences in usage are not necessarily inherent in the disciplinary techniques themselves. Therefore, studies assessing the effectiveness of the disciplinary action that parents take in socializing their children may reflect differences in the way the techniques are used, rather than differences in the techniques themselves.

Reasoning: Experimental Studies

Some of the difficulties of interpreting results from correlational studies do not exist for studies in which an experimental paradigm is employed. However, the few studies in which the effectiveness of reasoning has been compared with that of punishment have not yielded results consistent with the findings obtained in naturalistic studies of socialization. La Voie (1973a and b), for example, found that the sound of a loud buzzer, a rationale, and a combination of the two were equally effective in preventing children and adolescents from playing with a toy, even when they thought that they were alone and therefore no one would know what they had done. Even more surprising results were obtained in another study in which the sound of a loud buzzer produced more response suppression than did a rationale, the loss of six pennies, or withdrawal of the experimenter's attention (La Voie 1974c). La Voie's rationale was not generally other-oriented, however. Instead, he explained that the prohibited toy might break or that it should not be played with without the permission of its owner. Moreover, in these studies, arbitrary intensities of various disciplinary techniques were selected for comparison. Suppose that the children in La Voie's later study had lost sixty pennies rather than six, or that it had been a parent's attention that had been withdrawn rather than that of the experimenter, or that the noise level produced by the loud buzzer had been 80 decibels rather than 104. The comparative effectiveness of the various techniques could well have been different.

What perhaps merits more investigation is the effect of different disciplinary techniques on variables other than immediate resistance to temptation. La Voie (1974a) reported that the use of reasoning produced greater generalization of the experimenter's prohibition than did punishment, although, in the earlier study (1974c), he found no difference. The side effects of various disciplinary techniques are also worth comparing. For example, is the effect of reasoning on self-esteem less negative than, say, the withdrawal of love? Do children who are told why they should not behave in a particular way feel less hostile toward the agent of discipline than do those who are punished by being subjected to the sound of a loud buzzer or by having material rewards withdrawn? And what about the stability of response suppression through time? In all cases, of course, it would be desirable to assess the effects of discipline over a range of intensities of punishment and for different kinds of rationales. The systematic manipulation of variables is as necessary in child-development studies as it is in animal learning studies, but it is only in the latter that it has been achieved.

Reasoning as a Source of Information

Parents who use reasoning as a means of modifying behavior may simply convey more information about misbehavior than do those who rely solely on punishment. In Chapter 3, we explained how the presence of cognitive structuring can dramatically alter the effects of punishment, often simply by making the contingencies of punishment clearer. Recall, also, that La Voie (1974a) found generalization of prohibition to be greater with the use of a rationale than with punishment. La Voie's result is not surprising: the subjects in his study who were given a rationale were not only instructed not to play with a specific toy, but also told that they should not touch another person's property without permission; those who were subjected to punishment were told only that they should not play with the toy. Because no permission was subsequently granted for playing with other, similar toys, it is quite likely that, to boys who were given the rationale, the prohibition was thought to include these other objects, whereas, to those who had been subjected to punishment, it was not. By its very nature, an interaction between parent and child that includes some form of explanation no doubt supplies the child with more information than does punishment for a specific response. A child who is told that a given behavior is bad "because you shouldn't touch another person's belongings" or "because what you did hurts other people" learns a general principle, as well as the fact that a specific act just committed is unacceptable. On the other hand, a child who is punished for a particular act learns only that that act is wrong. Thus reasoning seems to aid in generalization by applying not only to the current misdeed but also to possible future related misdeeds. A similar point has been made by Burton (1963) and Cheyne and R. Walters (1970).

Reasoning also enables children to generalize the suppression of misbehavior in the presence of the punishing agent to misbehavior in the agent's absence. They learn not only that a given act is unacceptable to the punishing agent, but that it is unacceptable to other people as well. "Don't play with that vase!" accompanied by a slap can be most easily interpreted to mean, "*I* don't like it when you play with that particular vase." "Don't play with that vase!" followed by "You should not touch another person's property" has to be interpreted as "Anybody will become upset if you play with things that belong to him." In this way one of the conditions of internalization that might not be satisfied by the use of punishment is satisfied by the use of reasoning—response suppression is more likely to continue in the absence of the socializing agent. This is not due, however, to any "incorporation" of standards, or adopting another's standards as one's own, in the sense that the concept of internalization usually implies. Rather, it is just that something has been learned about the negative reactions that others might have to similar misdeeds.

Varieties of Rationales and Response Suppression

Virtually all the studies that deal with the effects of different kinds of rationales on behavior have been done within a developmental framework. The primary assumption underlying these studies is that certain kinds of reasons are necessarily more effective with certain age groups because dramatic changes in cognitive capabilities and comprehension are taking place in relatively short spaces of time during childhood. The sources of these variations in ability to comprehend and respond to different rationales are as yet unclear. As children mature, they become capable of more complex kinds of moral reasoning—this is well documented by cognitive-developmental theorists who have described stages of development in the making of moral judgments (see Kohlberg, 1964; Piaget, 1965). Such theorists assume that the sequence and duration of these stages are relatively independent of environmental effects, an assumption that is questioned by social-learning theorists. The latter stress the importance of changing child-rearing practices as children become older (e.g., the kind of rationale that parents give for suppressing behavior) and of environmental variables that produce changes in responsivity to disciplinary rationales. It is the extent to which environmental variables contribute to the effectiveness of reasoning that separates the two points of view. The present discussion will simply deal with age differences and the effectiveness of rationales, however, ignoring the problem of what causes them.

The majority of studies comparing various rationales for resistance to temptation have been carried out by Ross Parke and his students. Parke and Murray (see Parke, 1974), for example, compared the effectiveness of an object-oriented rationale that stressed the possibility that a toy might break if touched with a possession-oriented rationale that stressed that a toy should not be played with because it belonged to someone else. The object-oriented rationale was more effective for four-year-old children than the possession-oriented rationale, presumably because the physical consequences of an act were more easily understood by these children than were abstract judgments about the rights of others. Moreover, as should be expected, the two kinds of rationales were equally effective for seven-year-olds. In a later study, Parke found that the shift in effectiveness from concrete to abstract rationales occurs during the last half of the fourth year, somewhat earlier than the parallel shift from making concrete moral judgments to making abstract ones. He suggested that there may be a lag between recognition and production, which means that children can respond to a rationale to control their own behavior before they are able to use that rationale to justify their moral decisions. Perhaps by hearing adults use rationales in their attempts to control them, children eventually employ the same rationales in making moral judgments when they are called upon to explain the reason for the rightness, or wrongness, of a specific behavior.

Other kinds of rationales also have different effects on different age groups. Telling a seven-year-old not to play with a toy because it might get broken is just as effective as telling that child not to play with it because it is wrong to want to do so. The latter rationale becomes increasingly more effective, however, as the child grows older (La Voie 1974b). Once again a parallel can be drawn between how well a particular rationale can inhibit behavior and the child's stage of moral reasoning. Seven-year-olds are entering the stage of development at which they begin to make moral judgments that have to do with intent—a more mature kind of judgment than one that deals merely with fear of the consequences of deviation.

Further comparisons of the effectiveness of different kinds of rationales have been undertaken by Kuczynski and Grusec (1976). They found that six-and eight-year-old children deviated less when they were told not to play with a toy because it might break and make the experimenter unhappy than they did when they were told that it might break and then they would be unhappy. Apparently, reasoning that arouses empathy for others is more likely to suppress behavior than is reasoning that focuses on the personal consequences of misbehavior. This difference is already apparent by the age of six.

Studies of the effectiveness of rationales in suppressing behavior have been undertaken only quite recently. This is partly because the belief that there is little relationship between the development of moral behavior and the ability to make moral judgments has been widely held for a long time. In 1928, Hartshorne and May argued for the specificity of various aspects of morality. Moral behaviors such as resistance to temptation have been assumed to be age-independent (Grinder 1964), whereas it has been demonstrated that the degree to which a child is capable of moral reasoning is very much age-related. Thus, although a particular behavior may itself remain unchanged through time, the kind of explanations that children give for that behavior changes as they grow older. It was for this reason, then, that studies of moral behavior and moral judgment remained largely divorced from each other, being considered by many to be two unrelated aspects of development. However, it is apparent that the separation between them is not as complete as some may have thought.

How Rationales Become Effective

What makes rationales effective in suppressing behavior, and what conditions for socialization are necessary to make them work? Why should a child who is told not to play with a toy because it might break, or because it belongs to someone else, subsequently not play with that toy? It is certainly not because the child has been threatened with punishment for deviating. What accounts for suppression of responding then?

A number of mechanisms by which rationales become effective have been suggested (e.g., Aronfreed, 1968; Cheyne and R. Walters, 1970; R. Walters and Parke, 1967), all of which can be understood within a conditioning framework. Verbal rationales may acquire their capacity to suppress behavior by having been paired initially with anxiety-arousing stimuli. For example, a parent may punish a child for misbehavior, accompanying the punishment with an explanation of why what the child has done is wrong. Through classical conditioning, the child eventually suppresses responding whenever it hears the rationale that has thus become a conditioned stimulus for anxiety about punishment. Or a parent may punish a child for not complying with a prohibition only when that prohibition has been accompanied by a rationale—the rationale serves as a stimulus signalling that punishment will be administered for misbehavior. In this case, subsequent suppression is simply to avoid punishment. (Given our discussion in the preceding section about the relationship between age and the effectiveness of different rationales, we must assume that the child is capable of comprehending that a particular statement does constitute a rationale for good behavior.) These proposals sound plausible, but what evidence is there that this is what is happening? There are studies that indicate that parents who employ reasoning in the socialization of their children often do so in conjunction with the use of punishment. Baumrind

(1973) found that mothers of children who were socially responsible, self-controlled, independent, achievement-oriented, and energetic tended to rely more on power assertion and reasoning to gain compliance than did mothers of children who were less inclined to exhibit these characteristics. The latter were more likely to employ withdrawal of love and ridicule when they were disciplining their children. Similarly, Hoffman (1970a) reported that mothers who relied on reasoning that pointed out to their children what the consequences of their misbehavior would be for others were more inclined to use power assertion when their children refused to comply than were mothers who frequently used withdrawal of love for misbehavior, calling attention to the harm done to themselves. These studies do not portray a parent who always relies on reason itself in dealing with a deviating child—it is reason backed up by the threat of unpleasant consequences for lack of conformity. Hoffman suggested that the function of power assertion is primarily a discriminative one, making the child attend to the parent's request and reason: "Some power assertion may be needed for the voice of reason to be heard." Taking a somewhat different point of view, we suggest that the parent who uses reasoning effectively is one who has, in the past, made punishment contingent on noncompliance with a request accompanied by a rationale, or who has paired punishment with a rationale.

In addition to learning to behave in accord with the rules established and explained by their parents, children learn to comply with rules that they observe inhibiting the behavior of others (Bandura and Kupers 1964; Bandura, Grusec, and Menlove 1967). Liebert, Hanratty, and Hill (1969) have also demonstrated that the amount of cognitive structuring supplied by a model affects the observer's adherence to that model's standards of self-reward. Earlier, we explained how vicarious learning affects the development of response suppression. Presumably, in observing the effects of rationales on the behavior of others, children learn that there is a good chance that rules that apply to others can also apply to them. Noncompliance with such rules, in that case, may produce the same kinds of negative consequences as those received for noncompliance with rules that did apply directly to them.

In summary, if our analysis is correct, what makes the use of rationales effective can be comprehended quite well in terms of respondent and operant conditioning. Children respond to reasoning either to reduce anxiety or to not be punished. A parent who relied solely on reasoning as a disciplinary technique would not be very successful in obtaining response suppression. Reasoning becomes effective only when it is supported by a history of punishment.

Reasoning and Long-term Suppression

If the effectiveness of reasoning depends on previous punishment, why are parents who rely on reasoning (occasionally accompanied by power assertion) more successful as socializing agents than those who rely on power assertion alone, or on the withdrawal of love, or on ridicule? Recall that, for socialization to be considered successful, children must internalize prohibitions; that is, they must suppress behavior in the absence of those who disciplined them. It has been suggested (e.g., Cheyne and R. Walters, 1970; Hoffman, 1970b) that reasoning serves to focus a child's attention on the act rather than on the punishing agent and that this is what promotes internalization. If it is assumed, however, that rationales are effective because previous noncompliance was punished, then their use does not completely remove the child from the influence of the punishing agent. It may cause the child to think about abstract principles—the rights of others, for example—but in the end compliance is mediated by fear of punishment. If this is so, why should reasoning be any better than any other kind of disciplinary technique? Parke (1974) offered some interesting observations on this point. He suggested that an important aspect of internalization is permanence, or stability, of suppression, and cites research (Cheyne and R. Walters 1969; Parke 1969) showing that, although rationales and punishment may be equally effective in the production of short-term suppression, the former is superior for the production of long-term response suppression. According to Parke's analysis, long-term suppression is achieved because children who are supplied with a rationale repeat the rationale and accompanying rules to themselves, thereby reinstating relevant cues and anxiety, which can be reduced only when they comply with the prohibition. If punishment is used alone, they forget a prohibition, or they may not remember that it is still in effect after some time has elapsed; if they have been given a rationale, they have something to rehearse, which will continue to remind them of the relevant contingencies. The rationale, however, must make sense. Parke described a study in which children were told they should not play with a toy because it was fragile and might break. They soon discovered that the toy was, in fact, not fragile and therefore not likely to break; consequently, they resumed playing with it.

The effect that the repetition of a prohibition can have has been demonstrated in several studies. O'Leary (1968) reported that first-grade boys who had been told to instruct themselves about whether to respond to a "right" or "wrong" stimulus deviated less than subjects who had not been told to self-instruct. Similarly, Hartig and Kanfer (1973) found that three- to seven-year-old children were better able to resist temptation when they had been instructed to say to themselves, "I must not turn around and look at that toy," than when they had been given no instructions to verbalize or had been told to say, "Hickory dickory dock, the mouse went up the clock."

Some statements that children are instructed to repeat to

themselves are likely to be more effective than others (there may, for example, be a relationship between their efficacy and the level of moral judgment of which a child is capable). Parke's position suggests, however, that *any* rationale should be better than none at all. It is interesting to note that the addition of self-evaluation ("If I do [do not] look at the toy I will be a bad [good] boy/girl") to self-instruction does not lead to greater resistance to temptation (Hartig and Kanfer 1973).

Assuming that the use of rationales by socializing agents is more likely to lead to self-instruction than is punishment alone, then rationales should be a particularly effective means of behavioral control. For example, a rationale such as "Don't touch that. That belongs to someone else" supplies more material on which to model self-instructions that are relevant to a situation in which a child is tempted to deviate than does "Don't touch that. You can't watch television for a week" or "Don't touch that. Go straight to your room." The key word here is *relevant*. A child who is given a rationale can recall it each time that particular temptation presents itself, whereas a punished child may simply be distracted by the thought of a week without television or by the boredom of being alone. And irrelevant verbalizations, as mentioned earlier, do not have a response suppressing effect.

Maurer (1974) has indicated that there is clinical evidence for the distracting aspects of punishment. She describes the well-known phenomenon that children are rarely able to identify the behavior that preceded a particular punishment although they are able to remember the punishment itself. It is entirely possible that the events of the punishment are so distracting that they prevent a child from learning what a particular response-punishment contingency is, whereas, in reasoning with a child, there is less *irrelevant* material to interfere with the retention of what the socializing agent is trying to teach. Related to this is the fact that punishment increases the degree to which a child becomes aroused; if arousal is too high, the learning of response-punishment contingencies becomes impaired. Such impairment should be less likely to occur with reasoning.

Attribution Theory and Internalization

If internalization is defined as response suppression in the absence of a socializing agent, then a goal that the socializing agent must have is to become unnecessary. One way of accomplishing this is to reduce the importance of that person in the punishment process. How this might occur has been the subject of recent research by social psychologists on attribution processes—that is, on the ways in which individuals perceive the causes of both their own behavior and that of others. One set of notions put forth by attribution theorists that seems particularly relevant to what is being considered in this chapter is that of *insufficient justification* and *overly sufficient justification* (Nisbett and Valins 1971). If people perceive that they have behaved in a certain way because of strong external pressure to do so, their value systems will not change as much to conform with that behavior as they would if they were unable to perceive any external pressure. We suggest that children who perceive that they have been coerced into conformity should be much less likely to bring their attitudes and values into line with their behavior, and hence to continue to conform in the absence of pressure, than should children who are less conscious of being coerced. And reasoning minimizes the intrusiveness of external pressure. For a child who believes that it has not hit another child because of concern about the well-being of others there is much less obvious (the implied threat for nonconformity is there, but in the background) external justification for response suppression than there is for a child who believes that it has refrained from doing so to avoid being spanked. The child who finds little external justification may well come to believe that the reason for the behavior was that it was the "right" thing to do.

Recently, Dienstbier, Hillman, Lehnhoff, Hillman, and Valkenaar (1975) have taken a similar position. They maintain that the negative emotional states associated with punishment remain much the same throughout a person's life, but the causal attributions made about these states can change, and it is these attributions that determine subsequent behavior. Suppose that a young child is punished for telling a lie. In the future, the temptation to lie should be followed by anxiety that had its beginnings in the original punishment-training situation. But the cause of anxiety can be attributed to different things. On one hand, the child could believe that the anxiety was due to fear of being found out and punished, whereas, on the other hand, the anxiety could be attributed to the knowledge that good people do not tell lies. The child should not be expected to tell the truth if fear of being found out was the perceived reason for anxiety when there was no chance of detection, whereas, if the perceived reason was knowing that not to lie was associated with goodness, expecting honesty, even in the absence of surveillance, would be justified. In this way, it could be said that a rule about being honest had been internalized.

Considering that a great deal of laboratory data seem to be organized very nicely by attribution theory, this may prove to be a useful approach in understanding the concept of internalization. In the area of response suppression, for example, Lepper (1973) found that children who complied with a prohibition under mild threat, and who presumably justified their obedience by inferring they must be the kind of people who typically engage in good behavior, cheated less three weeks later than did children who complied with a prohibition under severe threat of punishment. The latter children, it is assumed, were more likely to attribute their initial compliance to fear of punishment. Attribution theory supplies a convenient framework within which to understand how it is that responses may be suppressed even in the absence of the possibility of punishment. And it supplies a way of seeing how reasoning—

augmented by punishment—can be a useful and effective means of suppressing behavior.

Age and the Effectiveness of Rationales

There are a number of reasons for believing that reasoning may not be as effective as punishment for very young children. First, if parents pair rationales with punishment, then rationales will be completely ineffective until this pairing has taken place. It can be assumed that most parents do not begin to give their children reasons for conformity, nor do they punish them for nonconformity to prohibitions that had been accompanied by reasons, until they believe that their children are old enough to understand them. Therefore, the kind of learning experience to which a child is exposed depends on the child's level of maturation.

In addition to having difficulty in understanding the meaning of rationales, young children also exhibit what has been labelled a "production deficiency" in language use (Flavell, Beach, and Chinsky 1966). Although they know the words that are relevant to a particular act, they are not able to produce them at the appropriate time to guide their behavior. If one function of a rationale is to serve as a cue that reminds a child not to deviate, then the child must be capable of verbalizing the relevant rule at the appropriate time. If young children cannot do this, then rationales should be much less effective in suppressing their behavior than they are in suppressing the behavior of older children. It should be noted, however, that children who do not engage in spontaneous verbal mediation can be taught to do so (Keeney, Carnizzo, and Flavell 1967; Hagen and Kingsley 1968). To do this requires more than a simple instruction to repeat to themselves what they are supposed to be doing, because they apparently stop repeating instructions to themselves when they are told that it is not necessary to continue (Keeney, Carnizzo, and Flavell 1967). A more substantial procedure that includes the modeling of self-instruction and reinforcement for appropriate verbalization ought to produce successful long-term suppression of behavior. This is certainly a proposition that can be easily tested.

Another reason for believing that, relative to punishment, reasoning should be more effective for older children than for younger ones has as its basis an observation by Cheyne and R. Walters (1970). They reported that, although eight-year-old children are more responsive to rationales than are five-year-olds, the older ones may be *more* deviant than the younger ones when rationales have not been provided. Older children may come to expect that they should be given a reason for response suppression. In the absence of a rationale they may be less willing to acquiesce to the requests of others than are young children. One goal of socialization, presumably, is to discourage blind obedience to authority. Therefore, it should not be surprising to find that, as children grow older, they come to expect that they will be given reasons for why they should conform to adult commands.

Teaching Self-control

In his novel *Walden Two*, Skinner related several ways for developing self-control. The children in *Walden Two* learned to drink cocoa with less and less sugar in it until they no longer reacted to the bitterness. And, when tired and hungry, they had to stand for five minutes in front of steaming bowls of soup before eating, bridging the delay with jokes or singing; later on these social devices were prohibited, and the children were forced to find their own devices—silent ones—for dealing with the frustration. For many years, there was little interest on the part of child-development researchers in these methods of teaching self-control. Researchers in animal learning did investigate similar phenomena when they studied DRL schedules. (Recall from Chapter 3 that, in this procedure, animals are reinforced only when they have delayed responding for a specified period.) It has long been evident that it is possible to train rats and pigeons to delay responding for given periods, and in this way they can be taught to engage in self-control. Recently, however, a variety of ways for teaching children to control their own behavior have been studied in the laboratory.

The advantages of self-control are twofold. First, it is an economical means by which to change behavior: some of the work necessary in suppressing a response can be transferred from the socializing agent to the child, assuming that the child is still motivated to avoid punishment. Second, self-control helps to minimize the intrusiveness of external pressure in the maintenance of behavior. The employment of various techniques for the purpose of self-control should make it less likely that a child will perceive a change in behavior to be due to fear of external consequences than if that behavior is obviously being manipulated by someone else. Consequently, the child should be more likely to continue to resist temptation even when the chances of detection are slight or virtually nonexistent.

Training in Self-punishment

Perhaps the most obvious way in which to instill self-control is to train a child to administer its own punishment. Continued surveillance by an external agent would then no longer be necessary, for it would no longer be possible for the child to make a decision about whether or not to deviate based on the probability of detection; detection would be certain and so punishment would certainly follow. Nor would the kind of punishment be of great importance. Although it might be difficult, but not impossible, to train children to administer corporal punishment to themselves, it certainly would not be difficult to train them to withhold privileges or material rewards from themselves or to engage in some form of physical self-deprivation. What is being suggested is the possibility that *any* form of discipline that is self-administered is more effective in suppressing behavior than are disciplinary measures taken by an external agent.

Self-administered punishment could be considered a form of guilt. Although convincing evidence has been obtained that indicates that resistance to temptation and guilt are not correlated (e.g., Solomon, Turner and Lessac, 1968), we suggest that guilt produced by teaching children to punish themselves might well be a successful technique for suppressing behavior. However, whether it is even possible to train people to administer punishment to themselves must be considered first.

How might children be taught to punish themselves? First, to be consistent with attribution theory, this teaching should be done in such a way that the child perceives the punishment to be voluntarily self-administered; that is, by choice rather than parental dictate. There are several ways in which this might be accomplished. Social psychologists have developed a number of social-influence procedures that give subjects an "illusion of freedom" (Kelly 1967), a feeling that they have acted in a given way because they have elected to do so. These procedures provide indications of how children might be successfully taught to administer punishment to themselves. One manner of doing this might be to supply models of self-punishment: observation of models seems a less coercive way of influencing behavior than does direct instruction. In another procedure, children could be trained to punish themselves by being advised and encouraged to do so. The greater the subtlety with which this is done, the more effective it ought to be. A child's decision to self-punish might then be labelled a free choice ("It's up to you to decide what you want to do"), or pressures and constraints applied so diffusely that they never attract the attention of the child ("You may do what you wish, but I would like to ask you. . . . Do you think you could do it for me"). A child could be made to feel that self-punishment is praiseworthy ("That would be an admirable thing to do"). Or socializing agents might suggest that children be responsible for their own punishment, hinting that deviation would surely be followed by self-punishment ("If you do that you will feel very bad about it afterward"). Parenthetically, it should be noted that most of these techniques include some kind of reasoning or explanation and that an observer of naturalistic child-rearing practices might be inclined to call them inductive. This could be misleading, however, for the important element in them is the attempt to make children their own punishers, rather than calling on some empathic faculty or cognitive ability.

Recently, Grusec and Kuczynski (1975) have demonstrated that children can be trained to punish themselves. Boys and girls were given a large bowl of pennies and told they could take some away from themselves, if they wished, when they performed poorly in a game. This method was no more successful than the somewhat more direct one of *instructing* children to take pennies away from themselves, but both techniques were better than one in which the experimenter took the pennies away, in which case there was little evidence of self-punishment, either in the experimenter's presence or in her absence. The two self-punishment groups differed, however, in one important respect: the children who had "freely" punished themselves were more compliant when the experimenter subsequently requested that they not play with some toys than were those who had been instructed to punish themselves. This is an argument for the use of a voluntary punishment-training procedure, although, technically, the effects are indirect rather than direct.

The Use of Self-instruction

Besides being taught to administer their own punishment, children can be trained in self-control in other ways. As noted earlier, children who have been instructed to remind themselves not to deviate, by making appropriate verbalizations, resist temptation longer than those who engage in irrelevant verbalizations (Hartig and Kanfer 1973). And it seems that this is more easily done if external control is minimized during training. Kanfer and Zich (1974), for example, told children not to look at a display of toys. Each child listened, either alone or with the experimenter, to tape-recorded instructions ("If you do not turn around and look at the toys you will be a very, very good boy/girl") that were in either the child's own voice or that of the experimenter. They were then instructed not to look at a caged hamster that had been placed next to the toys and were left alone. Those who had heard the prohibition in the experimenter's voice and in the experimenter's presence looked at the hamster just as much as did children who had not heard tape-recorded instructions at all. Those who had been subjected to less external control did not deviate as much. From these results, it can be concluded that too much apparent control is detrimental to the teaching of self-control, both because it reduces willingness to cooperate with the socializing agent (Grusec and Kuczynski 1975) and because it may reduce training effectiveness under particular circumstances.

The question of the obviousness of external control in the learning process aside, how else have researchers attempted to teach self-control to children? Meichenbaum and Goodman (1971) maintained that the critical step in a child's development of voluntary control of behavior consists of the internalization of verbal commands. Initially, a child's behavior is controlled by the speech of others, generally adults; then it is controlled by the child's own overt speech; and, finally, by the child's covert speech (Vygotsky 1962). By guiding them through these three stages, Meichenbaum and Goodman attempted to modify the behavior of impulsive children. First, the children observed a model who completed a task in a nonimpulsive manner while engaging in verbal behavior that included listing the requirements of the task, self-guidance, and self-reinforcement. This kind of modelling by itself was not successful in inducing greater self-control; after observation, it was necessary to have the subjects perform a task while being instructed by the experimenter, and then to do it while engaging in self-instruction, overtly at first and, finally, covertly. Using this procedure, Meichenbaum and Goodman were able to develop in young children the ability to size up the demands of a task, mentally rehearse their actions, guide their performance by self-instruction, and reinforce themselves when appropriate. Part of this procedure is very much like that employed by Hartig and Kanfer (1973) in teaching children to instruct themselves not to deviate. That all the steps from external to internal control in the procedure used by Meichenbaum and Goodman are necessary seems doubtful in view of the Hartig and Kanfer findings. Nevertheless, the findings of Meichenbaum and Goodman give further evidence that self-control can be taught in the same way that any other behavior can be taught. Undesirable responses can be suppressed in the absence of external surveillance and directions if children are given the tools for self-guidance.

Participation in Rule Enforcement

Bosserman and Parke (in Parke, 1974) reported that children who participate in the enforcement of rules deviate less than those who do not. They found that six- and seven-year-old boys who were made responsible for punishing other children for touching forbidden toys subsequently played less with these toys themselves than did boys who simply observed offenders being punished by an adult. Resistance to deviation was even greater for those who, in addition to being made responsible for enforcing the rules, had to choose which type of punishment to administer. Apparently, participation in administering negative consequences facilitates one's own compliance. It is not clear, however, whether the relationship between acceptance of responsibility and self-control is general or specific: that is, to ensure suppression of a given response, should a child be assigned the task of suppressing that particular response in others, or will the effects of accepting responsibility for enforcing rules generally facilitate self-control in new situations?

Learning to Delay Gratification

Most of the work on response suppression discussed so far has consisted of getting children not to engage in a particular activity such as playing with a forbidden toy. Several studies, however, have been addressed to another aspect of self-control, that of learning to delay gratification by giving up immediate rewards for the sake of larger, delayed ones. In these studies, one response must be suppressed in order to obtain a more substantial reward at a later time. In recent years, Walter Mischel and his students have attempted to determine whether certain cognitive strategies will enable young children to wait for a delayed reward rather than engaging in impulsive behavior whose goal is immediate gratification. In a summary of this work, Mischel (1974), concluded that the *manner* in which children attend to the rewards is crucial to whether or not they are able to delay. Thinking of these rewards can have both motivational (arousal) and cue (informative) functions. If children dwell on the concrete aspects of rewards—how good the candy will taste, for example—then they will be frustrated and self-control will be undermined. If, on the other hand, they concentrate on the informative aspects of the situation—reminding themselves of the relevant contingency, thinking of what they will get if they delay—they may be more likely to engage in covert self-instruction to wait and self-reinforcement for waiting. It can be concluded, then, that training children to focus their attention on the more abstract aspects of a delay situation and not to think about the concrete qualities of rewards should enable them to achieve greater self-control. In a similar vein, C. Patterson and Mischel (1975) told young children how to resist being distracted from a boring task. Children who had been told to respond to a distracting "Clown Box" by saying, "No I can't, I'm working" or "I'm going to keep working so I can play with the fun toys and Mr. Clown Box later," or who had been told to imagine a brick wall between themselves and the Clown Box, worked longer at the boring task than those who had not been told how to resist being distracted. Further, C. Patterson and Mischel (1976) found that children who were instructed not to pay attention to the temptation were better able to avoid distraction than were children who were instructed to pay attention to the boring task.

Newman and Kanfer (1974) have suggested another technique for fostering self-control in the form of delaying gratification. Children learned a discrimination task in which the length of time between responding and reinforcement was gradually increased from 0 to 60 seconds, decreased from 60 to 0 seconds, or remained a constant delay. Their ability to delay gratification was then tested. The children who had learned the discrimination task with increasing delay of reward were able to delay gratification longer than those for whom the time between responding and reinforcement gradually decreased, and than those for whom the delay was constant. The mechanism by which exposure to delay of reward facilitated ability to wait is not clear. It is interesting, however, that only exposure to increasing delays was effective: children trained with constant delay did not increase their self-control. Just as exposure to fear-producing stimuli must be gradual in order to reduce phobic behavior, gradual exposure to frustration-producing stimuli seems necessary to facilitate delay of gratification. Newman and Kanfer suggested that experience with increasing delay of reward also facilitated responding that enabled their subjects to cope with frustration—the kind of responding that Mischel has noted in his subjects. In Mischel's experiments, children cover their eyes with their hands, rest their heads on their arms, sing songs, play games, and even go to sleep, presumably in an effort to distract themselves from the frustrating aspects of delay. If Newman and Kanfer's subjects had employed these kinds of coping mechanisms between response and reward during the training task, increasing delay would have been the optimal condition for strengthening them.

Conclusion

It is evident that children can be taught to control their own behavior. A variety of techniques have been demonstrated to be useful and, no doubt, more will be added to the list as investigators continue to pursue the problem of self-control. The techniques discussed in this section include self-punishment, verbalization remindful of the behavior in which a child is supposed to be engaging, responsibility for ensuring nondeviant behavior in others, and exposure to graduated frustration-producing delays. All these techniques enable those who practice them to alter or maintain behavior in the absence of immediate external control. And, although our evidence is not yet that strong, we suggest that children are more likely to continue to employ techniques that enable them to control their own behavior if the training they originally received minimized the role of the training agent.

To what extent parents employ these techniques to encourage the development of self-control is irrelevant to the present purpose. Should it be the case that few socializing agents do, in fact, train children to use the kind of self-control mechanisms that we have described, then we may well be discovering in the experimental literature some potentially very useful response-elimination techniques for application to the practical problems of child-rearing.

Summary

Quite clearly, alternative techniques for eliminating behavior have been of much greater interest to child-development researchers than has punishment—the existence of the large body of evidence reviewed in this chapter attests as well as anything to the attraction of nonpunishment procedures for those interested in child-rearing processes. Yet it has also been evident that punishment may constitute a significant part of training that on the surface seems to rely on a nonpunitive approach. In this sense, then, psychologists have not moved as far as they might have thought from a punitive approach to behavioral change.

6

OVERVIEW AND FUTURE DIRECTIONS: SOME THOUGHTS ABOUT PUNISHMENT

The Nature of Punishment

Direct Effects

If the effectiveness of punishment is assessed in terms of the rapidity and degree of suppression that can be achieved during its application, then there is no doubt that it can be a potent modifier of behavior. Moreover, current knowledge of the effects of such stimulus variables as intensity, duration, and delay is such that they can be related to varying degrees of response suppression in the laboratory and in certain applied settings. The greater the intensity of the punishing stimulus and the longer that stimulus lasts, the greater its effectiveness; if the recipients are human beings, obviously some degree of effectiveness must be traded for a reasonable degree of moderation in intensity.

Consistency has always been advocated by child-development psychologists as an extremely important component of effective socialization. And it has been seen, primarily in learning studies, that continuous punishment is indeed more effective in response suppression than is intermittent punishment.

Delay between a response and the onset of punishment has been of much concern to learning researchers, and their recommendation is that punishment should be administered as soon after an undesirable response as possible. Children, however, because of their capacity for language, are capable of spanning long periods between a response and punishment contingent on, although not contiguous with, that response. Nevertheless, the immediacy of punishment could be of importance in suppressing responding in autistic and mentally retarded children who have suffered impairment in their ability to function symbolically—to reason and talk.

A great deal of emphasis has been placed on the study of the interaction of punishment and positive-reinforcement variables, because it is assumed that much of human behavior is established and maintained by these variables. Although this may be so, it is important to remember that behaviors other than learned operants may be affected differently by punishment. This problem will be considered later in this chapter.

Indirect Effects

Under certain conditions, the application of punishment can have undesirable results. However, what are considered to be its side effects are not nearly so potent as has been suggested. If the intensity of the punishment administered is moderate and if the contingencies between behavior and its consequence are clear, there is no evidence that it produces neurotic or maladaptive behavior. Nor does it inevitably lead to inappropriate suppression of related behaviors. Further, it does not seem to promote avoidance of the agent who administers the punishment unless that agent is solely a source of punishment and not of reinforcement as well. There is also evidence that suggests that nonphysical punishment does not lead to aggressive behavior.

There is no question that, under certain circumstances, punishment can produce undesirable results. It has been suggested that physical punishment supplies a model for aggression—behavior that is intended to injure. If the administration of punishment emphasizes its coercive aspects, hostility may be aroused. As yet, however, little is known about how to prevent the hostile reactions of those who are punished. The relationship between the punishing agent and the recipient of punishment may be important perhaps, with friendly punishers less likely to evoke hostility than unfriendly ones. The attractiveness of the punished behavior to the performer may also effect hostility, as may the lack of an alternative reinforced response. Response-cost punishment could be expected to produce greater hostility as the value of the reward being withheld increases. Perhaps punishment that is logically related to a misbehavior rather than arbitrarily—one that expresses the reality of the social order rather than the power of a personal authority—may be less detrimental to the relationship between the punished person and the socializing agent than punishment administered vindictively and in the context of a struggle. Dreikurs and Grey (1968), for example, suggested that children who refuse to hurry in the morning should not be nagged to speed up their activities or threatened with unrelated punishment for slowness, but should instead be allowed to experience the unpleasantness of being late for school—a direct and logical consequence of misbehavior.

Although punishment can sometimes be administered in such a way as to do more harm than good, it is not necessary to conclude that, for that reason, it should not be used as a means of changing behavior. If it is employed so as to minimize anger—in combination with reasoning, for example, or suggestion, or as a logical consequence administered in a matter-of-fact manner—it could well be very powerful in its suppressive effects. These possibilities have received little attention in either the learning or the child-development laboratory.

In our review of punishment we have been impressed by the continued rejection of punishment as a socializing technique by those centrally involved in the child-development tradition. As noted in Chapter 1, psychologists in both lines of research were at one time united in their rejection of punishment as a viable tool for behavioral change. The great surge of interest in punishment, combined with repeated demonstrations of its effectiveness, has led many learning researchers to take the opposite point of view. A parallel surge of interest and change in viewpoint about punishment effectiveness has not occurred among those interested in the socialization of children. The number of articles about punishment published in journals that report the work of learning researchers increased dramatically after 1960, whereas the number published by child-development researchers did not. The brief flurry of interest in punishment from about 1965 to 1970, touched off by Solomon's study of the timing of punishment, seems to have subsided, and Parke (1974) is not alone in writing that

> there is a growing body of evidence which suggests that punitive inhibitory tactics can have deleterious side effects. . . . Although I still believe that punishment plays a role in childhood socialization, our focus has shifted to an examination of alternative inhibitory techniques which may be effective and may avoid some of the disadvantages of punishment. (p. 111)

Although we agree that more effort should be directed toward the study of alternative suppressive techniques, we also feel that much more attention should be paid to punishment as a socializing technique. Parents use it and it works, and many of the so-called alternative techniques probably derive their effectiveness from the fact that they are based on punishment. It may be more palatable for researchers who are concerned with the normal course of child development to focus their attention on ways in which punishment can be administered so as to minimize those side effects that occur in certain situations. But it is clearly wrong to assert that punishment is a procedure for which we have no practical use; it merits much greater attention from child-development researchers than it has received or, at present, seems destined to receive.

Durability of Punishment

What happens to punished behavior when the punishing stimulus is terminated? In the learning laboratory, after shock no longer follows a lever-press, a rat eventually resumes lever-pressing. As already noted, there are two important exceptions to this generalization. First, if the intensity of the punishment is sufficiently high, response suppression is maintained even after the original punishing stimulus is no longer in effect. The intensity required to accomplish this, however, is well outside the range normally employed in a typical laboratory study of punishment. Second, and of more interest, it is known that, when it is possible to reinforce alternative behaviors, the effects of punishment can be extremely durable. It could be said that the point of punishment is not simply to stop an organism from engaging in a prohibited behavior, but to provide an opportunity for the controlling agent to build in new behaviors or strengthen already existing ones so that there is no longer an opportunity for engaging in the prohibited one. Thus the "transient" suppressive effect produced by punishment (i.e., not responding) can be turned into a durable behavioral change under the appropriate circumstances.

In the absence of such circumstances, however, punishment, like reinforcement, is usually found to be transient in its effects. Yet, there are instances in which a behavioral change, no longer supported by primary reinforcement or by primary punishment, is maintained for very long periods. Researchers working in operant conditioning have attempted to explain this maintenance by calling attention to the operation of generalized conditioned reinforcing and punishing stimuli. They have suggested that behavioral changes are maintained because stimuli that have been paired with primary reinforcement or punishment have taken over the functions of the original reinforcing or punishing stimuli. Certainly, there is a long and well-documented history of empirical studies of conditioned reinforcement that lends credibility to its use as an explanatory mechanism (e.g., Nevin, 1973). Much is known about the parameters that affect its acquisition, maintenance, and generality. By contrast, however, few such studies have been made of conditioned punishment. Although the phenomenon was demonstrated as early as 1954 (Mowrer and Solomon), we know very little about its operation.

A related mechanism used to account for the durability or maintenance of behavior is the concept of stimulus generalization. Stimuli that are similar to, although not identical with, those associated with punishment may, through the process of stimulus generalization, come to serve a suppressive function. However, as is true for conditioned punishing stimuli, there is little empirical evidence to draw upon. Aside from the Honig and Slivka (1964) study (see Chapter 4), there is little known about the specific conditions most likely to lead to generalization of response suppression.

Durability in Practical Settings

Durability of responding is not very easily attained in practical settings employing operant techniques. Psychologists studying behavior modification have found that changes that have been successfully effected in a treatment environment generally do not carry over to a person's regular environment, and therapists have had to accept the fact that generality and maintenance of a behavioral change must be programmed (Birnbrauer, in press). One approach to solving the problem of transferring behavior to a different setting is to train parents, teachers, and even peers in the principles of behavioral change so that reinforcement and punishment contingencies in the regular environment could conform to those used in the clinical one. In this way, punitive contingencies would not be discontinued. Another approach is to teach a person who is being treated skills that will bring about reinforcement in the regular environment. The latter approach is more economical in that it takes advantage of control techniques that already exist in that environment. Behaviors that are particularly repellent to the social community should be those whose suppression is most easily transferred: presumably, self-mutilation and certain forms of aggression, for example, are so unpleasant to observe that children who engage in such behaviors are avoided and, hence, are less likely to receive positive reinforcement for desirable behavior. If, after a program of behavior modification, these responses are at least temporarily suppressed, positive reinforcement for acceptable alternative behavior is more likely to be forthcoming from those with whom long-term interaction must take place. Neither of these approaches is completely satisfactory. Training those people who play significant roles in a child's life to use techniques for controlling behavior may be difficult. The nature of the behaviors to be suppressed may not be such that they affect a child's interaction with the environment.

A third approach to behavior maintenance that has become increasingly popular includes self-evaluation and self-reward or self-punishment. Those undergoing treatment are assisted in setting up their own programs of behavior modification and in devising a system for deciding whether they have earned a predetermined amount of reinforcement (Watson and Tharp 1972).

Or they enter into contracts with parents, spouses, or therapists that specify the behaviors that each party to a contract must engage in, what the rewards are for fulfillment, and what the sanctions are for nonfulfillment (Kanfer and Karoly 1972). Such procedures necessitate a desire for behavior modification by the participant, as well as ultimate control of reinforcement and punishment by an external agent. Yet when these conditions hold, the approach seems to be effective, and the behavioral changes that result are just as marked as those obtained by means of external evaluation and reinforcement. It is by no means evident, however, that self-control procedures will continue to be employed in the absence of surveillance or without the cooperation of external agents: it is not that difficult for a person to discriminate between situations in which punishment contingencies are in effect and those in which they are not.

The Concept of Internalization

One should not be discouraged by the fact that long-term response suppression is difficult to obtain or that generalized conditioned punishing stimuli do not seem to be operating that obviously in real life. From a functional point of view, it is adaptive for organisms to discriminate between situations in which punishment is likely to occur and those in which it is not. Socializing agents make mistakes, and if their mistakes could not be undone the consequences would be serious indeed. Yet socializing agents do wish to build in effects that will endure after punishment is no longer administered and will enable a person to resist counter pressures. (Hoffman [1970b] has noted that the need for durability and resistance may be peculiar to the middle classes; a mechanism for transfer makes less sense for lower class children and their parents who have much less stake in the social order and who are subject to much direct supervision.) Permanence of behavior suppression under all conditions for all time is undesirable, although a degree of stability greater than that which has been achieved so far by using punishment would seem desirable. That is why the concept of internalization has been so prevalent in the writings of those interested in the socialization process.

Although it was noted in Chapter 5 that one characteristic of internalization is long-term suppression, the main point stressed in socialization theories is that such suppression is maintained in the absence of fear of external punishment. Many have argued that internalization is unnecessary for the maintenance of suppression. They point to the vulnerability of moral standards to external pressures and to the fact that there is so much external surveillance in our lives that the suppression of behavior can be quite successfully maintained. William Golding, in his novel *Lord of the Flies,* presents a rather chilling description of the breakdown of morality in a group of English schoolboys marooned on an uninhabited island far from the civilizing influences of home and school. Perhaps this would be everyone's fate under similar circumstances. Perhaps the reason that people continue to act in accord with a given moral code even when it is unlikely that deviation will be detected is that they are never certain that they will not be found out. A great advantage that parents have is that they are more clever, on the average, than their charges. Children who deviate may feel certain they have covered their tracks completely and that the deviation will go undetected, and yet it is inevitably discovered. Thus parents are undeceived by outrageous lies that seem to their children to be perfectly reasonable statements, or they can detect subtle changes in behavior that go along with deviation. Basically, parents are good detectives: the repeated experience of being punished for "crimes" that one thought were perfect may be sufficient to shake one's faith in undetectability for life.

Perhaps a discussion of internalization should be terminated at this point. Although we could go on to cite examples of what seems to be "truly moral" behavior (i.e., response suppression in the absence of possible detection), all of them could probably be explained away without internalization. We simply do not seem to be asking the question correctly. Rather than pursue the question of whether a concept of internalization is necessary, we will outline the ideas put forward about how internalization occurs and, using this as a framework, indicate conditions under which the maintenance and transfer of response suppression may be more efficiently accomplished.

Internalization and Fear Conditioning. Learning theorists have dealt with internalization by talking about it in terms of fear conditioning. Mowrer (1960b) suggested that, because of repeated punishment for a deviant act, the kinesthetic cues produced by that act arouse conditioned fear or anxiety. The only way in which this anxiety can be terminated is by suppression of the behavior. Although this explains why behavior that was once punished may continue to be suppressed when punishment is discontinued, it does not take into consideration the fact that conditioned fear will eventually extinguish if there are not at least a few pairings of that behavior and punishment.

Internalization and Identification. Internalization can be thought to take place because of a person's positive orientation toward someone, or toward a group, not present. The person continues to behave in accord with the standards of the respected figure because of a desire not to hurt that person and/or a desire to be like that person. This introduces the concept of identification and the assumption that people adopt the moral standards of those whom they admire, love, or envy. But it is difficult to see how the gratification derived from acting like someone else is not offset by the unpleasant-ness of suppressing a behavior in which a person would like to engage. And, if the motivation for internalization of standards is a desire not to hurt a revered person, this could be reduced to a fear of incurring the disapproval of that person; that is, a fear of external punishment. As seen in Chapter 5, there is nothing as yet from the many studies of imitation to indicate that the effect of a model's behavior on an observer's suppression of responding is tied to anything other than fear of punishment from external sources.

Internalization and Attribution Theory.   A final version of the internalization concept accounts for transfer of suppression in terms of people believing that they are suppressing behavior because it is the right thing to do. Recall that in Chapter 5 the suggestion was made that punishment adminis-tered in a way that minimizes the role of the external agent may be more effective in suppressing behavior than if it were administered in a way that makes external control more obvi-ous; it was also suggested that a mechanism for handling this relationship is provided by attribution theory. According to this theory, persons who perceive that they have suppressed particular responses without having been subjected to exter-nal control attribute that suppression to their own morality rather than the external pressure, and hence are more inclined to continue to suppress the response. Those who perceive that they have been forced to conform by external pressure would be much more inclined to lapse into old behavioral patterns after external surveillance was discontinued. Any way of ad-ministering punishment that minimized the perception of ex-ternal control should thereby facilitate transfer. This view of internalization seems to be applicable only to human beings, as is that in which identification is the underlying mechanism for internalization. (It might be possible to develop analogues of the attribution process in the animal laboratory, but the usefulness of such a procedure is not immediately evident.)

To what extent could a procedure that minimizes the obviousness of external control be used in treating autistic and mentally retarded children, as well as children who are generally disruptive? Certainly, compliance that is not perceived as forced is easier to obtain from well-socialized children who are generally willing to behave in accord with polite suggestions from authority figures. Therefore, the first stage in dealing with children who are not well socialized may be to train them to be cooperative and compliant. The processes referred to by attribution theorists may emerge only after a particular kind of socialization to which an autistic or mentally retarded child is unlikely to have been exposed.

The Question of Integration

A fundamental difference between the work that has been done on punishment by learning researchers and that which has been done by child-development researchers lies, with few exceptions, in the objectives of the two lines of research. When Thorndike raised the question whether annoying consequences affect behavior, he set the tone for subsequent research on punishment in learning. The task that punishment researchers took to their laboratories was to determine the conditions, if any, under which punishment was effective and the kinds of behavioral changes that characterized its application. Interest centered on the suppression of behavior in the presence of an external agent. Quite different questions were being asked by child-development researchers concerned with problems of socialization. They focused their attention on internalization, or response suppression in the absence of surveillance. Because of these different approaches, there has been little integration of the two lines of research.

It is the research of learning psychologists working within a nonoperant framework that is most directly related to the concerns of child-development researchers. Recall that the punishment research conducted by Aronfreed, R. Walters, Parke, Cheyne, and others was directly inspired by Solomon's work on the timing of punishment. And Solomon *was* concerned with the ability of his dogs to resist temptation when they were left alone. Thus it is not surprising that his paradigm should have been borrowed by researchers whose subjects were children. What is difficult to understand is why learning psychologists have not pursued Solomon's resistance-to-temptation paradigm, and why systematic attempts have not been made to use the laboratory to study animal analogues of socialization practices such as punishment. Perhaps it is because, in a very real sense, the operant paradigm has dictated the research to be undertaken. And, although this research has revealed variables that influence punishment's effectiveness, it may well be that they are paradigm-bound. There has also been a corresponding lack of concern on the part of child-development researchers interested in socialization to attend to many of the problems of interest to learning researchers—definitional matters, systematic investigation of variables affecting punishment, and so forth. The fact that investigators from the two major lines of research have approached the study of punishment so differently is why different ends have been attained by quite different means.

It is perplexing to find this discrepancy in the study of a phenomenon as ubiquitous as punishment; it seems that the two lines of basic research should have merged at some point. But they did not because child-development researchers were preoccupied with the concept of internalization and convinced that punishment did not serve this function, and the problem of socialization did not fit into the paradigms in which punishment was studied in the learning laboratory. The assumption that researchers in the two disciplines, with few exceptions, did not read one another's literature is probably not far from the truth either.

Other differences aside from that of an interest in different dependent variables also contribute to difficulties in integration. Learning researchers have relied almost exclusively on one behavior—the arbitrary operant—and one punishing stimulus—electric shock. The interests of child-development psychologists, on the other hand, have ranged over a wide variety of behaviors and a wide variety of punishing stimuli, none of which has been nearly as systematically explored as has the suppression of operant behavior of rats and pigeons in a Skinner box by means of shock.

Studies that employ the free operant paradigm tend to be focused on the maintenance, rather than the acquisition, of behavior. In studies of punishment, concern has centered primarily on the suppression of behavior after a great number of punished trials, and to a much lesser extent on the effects of punishment during initial training. The emotional, disrupted behavior characteristic of early trials tends to be ignored or dismissed as unimportant in the long run. The compelling thing to animal researchers is that behavior under most conditions eventually becomes stable, organized, and, at the intensities of punishment usually employed, unemotional. Child-development researchers, on the other hand, may have their subjects undergo five or six punished trials in the course of an experiment. In real life, children are not punished very frequently: Clifford (1959) reported that three-year-olds are punished approximately once every other day and nine-year-olds once every fourth day. Given the number of behaviors that parents attempt to suppress, it is evident that no child will ever undergo punishment for a specific behavior as consistent and lengthy as that administered to a rat in an operant-conditioning study. Thus it would seem that learning research yields very little information about what takes place during the acquisition of suppression—information that is certainly relevant to problems of socialization. The disruptive properties of a punishing stimulus may well dissipate in time so that its value is only as a cue, but the situation that produces this evidence is artificial indeed. Undergoing mild punishment hundreds of times may eventually lead to a state of apparently unemotional responding, but such repeated subjection to punishment seldom occurs in the real world except, perhaps, under the most grim and inhumane circumstances. Perhaps because punishment is not administered to human beings so frequently, the presentation of a punishing stimulus continues to have a disruptive effect on most people, and the anxiety and emotionality that this produces is a very important factor affecting human behavior.

Another factor contributing to the difficulty of integrating the work in learning and child development has to do with the ethics of psychological research and with what our society permits investigators to do. Although an increasing interest in the welfare of animals in the research laboratory is certainly being expressed, the restrictions placed on the activities of psychologists who are using children as their subjects are much greater than those that apply to the work of animal researchers. As a result, most investigations of punishment in the child laboratory employ response-cost punishment, verbal reprimands, and loud buzzers. In field studies, particularly those in which the subjects are unruly, disturbed, or deviant children, the use of time-out as a punishing stimulus is permitted. But the investigation of physical punishment can be conducted only in naturalistic studies. Contrast this situation with the typical learning study in which electric shock is employed because of its virtues as a punishing stimulus (see Chapter 2). It will always be impossible to integrate the two lines of research in the study of the effects of physical punishment: child-development researchers cannot follow the direction taken by learning researchers; therefore, the change in focus must be made by the latter.

A punishing agent has a definite social relationship with the child being punished, one that is bound to affect the child's perception of the punishment situation. Punishment that seems arbitrary to the child may well produce hostility and a reduction in subsequent cooperative and compliant behavior, a result not likely to occur in a typical laboratory study using animals. We assume that animals react to electric shock received through grids and electrodes implanted in the skin in the same way that children react to such natural punishment contingencies as being shocked while probing an electrical outlet with a metal object. Punishment that *is* obviously mediated by an agent can be studied in the animal laboratory: recall the study by D. Freedman (1967), described in Chapter 4, in which an experimenter nurtured some puppies and treated others in a negative way. The initial social interactions had a definite effect on reactions to the punishment that was subsequently administered by the experimenter. For the most part, however, the data from the two lines of research in terms of the social implications of punishment are extremely different, creating an imbalance that certainly limits integration.

The social relationship between punishing agent and the recipient of punishment, moreover, is not unidirectional. Children (and animals) in natural settings affect their socializing agents. Investigation of this interrelationship has only begun. Sawin, Parke, Harrison, and Kreling (1975) reported that the disciplinary action taken by an adult is affected by a child's previous reactions to punishment. Their study revealed that children who react by being defiant or by ignoring the adult are subsequently punished more severely than are children who plead for less severe punishment. Those who apologize and promise to behave better are not punished at all but generally rewarded. The physical characteristics of a child also affect the punitive behavior of an adult. Dion (1974), using an experimental learning situation, reported that women, but not men, are less punitive toward attractive boys than they are toward either attractive girls or unattractive children of either sex. Such relationships between punishing agent and recipient are virtually nonexistent in the laboratory, either animal or child. No matter how the organism appears or responds, experimenters continue with their preplanned programs. Any frustration, anger, or pleasure they experience is communicated later to colleagues, friends, or family, and never to the objects of their manipulations. So one-sided is the relationship in the laboratory that it has fairly blinded many researchers to the fact that, outside the laboratory, people are influenced by the reactions of those whose behavior they attempt to change or modify, and these reactions have an effect on subsequent attempts to punish.

The implications of many of the differences between the two lines of research in the study of punishment became clear quite early in the writing of this book. When we began this undertaking we expected to find greater possibilities for integration than actually emerged. In a sense, this is disappointing. On the other hand, the discrepancies that have impeded our attempt at integration have helped us to see quite clearly where we think research on response suppression *should* be heading.

Future Directions

The fact that integration has proved more difficult than we had originally expected makes it apparent that scientific inquiry about punishment is not near an end (cf. Bolles, 1975b). The question that must now be entertained is whether investigators are headed in the right direction and should simply keep on going. The answer is probably not.

The Rejection of Punishment as a Socialization Tool

The concern of child-development psychologists with internalization led to a comparison of different punishment techniques, all of which were subsequently rejected in favor of more cognitive approaches—the use of reasoning, for example—to response elimination. Even the flurry of interest in punishment in the late 1960s ended when it was thought that cognitive structuring could override the effects of such parameters as timing and intensity.

The rejection of punishment by researchers, because it supposedly does not lead to long-term suppression in the absence of surveillance and because the effects of various punishment parameters are attenuated by the introduction of cognitive manipulations, means that very little is known about its role in socialization. And it is unlikely that much more will be learned about it as long as its study is considered to be irrelevant to successful socialization. We think, however, that there are substantial reasons why this rejection ought to be reconsidered. Most important, if rationales are assumed to serve as cues signalling the possibility of punishment, then it is still necessary to know a great deal more about the parameters governing punishment's effectiveness. In what way do different kinds of rationales and cognitive structuring interact with different kinds of punishment? Although the work of Parke and others suggests that explaining the contingencies can attenuate the effects of intensity, timing, and delay of the sound of a loud buzzer in a laboratory, it seems premature to generalize from this to all kinds of punishment and all kinds of rationales. Even if the contingency between response and punishment is made clear, for example, we find it hard to believe that there are not situations in which the amount of punishment possible would have a definite effect on a child's decision about whether or not to engage in a prohibited behavior. And what about young children who do not have the intellectual apparatus to understand cognitive structuring?

As for the objection that punishment works only to suppress responding in the presence of the punishing agent, much of socialization in fact *does* consist of attempting to suppress behavior in the presence of socializing agents who do not really care whether the behavior is suppressed in their absence. Children who are excessively slow in getting ready for school, who fight and argue with their siblings, or who forget to take out the garbage or to clean up their rooms present the kinds of problems around which many parent-child interactions revolve. And they are certainly the kinds of problems addressed by columnists giving advice on raising children, for they are of great practical importance. Thus the preoccupation with internalization to the detriment of all other aspects of response suppression seems to us unnecessary.

The Use of the Operant Paradigm

There is no doubt that a useful technology has been developed in the learning laboratory, a technology that has yielded extensive and reliable data about the punishment of certain behaviors in well-controlled situations. However, it is also true that a long-term goal of punishment research is to clarify the role of punitive interventions in a broad range of human behaviors. This raises the question whether the punishment paradigm that is used in the learning laboratory is appropriate to the achievement of this long-term goal.

One difficulty has already been noted, which is the fact that so little attention is paid to the acquisition of punished responses, even though the things that happen during the early stages of response suppression are interesting and important to child-development psychologists. There are other problems as well, however. It would be wrong to assert that there is nothing further to be gained from additional punishment research conducted within the standard operant paradigm. But our opinion is that a point has been reached in the pursuit of this problem at which the questions being investigated are bound too closely to that paradigm, or are perhaps even determined by it.

There are two basic questions here. The first is whether the study of punishment in the learning laboratory has revealed anything about its operation in a broader context: that is, in changing human behavior. It is true that some of the principles derived from studies using the operant paradigm have been successfully applied to problems outside the laboratory. There is a very evident interaction between the psychologists doing research on punishment in the animal laboratory who are working within the operant framework and those concerned with the application of operant-conditioning principles to a limited range of human problems in settings that afford a high degree of stimulus control. In fact, the same people are often working in both areas. The interchange is easy because problems have been conceptualized in similar terms, and the technology developed in the animal laboratory has been applied directly to the modification of behavioral deviations of both children and adults with notable success. It is also true that a parent or teacher can turn to a rather straightforward set of principles developed in the animal laboratory for precise suggestions for the suppression of certain unwanted responses. Because the technology associated with the operant approach can be effective, practitioners have been eager to borrow and apply it to human problems. Interestingly enough, we might add that research in child development has not afforded the same degree of help for those who need to solve practical problems. Advice to be friendly, consistent, and understanding, to employ nonauthoritarian democratic child-rearing methods, to be accepting, to be rational—all are the kinds of suggestions that emanate from much of this research. Their implementation, however, is a great deal more difficult than that of the suggestion that every time children are rude they should be told to go to their rooms and stay there for 15 minutes.

A demonstration of the applicability of a few basic principles to solving certain behavioral problems, however, should not be regarded as evidence of an increased understanding of the general phenomenon of punishment. For example, the demonstration that punishment is effective in suppressing the self-mutilating behavior of autistic children does not *extend* what is known about punishment or tell us the mechanism by which punishment exerts its suppressive effect: it simply demonstrates the efficacy of an already developed technology. Behavior modification, then, is simply an extension, albeit a significant one, of already established principles of operant conditioning; it does not represent an *advance* in our knowledge about the role of punishment in the socialization process.

The other basic question having to do with reliance on the operant paradigm is whether the principles of punishment generated in the learning laboratory have much generality outside of that which we have already noted in problems of behavior modification. With few exceptions, principles have been derived from studying one or two species of animal as if they were representative of all organisms. Further, the study of the effects of punishment on behavior translates to the study of the effects of response-contingent electric shock on the lever-pressing or the key-pecking of the hungry rat or pigeon. Are these arbitrary operants representative of all behaviors and is electric shock representative of all aversive stimuli? Will this approach continue to give us information that will eventually lead to a comprehensive understanding of the mechanism of punishment? There is reason to believe that this is unlikely.

The question of generality was briefly dealt with in Chapter 3 in considering the role of the nature of the response in determining the outcome of punishment. Other evidence developed in studying the phenomenon of poison-avoidance also presents a challenge to anyone wishing to generalize too broadly about the effects of aversive stimuli on behavior. Briefly, what this work has shown is that rats have a special facility for learning about the relationship between the taste of poisoned food and the subsequent (aversive) illness produced by poisoning. For example, Garcia and Koelling (1966) have shown that rats will learn to avoid distinctively flavored water even when the period between water ingestion and the onset of illness produced by poison or radiation is long. This "bait-shyness" does not occur if audio-visual cues are substituted for the taste cues. Further, when electric shock is made contingent on drinking flavored water, no aversion is produced, although drinking is suppressed if it is associated with shock in the presence of audio-visual cues (see also, Bolles, 1975a; Hinde and Stevenson-Hinde, 1973; Seligman and Hager, 1972). The specificity of cue and consequence has also been demonstrated for birds, although in this case the cues utilized in learning about the consequences of poisoning are visual and not gustatory. The general principle seems to be that the significant cues are the ones that the organism normally uses in foraging for food in its natural environment. Such behaviors are, of course, adaptive for the long-term survival of a given animal and its species.

We have not gone into greater detail in considering the bait-shyness studies because most investigators have rejected the notion that this phenomenon can be explained in terms of a punishment paradigm. The primary reason that this work is of interest to us is that it may indicate the existence of a special learning mechanism that is not accounted for by the established laws of learning that apply to arbitrary events such as lever-pressing followed by punishing electric shocks. It seems very likely that all organisms have such special facilities for learning certain things. Perhaps, for human beings, language and symbolic thought processes are especially selected for ease of learning. The point to be remembered is that the information about punishment that is derived from observations of hungry rats or pigeons studied in the context of the operant paradigm in which an arbitrary behavior is being acquired, maintained, and suppressed probably does not constitute general principles about punishment's effectiveness. Indeed, that this is true has already been seen in the attempts that have been made to compare the effects of punishment on different types of responses.

This is not an argument for the abandonment of the operant analysis of punishment. It is, however, a plea for greater diversity in approaching the study of punishment. Even if the kinds of questions to which operant technology has been addressed—questions relating to the management of behavior—have been dealt with adequately, the time has come to expand the approach beyond that of building in arbitrary behaviors and delivering electric shocks while changes in rate of responding are measured. More knowledge is needed about the effects of punishment on behaviors that are not arbitrary—those that have functional significance for the organism—in order to develop a more comprehensive understanding of the effects of punishment. Given the growing acceptance and influence of ethology in the animal learning laboratory, it would seem that now is an opportune time to begin *systematic* studies of punishment and socialization in animals. Now is also the appropriate time to take stock of what has been accomplished in the animal laboratory and to determine whether the direction being taken in the study of punishment is still valid. Although the criteria for making such judgments are not altogether clear in any area of inquiry, this is a task that must be carried out.

The Future of Child-Development Research

We have just pointed out that a consideration of the functional significance of a given behavior for an organism is imperative if we are to understand how that behavior is modified. Although this is a view that has received considerable attention from learning researchers in recent years, little formal attention has been paid to it by child-development researchers. Given the present state of knowledge, it is not easy to decide which human behaviors can be classified, for example, as arbitrary operants, as being examples of species-specific behaviors, or as having a functional significance for the organism. How, for example, should an act of aggression be classified? Is it innate, learned, or some complex mixture of the two? How is obedience to parental commands and prohibitions to be classified? Most psychologists have assumed that a child's natural disposition is to ignore commands and prohibitions, particularly when they interfere with the child's personal desires. A contrary viewpoint, however, has been put forth by Stayton, Hogan, and Ainsworth (1971). These researchers maintained that evolutionary adaptation has established in children a natural disposition to obey and to become socialized. If this is true, a rigorous regimen of reinforcement and punishment should not be necessary to establish compliance with the requests of parents and other socializing agents.

We can offer no answers at this point. Clearly, some of the behaviors that people attempt to suppress are at least partly learned. Take swearing, for example. Children learn to swear through observation or direct reinforcement because it attracts attention. Similarly, they learn to throw temper tantrums because tantrums induce compliance in others. Other behaviors— for example, impulsive acts—may have less of a learned component. Some behaviors, such as acts of obedience, may have greater functional significance than others. A comprehensive theory of punishment must take such variability into account. Learning researchers have been limited in this regard by their virtually complete reliance on the operant paradigm; child-development researchers may be in danger of falling into a similar trap. There was less likelihood of this so long as they conducted mainly naturalistic observational studies. But because they have come to rely on the use of experimentation in the study of punishment to such a great extent, they run the risk of locking into one particular research paradigm to the detriment of a more comprehensive approach to the problem.

It has become fashionable to call for a return to naturalistic observational studies. The study of punishment could well benefit from this advice. Although some child-development researchers have never stopped conducting naturalistic studies of child-rearing practices—and these studies have often yielded provocative and interesting data—there is room for a new approach to analysis of events occurring in natural settings. Rather than being content with describing general patterns of parental behavior and seeking to establish the relationship of these patterns to various indices of the social behavior of children, however, we suggest that researchers should seek to make a more precise analysis of what goes on between parent and child. If a parent relies on power assertion, are some kinds of power assertion (e.g., the withdrawal of privileges) more likely to be effective than others (e.g., mild physical punishment)? Is there an interaction between the type of punishment administered and the ease with which certain kinds of behaviors are suppressed? Is punishment more likely to be effective if arbitrariness is minimized? (For example, is "No television!" a more effective punishment for watching television instead of studying than it would be for running out into the street without looking?) How important is the personal interaction that takes place when a punishing stimulus is imposed? Is punishment more effective if children themselves are asked to suggest an appropriate punishment? Do particularly successful parents tend to accompany punishment with certain types of verbalizations? Do these verbalizations stress the importance of the child's concern for the effects of its behavior on others, or do they seem to mainly serve the function of drawing the child's attention away from the fact that someone is forcing it to do something? Do parents react to different undesirable behaviors with different disciplinary techniques? Are some approaches more effective than others in producing an immediate cessation of an undesirable activity? Do children seem to respond differently to different punishing stimuli? (For example, is it true that some children are unaffected by withdrawal of social approval and that other children are devastated by it?) What might some of the correlates of this differential sensitivity be?

Some beginnings have been made in naturalistic observational studies that pave the way for this more precise analysis of parental punishment. G. Patterson (1974), for example, outlined a procedure by which networks of stimuli controlling the occurrence of noxious, or antisocial, responses can be established: observers in a natural setting watch the behavior taking place during adult-child interactions and categorize it into discrete units as it occurs. These observations enable the investigator to establish which events are likely to be associated with an increase or decrease in the occurrence of certain categories of predetermined responses. Using this approach, Lytton and Zwirner (1975) were able to determine what kinds of parental behaviors facilitate compliance and noncompliance in two-and-a-half-year-old boys. They found, for example, that compliance was greatest after parental suggestion and became progressively less after commands and reasoning.

Such observational findings must be subjected to experimental tests in the laboratory or field before cause-and-effect relationships can be established. Another limitation of this approach is that it reveals only the immediate, not the long-term, effects of a particular parental behavior. But clearly the approach taken by such researchers as Patterson and Lytton is a promising one and can be expanded to give a more comprehensive picture of parent-child interactions and to help in finding answers to some of the questions that have been raised in our analysis of punishment.

We have argued that child-development researchers should study the effects of punishment that occur while a child is under the surveillance of a socializing agent. There is important information to be gathered here. Nor should the significance of the effects of punishment on the internalization of standards be underestimated. But, in the study of these effects, a change in the paradigm that has been traditionally employed, or an addition to it, might well be considered. Although it is interesting that punishment consisting of the sound of a loud buzzer continues to be effective when a child is alone in an experimental room, little attention has been paid by experimenters to the durability or generality of these effects. Would a child who was returned to the experimental setting a week or a month later continue to suppress responding? Would the effects of punishment generalize to new settings? Would a child who was punished for failing to share in the laboratory, for example, share more during a free-play period in the classroom? These are important questions that must be answered.

Ethical Considerations and Alternatives Reconsidered

We would like to turn in this section to a consideration of ethics and alternatives to punishment. This problem was discussed earlier, but, because of its importance, it seems appropriate to draw together a few final thoughts about it.

It is generally agreed that harsh corporal punishment, teasing, ridicule, and other attacks on self-esteem are bad for children. However, some forms of punishment seem to be valuable aids to socialization: verbal rebuke and social disapproval that do not attack a person's worth, withdrawal of privileges and material objects, even the occasional use of physical punishment. It is helpful to give the child an explanation for why a particular behavior is punished, to clarify the relationship between the child's response and the punishment, and to be consistent in applying the punishing stimulus.

It could be argued that an approach to socialization stressing the suppression of antisocial behavior, rather than placing the emphasis on engaging in prosocial behavior, could produce an individual who, although not actively involved in unacceptable behavior, would not be actively involved in acceptable behavior. The evidence suggests, however, that, even in the context of punishment, children can be induced to engage in prosocial behavior. For example, prescriptive parents who emphasize being good have children who are more generous than do proscriptive parents who emphasize not being bad. But parental reliance on reward or punishment seems to make no difference in the child's generosity (Olejnik and McKinney 1973).

In spite of this, it could still be argued that we would be better off relying as little as possible on punishment as a way of changing behavior, expending our efforts instead on finding alternative and more appealing approaches. Why not use extinction? reasoning? imitation? Why not turn to positive reinforcement, concentrating our efforts on building in desirable behaviors that will be incompatible with, and therefore decrease the incidence of, undesirable behaviors?

We have previously noted the limitations of extinction. And the efficacy of reasoning and vicarious processes seems to be very much determined by their relationship to fear of punishment. Also, recall from Chapter 3 that punishment for incorrect responding is more effective than reinforcement for correct responding. We suggested that this may occur because socializing agents tend to use reinforcement more in a noncontingent way than they do punishment. Interestingly enough, some support for this hypothesis comes from a class project carried out for one of us (Grusec). Undergraduates observed family interactions in a home setting and found that—at least for children between the ages of three and six—parents administer very little noncontingent punishment, but do give their children a fair amount of noncontingent reinforcement. This does not reflect simply a reluctance to employ punishment at all; there was a great reliance by parents on both reinforcement and punishment applied contingent on specific behaviors.

Further, it is important to note that all stimuli, whether reinforcing or punishing, have distracting properties. It follows logically that such stimuli, because they disrupt responding, would initially facilitate response suppression just as they would at first be detrimental to response acquisition. In this way punishment can be construed as having an advantage in the suppression of responding in that disruption works in the direction of the intended behavioral outcome, suppression; in reinforcement, these initial disruptive effects work against the desired goal, acquisition. Going one step further, recall the evidence cited in Chapter 3 that material reinforcers distract children from tasks in which they are supposed to be engaging *to a greater extent* than do punishing stimuli (see Penney, 1967; Witte and Grossman, 1971).

Additional difficulties with reinforcement are highlighted by recent evidence that, under certain circumstances, when children are given reinforcement for engaging in a behavior, unexpected consequences may occur. The quality of their behavior deteriorates relative to what it is like when they are not motivated by the expectation of reinforcement and, moreover, subsequent interest in the activity also declines (Garbarino

1975; Lepper, Greene, and Nisbett 1973). The mechanism producing this effect is not entirely clear. Attribution theorists suggest that children who are given reinforcement for their behavior perceive that they have done something because of the extrinsic reinforcement offered and not because of any intrinsic interest in the activity. In the absence of external reinforcement, then, interest declines. Reiss and Sushinsky (1975) argue that children offered external incentives are distracted by them, and so spend less time in the desired behavior and do it in a less efficient manner.

These considerations lead us to conclude that reinforcement has its own limitations as a technique of behavioral change and that these limitations may even, under certain conditions, make it less effective than punishment. In an attempt to find a viable alternative to punishment as a response-suppression technique, however, the possibility of trying to eliminate some of the deficiencies of reinforcement might be considered. Perhaps socializing agents should be urged to be less lavish in giving rewards, confining them to situations in which they are earned. We find the suggestion unappealing, however, that parents be discouraged from hugging, kissing, and praising their children, or giving them occasional gifts, regardless of whether these events have been earned. Spontaneity is an attractive aspect of human interaction. What then, about the distracting aspects of reinforcement? It may be instructive to study alternative ways of administering reinforcement, so as to alleviate this undesirable side effect. Recall our argument from Chapter 5 that punishment should be administered in such a way as to reduce the obviousness of the external agent. Why not a similar process in the administration of reinforcement? Rather than have children focus their attention on the fact that they are winning material objects or approval for a given behavior, why not supply them with rationales or reasons to which they can attribute their behavior? Compare the following two situations. In the first situation, Joey is told that he can win points for doing household chores and that the more points he gets the larger his allowance will be on Saturday. To this instruction is added, in the second situation, the information that this procedure is being instituted to help him develop a sense of responsibility and helpfulness, which will aid him in getting along with others for the rest of his life. In both situations, we are wagering that reinforcement will be necessary to get Joey started on the road to social responsibility. In the second situation, however, the way in which beds are made, dishes are washed, garbage is carried out, and the dog is fed should be of a higher quality and should be more likely to endure after the token system is ended. We doubt, however, that the approach would be as effective with reinforcement as a parallel approach would be with punishment, for the argument can be made that people apparently like to think about pleasant things, and so are distracted from what they are supposed to be doing, whereas they do not like to think about unpleasant things and would not be distracted.

These considerations lead us to two opinions. The first is that alternative techniques for behavioral change should be viewed with as much suspicion as is punishment; the assertion that punishment is bad and reinforcement good is a gross oversimplification. In some ways, we have come further in our understanding of how to apply punishment effectively than we have of how to apply reinforcement. The second is that a good case can be made that punishment is a more effective technique for behavioral change than is reinforcement. And this leads us to an inescapable conclusion: punishment will always be a necessary tool of behavioral change.

REFERENCES

Abel, E. L., and Walters, G. C. Reactions to punishment determined by infant experience with aversive stimulation. *Developmental Psychology,* 1972, 7, 1–3.

Adler, N., and Hogan, J. A. Classical conditioning and punishment of an instinctive response in *Betta splendens. Animal Behavior,* 1963, 11, 351–354.

Alcock, J. Punishment levels and the response of black-capped chickadees *(Parus atricapillus)* to three kinds of artificial seeds. *Animal Behavior,* 1970a, 18, 592–599.

Alcock, J. Punishment levels and the response of white-throated sparrows *(Zonotrichia albicollis)* to three kinds of artificial models and mimics. *Animal Behavior,* 1970b, 18, 733–739.

Allinsmith, W., and Greening, T. C. Guilt over anger as predicted from parental discipline: A study of superego development. *American Psychologist,* 1955, 10, 320 (Abstract).

Amsel, A. The role of frustrative nonreward in noncontinuous reward situations. *Psychological Bulletin,* 1958, *55,* 102–119.

Amsel, A. Positive induction, behavioral contrast, and generalization of inhibition in discrimination learning. In H. H. Kendler and J. T. Spence (Eds.), *Essays in neobehaviorism: A memorial volume for Kenneth N. Spence.* New York: Appleton-Century-Crofts, 1971.

Anderson, D. C., Cole, J., and McVaugh, W. Variations in unsignaled inescapable preshock as determinants of response to punishment. *Journal of Comparative and Physiological Psychology,* 1968, *65,* 1–17.

Andres, D. H. Modification of delay-of-punishment effects through cognitive restructuring. Unpublished doctoral thesis, University of Waterloo, 1967.

Appel, J. B. Punishment in the squirrel monkey *Saimiri sciurea. Science,* 1961, *133,* 36.

Appel, J. B. Punishment and shock intensity. *Science,* 1963, *141,* 528–529.

Appel, J. B., and Peterson, N. J. Punishment: Effects of shock intensity on response suppression. *Psychological Reports,* 1965, *16,* 721–730.

Aronfreed, J. Aversive control of socialization. In D. Levine (Ed.), *Nebraska Symposium on Motivation.* Lincoln: University of Nebraska Press, 1968.

Aronfreed, J., and Leff, R. The effects of intensity of punishment and complexity of discrimination upon the generalization of an internalized inhibition. Unpublished manuscript, University of Pennsylvania, 1963.

Aronfreed, J., and Reber, A. Internalized behavioral suppression and the timing of social punishment. *Journal of Personality and Social Psychology,* 1965, *1,* 3–16.

Azrin, N. H. Some effects of two intermittent schedules of immediate and nonimmediate punishment. *Journal of Psychology,* 1956, *42,* 3–21.

Azrin, N. H. Punishment and recovery during fixed-ratio performance. *Journal of the Experimental Analysis of Behavior,* 1959, *2,* 301–305.

Azrin, N. H. Effects of punishment intensity during variable-interval reinforcement. *Journal of the Experimental Analysis of Behavior,* 1960, *3,* 123–142.

Azrin, N. H. Punishment of elicited aggression. *Journal of the Experimental Analysis of Behavior,* 1970, *14,* 7–10.

Azrin, N. H., Hake, D. F., Holz, W. C., and Hutchinson, R. R. Motivational aspects of escape from punishment. *Journal of the Experimental Analysis of Behavior*, 1965, *8*, 31–44.

Azrin, N. H., and Holz, W. C. Punishment during fixed-interval reinforcement. *Journal of the Experimental Analysis of Behavior*, 1961, *4*, 343–347.

Azrin, N. H., and Holz, W. C. Punishment. In W. K. Honig (Ed.), *Operant behavior: Areas of research and application*. New York: Appleton-Century-Crofts, 1966.

Azrin, N. H., Holz, W. C., and Hake, D. F. Fixed-ratio punishment. *Journal of the Experimental Analysis of Behavior*, 1963, *6*, 141–148.

Azrin, N. H., Hutchinson, R. R., and Hake, D. F. Extinction-induced aggression. *Journal of the Experimental Analysis of Behavior*, 1966, *9*, 191–204.

Azrin, N. H., Hutchinson, R. R., and McLaughlin, R. The opportunity for aggression as an operant reinforcer during aversive stimulation. *Journal of the Experimental Analysis of Behavior*, 1965, *8*, 171–180.

Baenninger, R. Contrasting effects of fear and pain on mouse killing by rats. *Journal of Comparative and Physiological Psychology*, 1967, *63*, 298–303.

Baenninger, R., and Grossman, J. C. Some effects of punishment on pain-elicited aggression. *Journal of the Experimental Analysis of Behavior*, 1969, *12*, 1017–1022.

Bandura, A. Influence of model's reinforcement contingencies on the acquisition of imitative responses. *Journal of Personality and Social Psychology*, 1965, *1*, 589–595.

Bandura, A. *Principles of behavior modification*. New York: Holt, Rinehart and Winston, 1969.

Bandura, A., Grusec, J. E., and Menlove, F. L. Some social determinants of self-monitoring reinforcement systems. *Journal of Personality and Social Psychology*, 1967, *5*, 449–455.

Bandura, A., and Huston, A. C. Identification as a process of incidental learning. *Journal of Abnormal and Social Psychology*, 1961, *63*, 311–318.

Bandura, A., and Kupers, C. J. The transmission of patterns of self-reinforcement through modeling. *Journal of Abnormal and Social Psychology*, 1964, *69*, 1–9.

Bandura, A., Ross, D., and Ross, S. A. Imitation of film-mediated aggressive models. *Journal of Abnormal and Social Psychology,* 1963a, *66,* 3–11.

Bandura, A., Ross, D., and Ross, S. A. Vicarious reinforcement and imitative learning. *Journal of Abnormal and Social Psychology,* 1963b, *67,* 601–607.

Bandura, A., and Walters, R. H. *Adolescent aggression,* New York: Ronald Press, 1959.

Bandura, A., and Walters, R. H. *Social learning and personality development,* New York: Holt, Rinehart and Winston, 1963.

Banks, R. K. Persistence to continuous punishment and nonreward following training with intermittent punishment and nonreward. *Psychonomic Science,* 1966, *5,* 105–106.

Banks, R. K., and Vogel-Sprott, M. Effect of delayed punishment on an immediately rewarded response in humans. *Journal of Experimental Psychology,* 1965, *70,* 357–359.

Baron, A. Delayed punishment of a runway response. *Journal of Comparative and Physiological Psychology,* 1965, *60,* 131–134.

Baron, A., Kaufman, A., and Fazzini, D. Density and delay of punishment of free operant avoidance. *Journal of the Experimental Analysis of Behavior,* 1969, *12,* 1029–1037.

Barret, J. E., Hoffman, H. S., Stratton, J. W., and Newby, V. Aversive control of following in imprinted ducklings. *Learning and Motivation,* 1971, *2,* 202–213.

Baumrind, D. The development of instrumental competence through socialization. In Anne D. Pick (Ed.), *Minnesota Symposia on Child Psychology* (vol. 7). Minneapolis: University of Minnesota Press, 1973.

Beach, F. A., Conovitz, M. W., Steinberg, F., and Goldstein, A. C. Experimental inhibition and restoration of mating behavior in male rats. *Journal of Genetic Psychology,* 1956, *89,* 165–181.

Berkowitz, L. *Aggression: A social psychological analysis.* New York: McGraw-Hill, 1962.

Bernstein, A. Some relations between techniques of feeding and training during infancy and certain behavior in childhood. *Genetic Psychology Monographs,* 1955, *51,* 3–44.

Bertsch, G. J. Punishment of consummatory and instrumental behavior: Effects on licking and bar pressing in rats. *Journal of*

Comparative and Physiological Psychology, 1972, *78,* 478–484.

Birnbrauer, J. S. Mental retardation. In H. Leitenberg (Ed.), *Handbook of behavior modification and behavior therapy.* New York: Prentice-Hall, in press.

Black, A. H., and Morse, P. Avoidance learning in dogs without a warning stimulus. *Journal of the Experimental Analysis of Behavior,* 1961, *4,* 17–23.

Black, A. H., and Young, G. A. Constraints on the operant conditioning of drinking. In R. M. Gilbert and J. R. Millenson (Eds.), *Reinforcement: Behavioral analyses.* New York: Academic Press, 1972.

Boe, E. E. Bibliography on punishment. In B. A. Campbell and R. M. Church (Eds.), *Punishment and aversive behavior.* New York: Appleton-Century-Crofts, 1969.

Boe, E. E. Recovery from signaled shock as a function of response contingency in rats. *Journal of Comparative and Physiological Psychology,* 1971, *77,* 122–130.

Boe, E. E., and Church, R. M. Permanent effects of punishment during extinction. *Journal of Comparative and Physiological Psychology,* 1967, *63,* 486–492.

Bolles, R. C. Species-specific defense reactions and avoidance learning. *Psychological Review,* 1970, *77,* 32–48.

Bolles, R. C. *Learning theory.* New York: Holt, Rinehart and Winston, 1975a.

Bolles, R. C. *Theory of motivation* (2nd ed.). New York: Harper & Row, 1975b.

Bolles, R. C., and Seelbach, S. E. Punishing and reinforcing effects of noise onset and termination for different responses. *Journal of Comparative and Physiological Psychology,* 1964, *58,* 127–131.

Brethower, D. M., and Reynolds, G. S. A facilitative effect of punishment on unpunished behavior. *Journal of the Experimental Analysis of Behavior,* 1962, *5,* 191–199.

Boroczi, G., Storms, L. H., and Broen, W. E. Response suppression and recovery of responding at different deprivation levels as functions of intensity and duration of punishment. *Journal of Comparative and Physiological Psychology,* 1964, *58,* 456–459.

Brown, J. S. Factors affecting self-punitive locomotor behavior. In B.

A. Campbell and R. M. Church (Eds.), *Punishment and aversive behavior*. New York: Appleton-Century-Crofts, 1969.

Brown, J. S., and Farber, I. E. Emotions conceptualized as intervening variables—With suggestions toward a theory of frustration. *Psychological Bulletin*, 1951, *48*, 465–495.

Buchanan, G. U. The effects of various punishment-escape events upon subsequent choice behavior of rats. *Journal of Comparative and Physiological Psychology*, 1958, *51*, 355–362.

Bucher, B., and Lovaas, O. I. Use of aversive stimulation in behavior modification. In M. R. Jones (Ed.), *Miami Symposium on the Prediction of Behavior 1967: Aversive stimulation*. Coral Gables, Florida: University of Miami Press, 1968.

Bugelski, B. R. Extinction with and without sub-goal reinforcement. *Journal of Comparative Psychology*, 1938, *26*, 121–134.

Burton, R. V. The generality of honesty reconsidered. *Psychological Review*, 1963, *70*, 481–499.

Camp, D. S., Raymond, G. A., and Church, R. M. Temporal relationship between response and punishment. *Journal of Experimental Psychology*, 1967, *74*, 114–123.

Campbell, B. A., and Bloom, J. M. Relative aversiveness of noise and shock. *Journal of Comparative and Physiological Psychology*, 1965, *60*, 440–442.

Campbell, B. A., and Church, R. M. (Eds.). *Punishment and aversive behavior*. New York: Appleton-Century-Crofts, 1969.

Campbell, B. A., and Masterson, F. A. Psychophysics of punishment. In B. A. Campbell and R. M. Church (Eds.), *Punishment and aversive behavior*. New York: Appleton-Century-Crofts, 1969.

Carlsmith, J. M., Lepper, M. R., and Landauer, T. K. Children's obedience to adult requests: Interactive effects of anxiety arousal and apparent punitiveness of the adult. *Journal of Personality and Social Psychology* 1974, *30*, 822–828.

Chartier, G. M., and Weiss, R. L. Comparative test of positive control, negative control, and social power theories of identificatory learning in disadvantaged children. *Journal of Personality and Social Psychology*, 1974, *29*, 724–730.

Cheyne, J. A. Some parameters of punishment affecting resistance to deviation and generalization of a prohibition. *Child Development*, 1971, *42*, 1249–1261.

Cheyne, J. A., Goyeche, J. R., and Walters, R. H. Attention, anxiety, and rules in resistance-to-deviation in children. *Journal of Experimental Child Psychology,* 1969, 8, 127–139.

Cheyne, J. A., and Walters, R. H. Intensity of punishment, timing of punishment, and cognitive structure as determinants of response inhibition. *Journal of Experimental Child Psychology,* 1969, 7, 231–244.

Cheyne, J. A., and Walters, R. H. Punishment and prohibition: Some origins of self-control. In T. M. Newcomb (Ed.), *New directions in psychology.* New York: Holt, Rinehart and Winston, 1970.

Christy, P. R., Gelfand, D. M., and Hartmann, D. P. Effects of competition-induced frustration on two classes of modeled behavior. *Developmental Psychology,* 1971, 5, 104–111.

Church, R. M. The varied effects of punishment on behavior. *Psychological Review,* 1963, 70, 369–402.

Church, R. M. Response suppression. In B. A. Campbell and R. M. Church (Eds.), *Punishment and aversive behavior.* New York: Appleton-Century-Crofts, 1969.

Church, R. M., LoLordo, V., Overmier, J. B., Solomon, R. L., and Turner, L. Cardiac responses to shock in curarized dogs: Effects of shock intensity and duration, warning signal and prior experience with shock. *Journal of Comparative and Physiological Psychology,* 1966, 62, 1–7.

Church, R. M., and Raymond, G. A. Influence of the schedule of positive reinforcement on punished behavior. *Journal of Comparative and Physiological Psychology,* 1967, 63, 329–332.

Church, R. M., Raymond, G. A., and Beauchamp, R. D. Response suppression as a function of intensity and duration of a punishment. *Journal of Comparative and Physiological Psychology,* 1967, 63, 39–44.

Church, R. M., Wooten, C. L., and Matthews, T. J. Contingency between a response and an aversive event in the rat. *Journal of Comparative and Physiological Psychology,* 1970, 72, 476–485.

Clifford, E. Discipline in the home: A controlled observational study of parental practices. *Journal of Genetic Psychology,* 1959, 95, 45–82.

Corte, H. E., Wolf, M. E., and Locke, B. J. A comparison of procedures for eliminating self-injurious behavior of retarded adolescents. *Journal of Applied Behavior Analysis,* 1971, *4,* 201–214.

deCosta, M. J., and Ayres, J. J. B. Suppression of operant *vs* consummatory behavior. *Journal of the Experimental Analysis of Behavior,* 1971, *16,* 133–142.

Costantini, A. F., and Hoving, K. L. The effectiveness of reward and punishment contingencies on response inhibition. *Journal of Experimental Child Psychology,* 1973, *16,* 484–494.

Crider, A., Schwartz, G. E., and Shapiro, D. Operant suppression of electrodermal response rate. *Journal of Experimental Psychology,* 1970, *83,* 333–334.

Dardano, J. F. Fractional punishment of fixed-ratio performance. *Journal of the Experimental Analysis of Behavior,* 1970, *14,* 185–198.

Dardano, J. F. Preference for locus of punishment in a response sequence. *Journal of the Experimental Analysis of Behavior,* 1972a, *17,* 261–268.

Dardano J. F. Variable location of punishment in a response sequence. *Journal of the Experimental Analysis of Behavior,* 1972b, *17,* 433–441.

Dardano, J. F., and Sauerbrunn, D. Selective punishment of fixed-ratio performance. *Journal of the Experimental Analysis of Behavior,* 1964, *7,* 255–260.

Davitz, J. R. The effects of previous training on postfrustration behavior. *Journal of Abnormal and Social Psychology,* 1952, *47,* 309–315.

Deur, J. L., and Parke, R. D. Effects of inconsistent punishment on aggression in children. *Developmental Psychology,* 1970, *2,* 403–411.

Dienstbier, R. A., Hillman, D., Lehnhoff, J., Hillman, J., and Valkenaar, M. C. An emotion-attribution approach to moral behavior. Interfacing cognitive and avoidance theories of moral development. *Psychological Review,* 1975, *82,* 299–315.

Dinsmoor, J. A. A discrimination based on punishment. *Quarterly Journal of Experimental Psychology,* 1952, *4,* 27–45.

Dinsmoor, J. A. Punishment: I. The avoidance hypothesis. *Psychological Review,* 1954, *61,* 34–36.

Dinsmoor, J. A. Punishment: II. An interpretation of empirical findings. *Psychological Review,* 1955, *62,* 96–105.

Dion, K. Children's physical attractiveness and sex as determinants of adult punitiveness. *Developmental Psychology,* 1974, *10,* 772–778.

Dollard, J., Doob, L. W., Miller, N. E., Mowrer, O. H., and Sears, R. R. *Frustration and aggression.* New Haven, Conn.: Yale University Press, 1939.

Dove, L. D., Rashotte, M. E., and Katz, H. N. Development and maintenance of attack in pigeons during variable-interval reinforcement of key pecking. *Journal of the Experimental Analysis of Behavior,* 1974, *21,* 563–569.

Dreikurs, R., and Grey, L. *Logical consequences: A new approach to discipline.* New York: Hawthorn Books, 1968.

Dunham, P. J. Punishment: Method and theory. *Psychological Review,* 1971, *78,.* 58–70.

Dunham, P. J., and Klips, B. Shifts in magnitude of reinforcement: Confound factors or contrast effects? *Journal of Experimental Psychology,* 1969, *79,* 373–374.

Ebbesen, E. B., Bowers, R. J., Phillips, S., and Snyder, S. Self-control processes in the forbidden toy paradigm. *Journal of Personality and Social Psychology,* 1975, *31,* 442–452.

Eisenberg, J. F. A comparative study in rodent ethology with emphasis on evolution of social behavior. *Procedures of the United States National Museum,* 1967, *122,* 1–51.

Eron, L. D., Walder, L. O., Toigo, R., and Lefkowitz, M. M. Social class, parental punishment for aggression, and child aggression. *Child Development,* 1963, *34,* 849–867.

Estes, W. K. An experimental study of punishment. *Psychological Monographs,* 1944, 57 (3, Whole No. 263).

Estes, W. K. Outline of a theory of punishment. In B. A. Campbell and R. M. Church (Eds.), *Punishment and aversive behavior.* New York: Appleton-Century-Crofts, 1969.

Estes, W. K., and Skinner, B. F. Some quantitative properties of anxiety. *Journal of Experimental Psychology,* 1941, *29,* 390–400.

Fantino, E. Aversive control. In J. A. Nevin and G. S. Reynolds (Eds.), *The study of behavior.* Glenview: Scott, Foresman and Company, 1973.

Feirstein, A. R., and Miller, N. E. Learning to resist pain and fear: Effects of electric shock before versus after reaching goal. *Journal of Comparative and Physiological Psychology,* 1963, *56,* 797–800.

Ferster, C. B., and Skinner, B. F. *Schedules of reinforcement.* New York: Appleton-Century-Crofts, 1957.

Feshbach, S. Aggression. In P. H. Mussen (Ed.), *Manual of child psychology.* New York: Wiley, 1970.

Filby, Y., and Appel, J. B. Variable-interval punishment during variable-interval reinforcement. *Journal of the Experimental Analysis of Behavior,* 1966, *9,* 521–527.

Flavell, J. H., Beach, D. R., and Chinsky, J. M. Spontaneous verbal rehearsal in a memory task as a function of age. *Child Development,* 1966, *37,* 433–438.

Flory, R. K., and Lickfett, G. G. Effects of lick-contingent timeout on schedule-induced polydipsia. *Journal of the Experimental Analysis of Behavior,* 1974, *21,* 45–55.

Fowler, H. Suppression and facilitation by response contingent shock. In F. R. Brush (Ed.), *Aversive conditioning and learning.* New York: Academic Press, 1971.

Fowler, H., and Miller, N. E. Facilitation and inhibition of runway performance by hind- and forepaw shock of various intensities. *Journal of Comparative and Physiological Psychology,* 1963, *56,* 801–805.

Fowler, H., and Wischner, G. J. The varied function of punishment in discrimination learning. In B. A. Campbell and R. M. Church (Eds.), *Punishment and aversive behavior.* New York: Appleton-Century-Crofts, 1969.

Foxx, R. M., and Azrin, N. H. The elimination of autistic self-stimulatory behavior by overcorrection. *Journal of Applied Behavior Analysis,* 1973, *6,* 1–14.

Frankel, F. D. The role of the response-punishment contingency in the suppression of a positively-reinforced operant. *Learning and Motivation,* 1975, *6,* 385–403.

Freedman, D. G. The origins of social behavior. *Science Journal,* 1967, *3,* 69–73.

Freedman, J. L. Long-term behavioral effects of cognitive dissonance. *Journal of Experimental Social Psychology,* 1965, *1,* 145–155.

Gantt, W. H. *Experimental basis for neurotic behavior.* New York: Haeker, 1944.

Garbarino, J. The impact of anticipated reward upon cross-age tutoring. *Journal of Personality and Social Psychology,* 1975, *32,* 421–428.

Garcia, J., and Koelling, R. A. Relation of cue to consequence in avoidance learning. *Psychonomic Science,* 1966, *4,* 123–124.

Gelfand, D. M., Hartmann, D. P., Lamb, A. K., Smith, C. L., Mahan, M. A., and Paul, S. C. The effects of adult models and described alternatives on children's choice of behavior management techniques. *Child Development,* 1974, *45,* 585–593.

Glueck, S., and Glueck, E. *Unraveling juvenile delinquency.* Cambridge, Mass.: Harvard University Press, 1950.

Goodman, E. D., Dyal, J. A., Zinser, O., and Golub, A. UCR morphology and shock intensity. *Psychonomic Science,* 1966, *5,* 431–432.

Grabowski, J. G., and Thompson, T. Effects of shock on mirror reinforced behavior of *Betta splendens. Psychonomic Science,* 1969, *15,* 173–174.

Grinder, R. E. Relations between behavioral and cognitive dimensions of conscience in middle childhood. *Child Development,* 1964, *35,* 881–891.

Grusec, J. E. Some antecedents of self-criticism. *Journal of Personality and Social Psychology,* 1966, *4,* 244–252.

Grusec, J. E. Demand characteristics of the modeling experiment: Altruism as a function of age and aggression. *Journal of Personality and Social Psychology,* 1972, *22,* 139–148.

Grusec, J. E. Effects of co-observer evaluations on imitation: A developmental study. *Developmental Psychology,* 1973, *8,* 141.

Grusec, J. E., and Ezrin, S. A. Techniques of punishment and the development of self-criticism. *Child Development,* 1972, *43,* 1273–1288.

Grusec, J. E., and Kuczynski, L. Teaching children to punish themselves and effects on subsequent compliance. Unpublished manuscript, University of Toronto, 1975.

Grusec, J. E., and Simutis, Z. The effects of resisting and yielding models on resistance to temptation. Unpublished manuscript, University of Toronto, 1976.

Guthrie, E. R. *The psychology of learning* (2nd ed.). New York: Harper and Row, 1952. (First edition, 1935)

Gwinn, G. T. The effects of punishment on acts motivated by fear. *Journal of Experimental Psychology,* 1949, *39,* 260–269.

Hagen, J. W. and Kingsley, P. R. Labelling effects in short-term memory. *Child Development,* 1968, *39,* 113–121.

Hamilton, J., Stephens, L., and Allen, P. Controlling aggressive and destructive behavior in severely retarded institutionalized residents. *American Journal of Mental Deficiency,* 1967, *71,* 852–856.

Hamilton, M. L. Discrimination learning in children as a function of verbal-reinforcement combination and information. *Journal of Genetic Psychology,* 1969a, *114,* 283–290.

Hamilton, M. L. Reward and punishment in child discrimination learning. *Developmental Psychology,* 1969b, *1,* 735–758.

Hanratty, M. A., Liebert, R. M., Morris, L. W., and Fernandez, L. E. Imitation of film-mediated aggression against live and inanimate victims. In *Proceedings of the 77th Annual Convention of the American Psychological Association.* Washington, D.C.: American Psychological Association, 1969, 457–458.

Harman, R. E. Response elimination in concurrent and single operant situations with pigeons. *Learning and Motivation,* 1973, *4,* 417–431.

Hartig, M., and Kanfer, F. H. The role of verbal self-instructions in children's resistance to temptation. *Journal of Personality and Social Psychology,* 1973, *25,* 259–267.

Hartshorne, H., and May, M.A. *Studies in the nature of character. I. Studies in deceit.* New York: Macmillan, 1928.

Hearst, E., and Sidman, M. Some behavioral effects of a concurrently positive and negative stimulus. *Journal of the Experimental Analysis of Behavior,* 1961, *4,* 251–256.

Herman, R. L., and Azrin, N. H. Punishment by noise in an alternative response situation. *Journal of the Experimental Analysis of Behavior,* 1964, *7,* 185–188.

Herring, B. The effects of punishment on two different operants. Unpublished doctoral dissertation, University of Toronto, 1976.

Hill, W. F. Learning theory and the acquisition of values. *Psychological Review,* 1960, *67,* 317–331.

Hinde, R. A., and Stevenson-Hinde, J. (Eds.). *Constraints on learning.* New York: Academic Press, 1973.

Hoffman, M. L. Conscience, personality and socialization techniques. *Human Development,* 1970a, *13,* 90–126.

Hoffman, M. L. Moral development. In P. H. Mussen (Ed.), *Manual of child psychology.* New York: Wiley, 1970b.

Hoffman, M. L., and Saltzstein, H. D. Parent discipline and the child's moral development. *Journal of Personality and Social Psychology,* 1967, *5,* 45–57.

Hogan, J. A., and Roper, T. J. A comparison of the properties of different reinforcers. In J. S. Rosenblatt, R. A. Hinde, C. Beer, and M. C. Busnel (Eds.), *Advances in the study of behavior* (vol. 8). New York: Academic Press, in press.

Holz, W. C., and Azrin, N. H. Disriminative properties of punishment. *Journal of the Experimental Analysis of Behavior,* 1961, *4,* 225–232.

Holz, W. C., and Azrin, N. H. Recovery during punishment by intense noise. *Psychological Reports,* 1962, *11,* 655–657.

Holz, W. C., and Azrin, N. H. A comparison of several procedures for eliminating behavior. *Journal of the Experimental Analysis of Behavior,* 1963, *6,* 399–406.

Holz, W. C., Azrin, N. H., and Ulrich, R. E. Punishment of temporally spaced responding. *Journal of the Experimental Analysis of Behavior,* 1963, *6,* 115–122.

Honig, W. K. The role of discrimination training in the generalization of punishment. *Journal of the Experimental Analysis of Behavior,* 1966, *9,* 377–384.

Honig, W. K., and Slivka, R. M. Stimulus generalization of the effects of punishment. *Journal of the Experimental Analysis of Behavior,* 1964, *7,* 21–25.

Hull, J. H., and Klugh, H. E. Recovery from punishment related to movement and punishment severity. *Bulletin of the Psychonomic Society,* 1973, *1,* 110–111.

Hulse, S. H., Deese, J., and Egeth, H. *The psychology of learning.* New York: McGraw-Hill, 1975.

Hunt, J. McV., and Schlosberg, H. Behavior of rats in continuous conflict. *Journal of Comparative and Physiological Psychology,* 1950, *43,* 351–357.

Johnson, R. N. *Aggression.* Philadelphia: W. B. Saunders Company, 1972.

Jones, M. C. Albert, Peter and John B. Watson. *American Psychologist,* 1974, *29,* 581–583.

Kadden, R. M. Facilitation and suppression of responding under temporally defined schedules of negative reinforcement. *Journal of the Experimental Analysis of Behavior,* 1973, *19,* 469–480.

Kamin, L. J. The delay-of-punishment gradient. *Journal of Comparative and Physiological Psychology,* 1959, *52,* 434–437.

Kanfer, F. H., and Karoly, P. Self-control: A behavioristic excursion into the lion's den. *Behavior Therapy,* 1972, *3,* 398–416.

Kanfer, F. H., and Zich, J. Self-control training: The effects of external control on children's resistance to temptation. *Developmental Psychology,* 1974, *10,* 108–115.

Karsh, E. B. Effects of number of rewarded trials and intensity of punishment on running speed. *Journal of Comparative and Physiological Psychology,* 1962, *55,* 44–51.

Karsh, E. B. Changes in intensity of punishment: Effect on runway behavior of rats. *Science,* 1963, *140,* 1084–1085.

Karsh, E. B. Fixation produced by conflict. *Science,* 1970, *168,* 873–875.

Katz, R. C. Interactions between the facilitative and inhibitory effects of a punishing stimulus in the control of children's hitting behavior. *Child Development,* 1971, *42,* 1433–1446.

Keeney T. J., Carnizzo, S. R., and Flavell, J. H. Spontaneous and induced verbal rehearsal in a recall task. *Child Development,* 1967, *38,* 953–966.

Kelley, H. H. Attribution theory in social psychology. In D. Levine (Ed.), *Nebraska Symposium on Motivation.* Lincoln: University of Nebraska Press, 1967.

Kessen, W. *The child.* New York: John Wiley and Sons, 1965.

Kintz, B. L., and Bruning, J. L. Training, punishment and avoidance. *Psychonomic Science,* 1967, *7,* 387–388.

Kircher, A. S., Pear, J. J., and Martin, G. L. Shock as punishment in a picture-naming task with retarded children. *Journal of Applied Behavior Analysis,* 1971, *4,* 227–233.

Kohlberg, L. Development of moral character and moral ideology. In M. L. Hoffman and L. W. Hoffman (Eds.), *Review of child development research* (vol. 1). New York: Russell Sage Foundation, 1964.

Kohlenberg, R. J. The punishment of persistent vomiting: A case study. *Journal of Applied Behavior Analysis,* 1970, *3,* 241–245.

Konstantareas, M. M. Generalization and behavioral contrast in behavior change with children. Unpublished doctoral dissertation, University of Toronto, 1974.

Kramer, T. J., and Rilling, M. Effects of timeout on spaced responding in pigeons. *Journal of the Experimental Analysis of Behavior,* 1969, *12,* 283–288.

Kuczynski, L., and Grusec, J. E. Resistance to deviation as a function of age, sex, and orientation of induction. Unpublished manuscript, University of Toronto, 1976.

LaVoie, J. C. The effects of an aversive stimulus, a rationale, and sex of child on punishment effectiveness and generalization. *Child Development,* 1973a, *44,* 505–510.

LaVoie, J. C. Punishment and adolescent self-control. *Developmental Psychology,* 1973b, *8,* 16–24.

LaVoie, J. C. Type of punishment as a determinant of resistance to deviation. *Developmental Psychology,* 1974c, *10,* 181–189.

LaVoie, J. C. Aversive, cognitive, and parental determinants of punishment generalization in adolescent males. *Journal of Genetic Psychology,* 1974a, *124,* 29–39.

LaVoie, J. C. Cognitive determinants of resistance to deviation in seven-, nine-, and eleven-year-old children of low and high maturity of moral judgment. *Developmental Psychology,* 1974b, *10,* 393–403.

Leff, R. Effects of punishment intensity and consistency on the internalization of behavioral suppression in children. *Developmental Psychology,* 1969, *1,* 345–356.

Leitenberg, H. Is time-out from positive reinforcement an aversive event? *Psychological Bulletin,* 1965, *64,* 428–441.

Leitenberg, H. Punishment training with and without an escape contingency. *Journal of Experimental Psychology,* 1967, *74,* 393–399.

Lepper, M. R. Dissonance, self-perception, and honesty in children. *Journal of Personality and Social Psychology,* 1973, *25,* 65–74.

Lepper, M., Greene, D., and Nisbett, R. Undermining children's intrinsic interest with extrinsic reward: A test of the "overjustification" hypothesis. *Journal of Personality and Social Psychology,* 1973, *28,* 129–137.

Lichtenstein, P. E. Studies of anxiety: I. The production of feeding inhibition in dogs. *Journal of Comparative and Physiological Psychology,* 1950, *43,* 16–29.

Liddell, H. S. *Emotional hazards in animals and man.* Springfield, Illinois: Charles C. Thomas, 1956.

Liebert, R. M., Hanratty, M., and Hill, J. H. Effects of rule structure and training method on the adoption of a self-imposed standard. *Child Development,* 1969, *40,* 93–101.

Looney, T. A., and Cohen, P. S. Pictorial target control of schedule-induced attack in White Carneaux pigeons. *Journal of the Experimental Analysis of Behavior,* 1974, *21,* 571–584.

Lovaas, O. I., Schaeffer, B., and Simmons, J. Q. Experimental studies in childhood schizophrenia: Building social behavior in autistic children by the use of electric shock. *Journal of Experimental Research in Personality,* 1965, *1,* 99–109.

Lovaas, O. I., and Simmons, J. Q. Manipulation of self-destruction in three retarded children. *Journal of Applied Behavior Analysis,* 1969, *2,* 143–157.

Lytton, H., and Zwirner, W. Compliance and its controlling stimuli observed in a natural setting. *Developmental Psychology,* 1975, *11,* 769–779.

Maccoby, E. E. Role-taking in childhood and its consequences for social learning. *Child Development,* 1959, *30,* 239–252.

Mackintosh, N. J. *The psychology of animal learning.* New York: Academic Press, 1974.

Maier, N. R. F. *Frustration: The study of behavior without a goal.* New York: McGraw-Hill, 1949.

Mandler, G. The interruption of behavior. In D. Levine (Ed.), *Nebraska Symposium on Motivation.* Lincoln: University of Nebraska Press, 1964.

Maslow, A. H. Deprivation, threat, and frustration. *Psychological Review,* 1941, *48,* 364–366.

Masserman, J. H. *Behavior and neurosis.* Chicago: University of Chicago Press, 1943.

Masserman, J. H. *Principles of dynamic psychiatry.* Philadelphia: Saunders, 1946.

Masserman, J. H., and Jacques, M. G. Experimental masochism. *Archives of Neurology and Psychiatry,* 1948, *60,* 402.

Masserman, J. H., and Pechtel, C. Neurosis in monkeys: A preliminary report of experimental observations. *Annals of the New York Academy of Sciences,* 1953, *56,* 253–265.

Maurer, A. Corporal punishment. *American Psychologist,* 1974, *29,* 614–626.

McCord, W., McCord, J., and Zola, I. K. *Origins of crime.* New York: Columbia University Press, 1959.

McMillan, D. E. A comparison of the punishing effects of response-produced shock and response-produced time-out. *Journal of the Experimental Analysis of Behavior,* 1967, *10,* 439–449.

Meichenbaum, D., and Goodman J. Training impulsive children to talk to themselves: A means of developing self-control. *Journal of Abnormal Psychology,* 1971, *77,* 115–126.

Melvin, K. B. Vicious circle behavior. In H. D. Kimmel (Ed.), *Experimental psychopathology: Recent research and theory.* New York: Academic Press, 1971.

Melvin, K. B., and Ervey, D. H. Facilitative and suppressive effects of punishment on species-typical aggressive display in *Betta splendens. Journal of Comparative and Physiological Psychology,* 1973, *83,* 451–457.

Meyer, W. J., and Offenbach, S. I. Effectiveness of reward and punishment as a function of task complexity. *Journal of Comparative and Physiological Psychology,* 1962, *55,* 532–534.

Miller, N. B., and Zimmerman, J. The effects of a pre-time-out stimulus on matching-to-sample of humans. *Journal of the Experimental Analysis of Behavior,* 1966, *9,* 487–499.

Miller, N. E. The frustration-aggression hypothesis. *Psychological Review,* 1941, *48,* 337–342.

Miller, N. E. Theory and experiment relating psychoanalytic displacement to stimulus-response generalization. *Journal of Abnormal and Social Psychology,* 1948, *43,* 155–178.

Miller, N. E. Learning resistance to pain and fear: Effects of overlearning, exposure, and rewarded exposure in context. *Journal of Experimental Psychology,* 1960, *60,* 137–145.

Miller, N. E., and Bugelski, B. R. Minor studies in aggression: The influence of frustrations imposed by the in-group on attitudes expressed toward out-groups. *Journal of Psychology,* 1948, *25,* 437–442.

Milne-Edwards, A. Observations sur quelques manifers du Nord de la Chine. *Annals of Natural Science (Zoology),* 1867, *7,* 375–377.

Misanin, J. R., Campbell, B. A., and Smith, N. F. Duration of punishment and the delay of punishment gradient. *Canadian Journal of Psychology,* 1966, *20,* 407–412.

Mischel, W. Toward a cognitive social learning reconceptualization of personality. *Psychological Review,* 1973, *80,* 252–283.

Mischel, W. Processes in delay of gratification. In L. Berkowitz (Ed.), *Advances in experimental social psychology* (vol. 7). New York: Academic Press, 1974.

Mischel, W., and Grusec, J. E. Determinants of the rehearsal and transmission of neutral and aversive behaviors. *Journal of Personality and Social Psychology,* 1966, *3,* 197–205.

Mitchell, G. D., Arling, G. L., and Moller, G. W. Long-term effects of maternal punishment on the behavior of monkeys. *Psychonomic Science,* 1967, *8,* 209–210.

Morris, W. N., Marshall, H. M., and Miller, R. S. The effect of vicarious punishment on prosocial behavior in children. *Journal of Experimental Child Psychology,* 1973, *15,* 222–236.

Mowrer, O. H. On the dual nature of learning: A reinterpretation of "conditioning" and "problem solving." *Harvard Educational Review,* 1947, *17,* 102–148.

Mowrer, O. H. *Learning theory and personality dynamics.* New York: Ronald Press, 1950.

Mowrer, O. H. *Learning theory and behavior.* New York: John Wiley and Sons, 1960a.

Mowrer, O. H. *Learning theory and the symbolic processes.* New York: John Wiley and Sons, 1960b.

Mowrer, O. H., and Solomon, L. N. Contiguity *vs.* drive reduction in conditioned fear: The proximity and abruptness of drive reduction. *American Journal of Psychology,* 1954, *67,* 15–25.

Muenzinger, K. F. Motivation in learning: I. Electric shocks for correct responses in the visual discrimination habit. *Journal of Comparative Psychology,* 1934, *17,* 267–278.

Mulick, J. A., Leitenberg, H., and Rawson, R. A. Alternative response training, differential reinforcement of other behavior, and extinction in squirrel monkeys *(Saumiri sciureus). Journal of the Experimental Analysis of Behavior,* 1976, 25, 311–320.

Myer, J. S. Punishment of instinctive behavior: Suppression of mouse-killing by rats. *Psychonomic Science,* 1966, 4, 385–386.

Myer, J. S. Some effects of noncontingent aversive stimulation. In F. R. Brush (Ed.), *Aversive conditioning and learning.* New York: Academic Press, 1971.

Myer, J. S., and Baenninger, R. Some effects of punishment and stress on mouse-killing by rats. *Journal of Comparative and Physiological Psychology,* 1966, 62, 292–297.

Myer, J. S., and Ricci, D. Delay of punishment gradients for the goldfish. *Journal of Comparative and Physiological Psychology,* 1968, 66, 417–421.

Myer, J. S., and White, R. T. Aggressive motivation in the rat. *Animal Behavior,* 1965, 13, 430–433.

Myers, W. A. Observational learning in monkeys. *Journal of the Experimental Analysis of Behavior,* 1970, 14, 225–235.

Nevin, J. A. The maintenance of behavior. In J. A. Nevin and G. S. Reynolds (Eds.), *The study of behavior.* Glenview, Illinois: Scott, Foresman, 1973.

Newman, A., and Kanfer, F. H. Delay of gratification in children: The effects of training under fixed, decreasing and increasing delay of reward. *Journal of Experimental Child Psychology,* 1976, 21, 12–24.

Nigro, M. R. Punishment of an extinguishing shock-avoidance response by time-out from positive reinforcement. *Journal of the Experimental Analysis of Behavior,* 1966, 9, 53–62.

Nisbett, R. E., and Valins, S. *Perceiving the causes of one's own behavior.* Morristown, N. J.: General Learning Press, 1971.

O'Kelly, L. I., and Steckel, L. C. A note on long enduring emotional responses in the rat. *Journal of Psychology,* 1939, 8, 125–131.

O'Leary, K. D. The effects of self-instruction on immoral behavior. *Journal of Experimental Child Psychology,* 1968, 6, 297–301.

O'Leary, K. D., and Becker, W. C. The effects of the intensity of a teacher's reprimands on children's behavior. *Journal of School Psychology,* 1968–1969, *7,* 8–11.

O'Leary, K. D., Kaufman, K. F., Kass, R. E., and Drabman, R. S. The effects of loud and soft reprimands on behavior of disruptive students. *Exceptional Children,* 1970, *37,* 145–155.

Olejnik, A. B., and McKinney, J. P. Parental value orientation and generosity in children. *Developmental Psychology,* 1973, *8,* 311.

Paris, G., and Cairns, R. B. An experimental and ethological analysis of social reinforcement with retarded children. *Child Development,* 1972, *43,* 717–729.

Parke, R. D. Effectiveness of punishment as an interaction of intensity, timing, agent nurturance, and cognitive structuring. *Child Development,* 1969, *40,* 213–235.

Parke, R. D. Rules, roles, and resistance to deviation: Recent advances in punishment, discipline, and self-control. In A. Pick (Ed.), *Minnesota Symposia on Child Psychology* (vol. 8). Minneapolis: University of Minnesota Press, 1974.

Parke, R. D., and Deur, J. L. Schedule of punishment and inhibition of aggression in children. *Developmental Psychology,* 1972, *7,* 266–269.

Parke, R. D., and Walters, R. H. Some factors determining the efficacy of punishment for inducing response inhibition. *Monograph of the Society for Research in Child Development,* 1967, *32,* No. 109.

Pastore, N. The role of arbitrariness in the frustration-aggression hypothesis. *Journal of Abnormal and Social Psychology,* 1952, *47,* 728–731.

Patterson, C. J., and Mischel, W. Plans to resist distraction. *Developmental Psychology,* 1975, *11,* 369–378.

Patterson, C. J. and Mischel, W. Effects of temptation-inhibiting and task-facilitating plans on self-control. *Journal of Personality and Social Psychology,* 1976, *33,* 209–217.

Patterson, G. R. Parents as dispensers of aversive stimuli. *Journal of Personality and Social Psychology,* 1965, *2,* 844–851.

Patterson, G. R. A basis for identifying stimuli which control behaviors in natural settings. *Child Development,* 1974, *45,* 900–911.

Pearl, J., Walters, G. C., and Anderson, D. C. Suppressing effects of aversive stimulation on subsequently punished behavior. *Canadian Journal of Psychology,* 1964, *18,* 343–355.

Penney, R. K. Effect of reward and punishment on children's orientation and discrimination learning. *Journal of Experimental Psychology,* 1967, *75,* 140–142.

Perry, D. G., Bussey, K., and Perry, L. C. Factors influencing the imitation of resistance to deviation. *Developmental Psychology,* 1975, *11,* 724–731.

Perry, D. G., and Parke, R. D. Punishment and alternative response training as determinants of response inhibition in children. *Genetic Psychology Monographs,* 1975, *91,* 257–279.

Piaget, J. *The moral judgment of the child* (M. Gabain, Trans.). New York: Free Press, 1965.

Quinsey, V. L. Lick-shock contingencies in the rat. *Journal of the Experimental Analysis of Behavior,* 1972, *17,* 119–125.

Rachlin, H. Recovery of responses during mild punishment. *Journal of the Experimental Analysis of Behavior,* 1966, *9,* 251–263.

Rachlin, H. Summary of the discussion at the conference. In B. A. Campbell and R. M. Church (Eds.), *Punishment and aversive behavior.* New York: Appleton-Century-Crofts, 1969.

Rachlin, H. *Introduction to modern behaviorism.* San Francisco: Freeman, 1970.

Rachlin, H., and Baum, W. M. Effects of alternative reinforcement: Does the source matter? *Journal of the Experimental Analysis of Behavior,* 1972, *18,* 231–241.

Rachlin, H., and Herrnstein, R. J. Hedonism revisited: On the negative law of effect. In B. A. Campbell and R. M. Church (Eds.), *Punishment and aversive behavior.* New York: Appleton-Century-Crofts, 1969.

Rachman, S., and Teasdale, A. *Aversion therapy and behavior disorders: An analysis.* Coral Gables, Florida: University of Miami Press, 1969.

Rashotte, M. E., Dove, L. D., and Looney, T. A. Absence of shock-elicited aggression in pigeons. *Journal of the Experimental Analysis of Behavior,* 1974, *21,* 267–275.

Rawson, R. A., and Leitenberg, H. Reinforced alternative behavior during punishment and extinction with rats. *Journal of Comparative and Physiological Psychology,* 1973, *85,* 593–600.

Redd, W. H., Morris, E. K., and Martin, J. A. Effects of positive and negative adult-child interactions on children's social preferences. *Journal of Experimental Child Psychology,* 1975, *19,* 153–164.

Reiss, S., and Sushinsky, L. W. Overjustification, competing responses, and the acquisition of intrinsic interest. *Journal of Personality and Social Psychology,* 1975, *31,* 1116–1125.

Rescorla, R. A. Pavlovian conditioning and its proper control procedures. *Psychological Review,* 1967, *74,* 71–80.

Rescorla, R. A., and Solomon, R. L. Two-process learning theory: Relationships between Pavlovian conditioning and instrumental learning. *Psychological Review,* 1967, *74,* 151–182.

Riccio, D. C., and Marrazo, M. J. Effects of punishing active avoidance in young and adult rats. *Journal of Comparative and Physiological Psychology,* 1972, *79,* 453–458.

Risley, T. R. The effects and side effects of punishing the autistic behaviors of a deviant child. *Journal of Applied Behavior Analysis,* 1968, *1,* 21–34.

Roberts, C. L., and Blase, K. Elicitation and punishment of intraspecies aggression by the same stimulus. *Journal of the Experimental Analysis of Behavior,* 1971, *15,* 193–196.

Rosenkoetter, L. I. Resistance to temptation: Inhibitory and disinhibitory effects of models. *Developmental Psychology,* 1973, *8,* 80–84.

Rouda, R. A. Punishment of sexual behavior in the male rat. Unpublished master's thesis, University of Toronto, 1968.

Sajwaj, T., and Hedges, D. Functions of parental attention in an oppositional retarded boy. *Proceedings of the Annual Convention of the American Psychological Association,* 1971, *6,* 697–698.

Sawin, D. B., Parke, R. D., Harrison, A. N., and Kreling, B. The child's role in sparing the rod. Paper presented at the meeting of the American Psychological Association, Chicago, 1975.

Schachter, S., and Singer, J. E. Cognitive, social and physiological determinants of emotional state. *Psychological Review,* 1962, *69,* 379–399.

Schick, K. Operants. *Journal of the Experimental Analysis of Behavior,* 1971, *15,* 413–423.

Schuster, R., and Rachlin, H. Indifference between punishment and free shock: Evidence for the negative law of effect. *Journal of the Experimental Analysis of Behavior,* 1968, *11,* 777–786.

Sears, R. R., Maccoby, E. E., and Levin, H. *Patterns of child rearing.* Evanston: Row, Peterson and Co., 1957.

Sears, R. R., Rau, L., and Alpert, R. *Identification and child rearing.* Palo Alto, Calif.: Stanford University Press, 1965.

Sears, R. R., Whiting, J. W. M., Nowlis, V., and Sears, P. S. Some child-rearing antecedents of aggression and dependency in young children. *Genetic Psychology Monographs,* 1953, *47,* 135–234.

Segal, E. F. Induction and the provenance of operants. In R. M. Gilbert and J. R. Millenson (Eds.), *Reinforcement: Behavioral analysis.* New York: Academic Press, 1972.

Seligman, M. E. P., and Campbell, B. A. Effect of intensity and duration of punishment on extinction of an avoidance response. *Journal of Comparative and Physiological Psychology,* 1965, *59,* 295–297.

Seligman, M. E. P., and Hager, J. L. *Biological boundaries of learning.* New York: Appleton-Century-Crofts, 1972.

Seward, J. P. The role of conflict in experimental neurosis. In B. A. Campbell and R. M. Church (Eds.), *Punishment and aversive behavior.* New York: Appleton-Century-Crofts, 1969.

Seward, J. P., King, R. M., Chow, T., and Shiflett, S. C. Persistence of punished escape responses. *Journal of Comparative and Physiological Psychology,* 1965, *60,* 265–267.

Skinner, B. F. *The behavior of organisms.* New York: Appleton-Century-Crofts, 1938.

Skinner, B. F. *Beyond freedom and dignity.* New York: Knopf, 1971.

Solomon, R. L. Punishment. *American Psychologist,* 1964, *19,* 239–253.

Solomon, R. L., Kamin, L. J., and Wynne, L. C. Traumatic avoidance learning: The outcomes of several extinction procedures with dogs. *Journal of Abnormal and Social Psychology,* 1953, *48,* 291–302.

Solomon, R. L., Turner, L. H., and Lessac, M. S. Some effects of delay of punishment on resistance to temptation in dogs.

Journal of Personality and Social Psychology, 1968, *8,* 233–238.

Spence, J. T. Verbal discrimination performance as a function of instructions and verbal reinforcement combination in normal and retarded children. *Child Development,* 1966, *37,* 269–281.

Spence, J. T. The distracting effects of material reinforcers in the discrimination learning of lower- and middle-class children. *Child Development,* 1970, *41,* 103–111.

Spence, J. T. Verbal and nonverbal rewards and punishments in the discrimination learning of children of varying socioeconomic status. *Developmental Psychology,* 1972, *6,* 381–384.

Spinetta, J. J., and Rigler, D. The child-abusing parent: A psychological review. *Psychological Bulletin,* 1972, *77,* 296–304.

Staddon, J. E. R., and Simmelhag, V. L. The "superstition" experiment: A reexamination of its implications for the principles of adaptive behavior. *Psychological Review,* 1971, *78,* 3–43.

Stagner, R., and Condon, C. S. Another failure to demonstrate displacement of aggression. *Journal of Abnormal and Social Psychology,* 1955, *51,* 695–696.

Stayton, D. J., Hogan, R., and Ainsworth, M. D. Infant obedience and maternal behavior: The origins of socialization reconsidered. *Child Development,* 1971, *42,*1057–1069.

Stein, A. H. Imitation of resistance to temptation. *Child Development,* 1967, *38,* 157–169.

Steuer, F. B., Applefield, J. M., and Smith, R. Televised aggression and the interpersonal aggression of preschool children. *Journal of Experimental Child Psychology,* 1971, *11,* 442–447.

Stockman, C. L., and Glusman, M. Suppression of hypothalamically produced flight responses by punishment. *Physiology and Behavior,* 1969, *4,* 523–525.

Storms, L. H., Boroczi, G., and Broen, W. E., Jr. Effects of punishment as a function of strain of rat and duration of shock. *Journal of Comparative and Physiological Psychology,* 1963, *56,* 1022–1026.

Thomas, J. R. Fixed-ratio punishment by timeout of concurrent variable-interval behavior. *Journal of the Experimental Analysis of Behavior,* 1968, *11,* 609–616.

Thorndike, E. L. Animal intelligence: An experimental study of the associative processes in animals. *Psychological Monographs,* 1898, 2, 109.

Thorndike, E. L. *Animal intelligence: Experimental studies.* New York: Macmillan, 1911.

Thorndike, E. L. *Human learning.* New York: Appleton-Century-Crofts, 1931.

Thorndike, E. L. *The fundamentals of learning.* New York: Teachers College, 1932.

Thurston, J. R., and Mussen, P. H. Infant feeding gratification and adult personality. *Journal of Personality,* 1951, 19, 449–458.

Tolman, C. W., and Mueller, M. R. Laboratory control of toe-sucking in a young rhesus monkey by two kinds of punishment. *Journal of the Experimental Analysis of Behavior,* 1964, 7, 323–325.

Topping, J. S., and Larmi, O. K. Response elimination effectiveness of omission and two extinction training procedures. *Psychological Record,* 1973, 23, 197–202.

Topping, J. S., Pickering, J. W., and Jackson, J. J. The differential effects of omission and extinction following DRL pretraining. *Psychonomic Science,* 1971, 24, 137–138.

Trenholme, I. A., and Baron, A. Intermediate and delayed punishment of human behavior by loss of reinforcement. *Learning and Motivation,* 1975, 6, 62–79.

Tullis, C., and Walters, G. C. Punished and unpunished responding in multiple variable-interval schedules. *Journal of the Experimental Analysis of Behavior,* 1968, 11, 147–152.

Uhl, C. N. Eliminating behavior with omission and extinction after varying amounts of training. *Animal Learning and Behavior,* 1973, 1, 237–240.

Uhl, C. N., and Garcia, E. E. Comparison of omission with extinction in response elimination in rats. *Journal of Comparative and Physiological Psychology,* 1969, 69, 554–562.

Uhl, C. N., and Sherman, W. O. Comparison of combinations of omission, punishment, and extinction methods in response elimination in rats. *Journal of Comparative and Physiological Psychology,* 1971, 74, 59–65.

Ulrich, R. E., and Azrin, N. H. Reflexive fighting in response to aversive stimulation. *Journal of the Experimental Analysis of Behavior*, 1962, 5, 511–520.

Vygotsky, L. S. *Thought and language.* Cambridge, Mass.: M.I.T. Press, 1962.

Wagner, A. R. Frustration and punishment. In R. N. Haber (Ed.), *Current research in motivation.* New York: Holt, Rinehart and Winston, 1966.

Wahler, R. G. Setting generality: Some specific and general effects of child behavior therapy. *Journal of Applied Behavior Analysis,* 1969, 2, 239–246.

Wall, A. M., Walters, G. C., and England, R. S. The lickometer: A simple device for the analysis of licking as an operant. *Behavior Research Methods and Instrumentation,* 1972, 4, 320–322.

Walters, G. C. Frequency and intensity of pre-shock experiences as determinants of fearfulness in an approach-avoidance conflict. *Canadian Journal of Psychology,* 1963, 17, 412–419.

Walters, G. C., and Glazer, R. D. Punishment of instinctive behavior in the Mongolian gerbil. *Journal of Comparative and Physiological Psychology,* 1971, 75, 331–340.

Walters, G. C., and Herring, B. Effect of punishment on lever-pressing and non-consummatory licking. Paper presented at the meeting of the Psychonomic Society, St. Louis, November, 1976.

Walters, G. C., and Rogers, J. V. Aversive stimulation of the rat: Long-term effects on subsequent behavior. *Science,* 1963, 142, 70–71.

Walters, R. H. Delay of reinforcement gradients in children's learning. *Psychonomic Science,* 1964, 1, 307–308.

Walters, R. H., and Demkow, L. Timing of punishment as a determinant of response inhibition. *Child Development,* 1963, 34, 207–214.

Walters, R. H., and Parke, R. D. Influence of response consequences to a social model on resistance to deviation. *Journal of Experimental Child Psychology,* 1964, 1, 269–280.

Walters, R. H., and Parke, R. D. The influence of punishment and related disciplinary techniques on the social behavior of children: Theory and empirical findings. In B. A. Maher (Ed.), *Progress in experimental personality research* (vol. 4). New York: Academic Press, 1967.

Walters, R. H., Parke, R. D., and Cane, V. A. Timing of punishment and the observation of consequences to others as determinants of response inhibition. *Journal of Experimental Child Psychology,* 1965, *2,* 10–30.

Watson, D. L., and Tharp, R. G. *Self-directed behavior: Self-modification for personal adjustment.* Monterey, Calif.: Brooks/Cole, 1972.

Watson, J. B. Psychology as a behaviorist views it. *Psychological Review,* 1913, *20,* 158–177.

Watson, J. B. *Psychological care of infant and child.* New York: Norton, 1928.

Watson, J. B. John Broadus Watson. In C. Murchison (Ed.), *A history of psychology in autobiography* (vol. 3). Worcester, Mass.: Clark University Press, 1936.

Watson, J. B., and Rayner, R. Conditioned emotional reactions. *Journal of Experimental Psychology,* 1920, *3,* 1–14.

Weber, S. Positive and negative reinforcement of instinctive behavior in the Mongolian gerbil. Unpublished bachelor's thesis, University of Toronto, 1974.

Westbrook, R. F. Failure to obtain positive contrast when pigeons press a bar. *Journal of the Experimental Analysis of Behavior,* 1965, *8,* 269–278.

Wetzel, C. D. Delay of punishment in shock-elicited aggression. *Psychonomic Science,* 1972, *26,* 270–272.

White, G. D., Nielsen, G., and Johnson, S. M. Timeout duration and the suppression of deviant behavior in children. *Journal of Applied Behavior Analysis,* 1972, *5,* 111–120.

Whiting, J. W. M., and Child, I. L. *Child training and personality.* New Haven: Yale University Press, 1953.

Witte, K. L., and Grossman, E. E. The effects of reward and punishment upon children's attention, motivation, and discrimination learning. *Child Development,* 1971, *42,* 537–542.

Wittenborn, J. R. A study of adoptive children. *Psychological Monographs,* 1956, *70,* 1–115.

Wolf, T. M., and Cheyne, J. A. Persistence of effects of live behavioral, televised behavioral, and live verbal models on resistance to deviation. *Child Development,* 1972, *43,* 1429–1436.

Wolfenstein, M. Trends in infant care. *American Journal of Orthopsychiatry,* 1953, *23,* 120–130.

Woodworth, R. S., and Schlosberg, H. *Experimental psychology.* New York: Holt, 1954.

Yarrow, M. R., Campbell, J. D., and Burton, R. V. *Child-rearing: An inquiry into research and methods.* San Francisco: Jossey-Bass, 1968.

Zeiler, M. D. Eliminating behavior with reinforcement. *Journal of the Experimental Analysis of Behavior,* 1971, *16,* 401–405.

Zeiler, M. D. Positive reinforcement and the elimination of reinforced responses. *Journal of the Experimental Analysis of Behavior,* 1976, *26,* 37–44.

Zimmerman, J., and Baydan, N. T. Punishment of S$^\Delta$ responding of humans in conditional matching to sample by time-out. *Journal of the Experimental Analysis of Behavior,* 1963, *6,* 589–597.

Zimmerman, J., and Ferster, C. B. Intermittent punishment of S$^\Delta$ responding in matching to a sample. *Journal of the Experimental Analysis of Behavior,* 1963, *6,* 349–356.

INDEXES

AUTHOR INDEX

Abel, E. L., 53
Adler, N., 107
Ainsworth, M. D., 246
Alcock, J., 108
Allen, P., 43
Allinsmith, W., 45
Alpert, R., 17
Amsel, A., 74, 141, 144, 170, 173
Anderson, D. C., 53
Andres, D. H., 87
Appel, J. B., 61, 63, 73, 92
Applefield, J. M., 146
Arling, G. L., 145
Aronfreed, J., 65, 66, 67, 83, 84, 169, 205, 235

Ayres, J. J. B., 108
Azrin, N. H., 11, 24, 28, 29, 38, 40, 42, 58, 60, 61, 63, 71, 72, 75, 90, 91, 93, 94, 96, 98, 101, 104, 105, 107, 125, 128, 137, 138, 139, 141, 150, 151, 168, 181

Baenninger, R., 107
Bandura, A., 17, 18, 19, 84, 142, 144, 146, 175, 191, 206
Banks, R. K., 74, 82
Baron, A., 81, 82
Barrett, J. E., 108

Miller, N. E., 39, 70, 96, 97, 140, 164, 175
Miller, R. S., 77
Milne-Edwards, A., 109
Misanin, J. R., 82
Mischel, W., 20, 147, 148, 219–220
Mitchell, G. D., 145
Moller, G. W., 145
Morris, E. K., 154
Morris, L. W., 146
Morris, W. N., 77, 78
Morse, P., 111
Mowrer, O. H., 10, 33, 111, 126, 127, 140, 154, 228, 232
Mueller, M. R., 108
Muenzinger, K. F., 105
Mulick, J. A., 186
Murray, S., 203
Mussen, P. H., 17
Myer, J. S., 51, 80, 81, 107, 137, 138
Myers, W. A., 19, 187

Nevin, J. A., 228
Newby, V., 108

Newman, A., 220–221
Nielsen, G., 68
Nigro, M. R., 43
Nisbett, R. E., 210, 252
Nowlis, V., 144

Offenbach, S. I., 115
O'Kelly, L. I., 137
O'Leary, K. D., 54, 208
Olejnik, A. B., 250
Overmier, J. B., 70

Paris, G., 115, 120, 121
Parke, R. D., 4, 41, 54, 66, 73, 74, 83, 84, 85, 88, 101, 191, 203, 205, 208, 209, 218, 226, 235, 238, 240
Pastore, N., 140
Patterson, C. J., 220
Patterson, G. R., 89, 248
Paul, S. C., 147, 148
Pavlov, I., 6, 164
Pear, J. J., 41
Pearl, J., 53
Pechtel, C., 112, 162
Penney, R. K., 115, 121, 251

SUBJECT INDEX

Neurosis, 156–157
  and confinement, 164
  and conflict, 159–163
  experimental, 158–165
  and fixated behavior,
    159–161

Observational learning. *See*
  Imitation
Omission training, 181–187,
  213–214
  application of, 185–186
  combined with punish-
    ment, 185
  compared with extinction,
    182–185
  compared with punish-
    ment, 183, 185, 187
  definition of, 181
  and response competition,
    181, 186–187
Operant paradigm,
  limitations of, 236,
  241–246
Overcorrection, definition
  of, 42

Permanence of suppression,
  8–10, 23–25, 60,
  94–96, 129–131,
  207–210, 227–228
  programming of, 228–230
  and stimulus generaliza-
    tion, 228
Permissiveness, 3–4, 8, 14
  and strictness, 15
Physical punishment, imitation of, 145–149
Positive reinforcement
  and amount of pre-
    punishment training,
    96–98
  compared with punish-
    ment, 115, 120–124,
    250–251
  conditioned, 228
  distracting properties of,
    252–253
  limitations of, 121–124
  schedules of, and punish-
    ment, 90–92
Power assertion
  compared with love-